Imagining
the
Nation

Post-Communist Cultural Studies Series
Thomas Cushman, General Editor

Imagining the Nation

History, Modernity, and Revolution in Latvia

Daina Stukuls Eglitis

The Pennsylvania State University Press
University Park, Pennsylvania

Library of Congress Cataloging-in-Publication Data

Eglitis, Daina Stukuls.
   Imagining the nation : history, modernity, and
         revolution in Latvia / Daina Stukuls Eglitis.
      p.   cm.—(Post-Communist cultural studies series)
   Includes bibliographical references and index.
   ISBN 0-271-02203-5 (cloth : alk. paper)
      1. Latvia—Social conditions.
      2. Social change—Latvia.
      3. Post-communism—Latvia.
      4. Women—Latvia.
      5. Latvia—Politics and government—1940–1991.
      6. Latvia—Politics and government—1991– .
   I. Title. II. Post-Communist cultural studies.

HN539.8.A8 E37 2002
306′.094796—dc21   2002005415

Copyright © 2002 The Pennsylvania State University
All rights reserved
Printed in the United States of America
Published by The Pennsylvania State University Press,
University Park, PA 16802-1003

It is the policy of The Pennsylvania State University
Press to use acid-free paper for the first printing of all
clothbound books. Publications on uncoated stock satisfy
the minimum requirements of American National
Standard for Information Sciences—Permanence of
Paper for Printed Library Materials, ANSI Z39.48–1992.

For my husband, Raits, my mother, Silvia, and to the memory of my beloved grandmother, Nellija Kalniņš (1910–2002)

Contents

Acknowledgments

This project is the culmination of a long process of research, writing, and preparation. It is no surprise, then, that the list of those to whom I am indebted is long. I am thankful to have had the good fortune to study with many excellent faculty members at the University of Michigan. I am especially grateful to Michael D. Kennedy for many years of advice, critique, and encouragement. My association with Professor Kennedy, my first sociology instructor, has had a profound and positive effect on the direction of my life and career. I have also benefited greatly from the ideas and support of other faculty members: Mayer Zald, Julia Adams, Katherine Verdery, Fatma Muge Gocek, Rick Lempert, and Margaret R. Somers. Outside the University of Michigan, Professors Yuri Slezkine and Peggy Watson kindly read and commented on some of the work that appears here.

I am grateful to many people and organizations for the support that helped make this project possible. My research on the 1993 elections in Latvia was enabled by the John A. and Patricia Armstrong Travel Fellowship for the former Soviet Union. In the summer of 1995, the Social Science Research Council Workshop on Sociology and Anthropology offered a valuable opportunity to meet with faculty and students from various universities to discuss and strengthen my work. A travel grant from the Department of Sociology at the University of Michigan provided the opportunity for a final research visit to gather information and tie up some loose ends in 1997. I was able to complete the writing of my doctoral dissertation on Latvia's transition thanks to a 1997–98 Dissertation Fellowship from the American Council of Learned Societies, and I revised the work for publication as a book with the support of a short-term grant from the Woodrow Wilson International Center for Scholars in 1999. All of the photos I have included here are my own.

In Latvia, I benefited from the assistance of many people, including Pārsla Eglīte and Boris Tsilevich, who offered valuable help when I was in Riga and kindly responded to many E-mailed inquiries when I was not. As well, I thank Daina Bleiere, Ailona Dārzniece, Juris Krūmiņš, Inta Mežavilka, Feliciāna Rajevska, Mikhail Rodin, Anda Lodziņa, Aiva Soboļeva, Andrejs Vilks, and Ļubova Zīle for materials and interesting discussions. Many more have helped, and regretfully I cannot name them all.

In the process of preparing this manuscript for publication, the comments of the series editor, Thomas Cushman, and the reader, Andrejs Plakans, were very helpful. I am grateful as well to Peter Potter and numerous others at Penn State Press for their help and patience in answering the many questions of a novice author.

I owe a debt of gratitude to my mother, Silvia Kalniņš Stukuls, and my father, Edward Stukuls, and my grandparents on both sides, who introduced me to the Latvian language and culture. I appreciate the fact that the opportunity to learn was never accompanied by a demand to conform. In particular, I am grateful to my grandmother Nellija Kalniņš, who has been a source of endless love and inspiration for me. I thank as well my in-laws in Riga, Mirdza and Laimonis Eglītis, for their kindness, and my friend Anita Eglīte, who was of great help in gathering materials I had missed during my own visits.

Finally, I wish to thank my husband, Raits Eglītis, for his patient support throughout this time-consuming project. In the midst of this work, we took on another project of tremendous importance: raising our children, Niklāvs and Anna. To these two wonderful beings I am grateful for teaching me many important lessons that I could not have learned in school or from any book.

Illustrations

Figures

Tables

(Re)Constructing Normality in Post-Communism

> Eighteen years ago on this day
> A boat came ashore on the Daugava.
> Out of the boat climbed an honorable old man,
> Holding in his arms a tiny boy,
> With a youthful gait he strode to the castle
> And brought me this fateful tiding:
> This small boy take as your son,
> Raise him as your heir.
>   An honorable old man was Vaidelots
> And he said: he found in the depths of the woods
> This odd human child
> Suckling at the milky breasts of a mother bear.
> He said the boy was fated by the gods
> To become in time a hero of the nation,
> Before whose word alone would tremble
> All future persecutors of the nation!
>
> —Lielvārdis, adopted father of the Bearslayer[1]

The Bearslayer: Myth, Memory, and Modernization

The Bearslayer *(Lāčplēsis)* is a mythic hero of ancient Latvian lore, whose story was put to paper by Latvia's first epic poet, Andrejs Pumpurs, in 1888. The epic integrates many of the themes that dominate both Latvian literature and history in the twentieth century: an ambivalence and distrust toward Christian religion, which is imported rather than indigenous; a devotion to nature and the natural world; a central place for song in the maintenance and protection of the nation; a fierce desire to defend the nation from subjugation by outsiders; and a veneration of the countryside, particularly in contrast to a suspicion about the big city, which is perceived to be the product and haven of outsiders.

Though the Bearslayer is not linked to Christian religion, he is a quasi-religious figure. The Bearslayer is reminded at points in the story that his

1 Mother Latvia represented on the Freedom Monument in downtown Riga

fate is to fight and sacrifice for his nation, another strand of the religious theme, though the "religion" is the nation rather than Christianity.[2] He is also, like the figure of Christ, a man unlike others: born of a mother bear, he inherited a bear's strength and a bear's ears, which are the locus of his strength. When he falls in battle with the enemy, the nation awaits his resurrection from the depths of the Daugava River. From the beginning of the story, when the Bearslayer earns his name by killing a bear who attacks his adopted father, he demonstrates his heroism and strength in the service of others.

Though the original *Bearslayer* epic was published in 1888 and a play by the Latvian writer Jānis Rainis, *Fire and Night,* based on the story, appeared in 1905, the hero is still relevant in the twenty-first century. Indeed, representations of the Bearslayer abound, particularly in Riga (which, ironically, did not occupy a place of great favor in Pumpurs's epic): there one can stroll down *Lāčplēsis* Street, drink a *Lāčplēsis* beer, and examine the figure of the Bearslayer on the south side of the Freedom Monument. In the interwar period (1918–1940), the *Lāčplēsis* Order was a military decoration of highest regard. This award has been renewed in the post-Communist period. In 1988, fully one hundred years after Pumpurs's epic appeared, the rock opera *Lāčplēsis* opened to great acclaim, and a physical representation, Kārlis Jansons's interwar statue of the Bearslayer, broken and decapitated, was unearthed in the city of Jelgava after decades beneath the soil. Dainis Īvāns, an important figure in the opposition movement of the late 1980s, wrote of the statue: "With flowers in place of his severed head, without legs, but with the handle of the sword in his hand, with strength in his muscles and heart, which had survived destruction, he spoke to an unthinkable wonder of resurrection."[3] Īvāns, in fact, called 1988 "the year of the Bearslayer." That same year, on *Lāčplēša diena* (Bearslayer Day, November 11), the interwar Latvian flag was raised over Riga Castle for the first time since the Soviet occupation. During the demonstrations of the period of opposition, signs could be seen in crowds calling for the removal of *kangari* from posts of power: the word comes from a character in the epic, Kangars, who betrays his nation for personal gain.

As Pumpurs's epic comes to a close, the Bearslayer and the Dark Knight, a mythical soldier in the army of Bishop Alberts from the German lands, are locked in battle at the edge of the Daugava. Seeking to deprive him of his strength, the Dark Knight severs the hero's ears with his sword. As they struggle, the Bearslayer and his nemesis tumble into the river. The Bearslayer, however, is not dead "to his nation." He continues his epic battle to overcome the Dark Knight beneath the "mourning river waves." The story

ends unfinished, and the fate of the nation that the Bearslayer both protects
and represents is uncertain:

> From time to time the sailors,
> Traveling the Daugava,
> See two men at midnight
> Battling on the steep shore;
> At that moment, in the ruins of the castle,
> A dim light is reflected,
> Two men locked in battle
> Reach the very shore,
> Until from that shore they finally
> tumble into the water's depths;
> A woeful scream echoes from the castle,
> The light is extinguished—
> That is the Bearslayer that struggles
> With the enemy still,—
> Laimdota looks from the castle,
> And waits for the victory.—
> The sailors believe, that someday
> The Bearslayer will
> Hurl down his enemy alone,
> drowning him in the whirlpool.
> Then a new time will arrive for the nation,
> Then it will be free![4]

In 1986, the Daugava again became the site of a struggle that, while not
itself of epic proportions, was a catalyst in the mass Latvian mobilization
against Soviet power, which ended in the defeat of the Soviet regime in
Latvia and arguably contributed to the collapse of the empire itself, an epic
conclusion to be sure. The struggle began with an article in the progressive
weekly newspaper *Literatūra un māksla* (Literature and art): the piece, written
by the journalist Dainis Īvāns and the engineer Artūrs Snips, was a critique
of Soviet plans to build a hydroelectric station (HES) on the Daugava River
in southeastern Latvia. The writers deplored the lack of expertise and bureaucratic incompetence of those responsible for the project, suggesting that
the damming of the Daugava would flood the surrounding arable land and
forests and worsen pollution problems. The writers also invoked the spirit
of Latvian national consciousness, reiterating the significance of the Daugava
in Latvian culture, and writing that "we cannot allow technicians to deter-

mine single-handedly the future of our common home, our river of destiny."⁵ The protection of the Daugava also finds echoes in the epic of the
Bearslayer, in which the genesis of the river is described: in the story, the
Daugava is dug by the creatures—birds and animals—on the order of the
god of thunder. Though the devil tries to reroute the river into a bottomless
pit, the river is saved by the intervention of thunder, who drives the devil
away.

   In the weeks following the publication of the article on the Daugavpils
HES, letters bearing more than thirty thousand signatures in defense of the
Daugava poured into the offices of *Literatūra un māksla*. The authors of the
piece also received letters, a handful of which Īvāns quoted in his book: "I
think that I could not live if the campaign to stop the construction of the
HES failed. None of my personal problems have hurt as does the fate of the
Daugava," and "I was anguished, I thought that the nation had fully lost its
self-respect and any rights to defend the Daugava. I too am gathering signatures for its protection, though it is sometimes difficult to bear this hopeless
road."⁶ Īvāns and Snips were invited across the country to make their case
against the HES. While the public responded with letters and meetings, the
Latvian Council of Ministers responded by creating a commission to study
the Daugavpils HES project. In January 1987, the commission returned a negative evaluation of the project, questioning its economic and ecological feasi-
bility. In November of the same year, the Union of Socialist Soviet Republics
(USSR) Council of Ministers, noting that the impact on the ecosystem had
been improperly assessed, halted construction of the Daugavpils HES.

   The power of the issue of the Daugavpils HES to mobilize a hitherto
politically passive population in a context that was still far from risk free for
those who challenged the regime highlights one of the paradoxes that colored social change in Latvia. On the one hand, the mobilization around the
issue marked the genesis of an independent and expanded civil society and
the assertion of civic power. On the other hand, it also highlighted the power
of the nation and culture in shaping the civic project, for a significant part
of the mobilizational power of the issue lay in its relationship to precisely
those two elements. That the Daugava was not just a river, but a national
icon, was understood by those who initiated the campaign as well: in a 1991
interview, Īvāns commented: "At the time that I wrote about the building of
the Daugavpils HES, [about] the permanence of the catastrophic consequences [of this], I understood that this problem is political and that it
touched my homeland's economics, history, culture."⁷

   The period of mass opposition in Latvia, which lasted from the mobilization around the Daugavpils HES issue through the achievement of indepen-

dence in August 1991, was a dramatic demonstration of the population's desire for fundamental change. From the protests of thousands of Latvians for the historical recognition of events like the Soviet deportations of 1940, to the Baltic Way, a human chain of pro-independence demonstrators that stretched from Tallinn, Estonia, through Latvia, to Vilnius, Lithuania, the sentiment in favor of a radical break from the Soviet order reached through the populations of these states.

Like the break with the USSR, Latvia's illegal annexation into the Soviet Union in 1940 had, at least initially, taken place with little bloodshed. After two decades of independence, the first period of statehood in its history, in 1939 the USSR presented Latvia with an ultimatum demanding that Latvia's government permit the Soviet army to base troops on Latvian soil, ostensibly for the purpose of mutual protection. Following in the path of Estonia, the Latvian government agreed to the terms. By this time, Russia and Germany had signed the Molotov-Ribbentrop Pact. The agreement contained a secret protocol that provided for the division of the Baltic states (Latvia, Estonia, Lithuania) and Poland between the signatories: Latvia, together with Estonia and later Lithuania, was to go to the USSR, and, in June 1940, it did. In the middle of that month, the Soviet government presented the Baltic states with demands that they submit to the transformation of their governments as stipulated by the Soviets. It must have been relatively clear that the intention of this transformation was to pull the Baltic states decisively into the Soviet sphere: on July 2, 1940, Soviet Foreign Commissar Vyacheslav Molotov indicated to the Lithuanian Minister of Foreign Affairs that he "must finally confront reality and understand that all the small states will have to disappear." Molotov continued that "your Lithuania, and the other Baltic states . . . will have to be incorporated into the glorious family of Soviet Republics. Consequently, you should from now on prepare the Lithuanian people for the introduction of the Soviet system, which will sooner or later prevail in all of Europe."[8]

Fearing that resistance would be futile, particularly with thousands of Soviet troops already on their soil as the result of earlier pacts providing for the USSR's establishment of military bases on Baltic territory, the governments capitulated. In July the new governments, elected from a single slate of Communist candidates by voters compelled to participate in the balloting, requested "admission" to the USSR, decisively ending the independent existence of the Baltics. By this point, rivers of blood poured from the heart of the Baltic states, as the Soviets sought to brutalize the population into submission with arrests, deportations, and killings. By some estimates, during this "year of terror" (baigais gads), which stretched from mid-1940 through

mid-1941, Latvia lost more than 40,000 inhabitants to deportations and exe-
cutions.[9] Toward the end of this period, from June 15 through June 27, 1941,
eight hundred twenty-four cattle wagons packed well beyond capacity with
about 15,600 people left Latvia by rail for the Russian interior.[10]

The end of independent existence in 1940 did not end the widely shared
desire of indigenous populations for self-determination, a desire that remained vital fully half a century after occupation. The ascent of Mikhail
Gorbachev to power in the USSR in 1985 signaled the beginning of a process
that would open the doors to the manifestation of the desire of the Baltic
populations (and others) for fundamental change in the social order.

What happened in this region of the world has been called revolution in
both popular and theoretical literature, though the term is often paired with
adjectives like "velvet" and "gentle." In the Baltics, the events are popularly
called the singing revolutions. Although they had powerful domestic and
international effects like earlier revolutions, these qualifying adjectives suggest that the events that transpired in the Eastern European and Soviet space
were not revolutions in the style of the great revolutions: they were largely
without both the utopias and the violence that permeated earlier revolutions, like those in Russia and France.

Furthermore, there was not a particular ideological model for the construction of society in the wake of the death of the old order, aside from the
often-repeated but vague aspirations for an open society, democracy, markets, civil society, and, more generally, "normality." Part of the challenge of
post-Communist societies, then, was not just to realize the institution of a
new social order, but to construct models of what that social order should
be and to endow that social order with meaning. This point is nicely highlighted by the editors of a history volume on the periods of opposition and
early independence in Latvia:

> In this period [1991–93], Latvia had again become an independent
> country with an internationally recognized government. It turned
> out, however, that Latvian society was not ready to turn this free-
> dom, for which it had fought actively for many years and gained
> suddenly, into goal-oriented practice and constructive politics. In
> other words, when the outer "shell" of independence was to be filled
> with appropriate practical content, it became obvious that the "leg-
> acy" of the Soviet period—the institutional system of government,
> basic social values, political self-understanding, governing skills,
> and political culture—did not meet the needs of the new situation.
> During this time, there was a clash of different, more or less con-

trasting, opinions, and only gradually did views crystallize on the goals toward which the renewed Latvia should move in terms of building the country's system of government, economy, and society and constructing the orientation of its foreign policy.[11]

In this work, I examine the construction of and contestation between different models and notions of social change in Latvia and the endeavors to identify the directions of change in that country in the early post-Communist period. I suggest that, in part, social change can be understood as the product of a widely shared desire for "normality," which, on the one hand, contributed to the construction of a unified opposition and, on the other hand, also underpinned the postindependence contest over how a post-Communist state and society should be imagined and (re)constructed.

Although the focus of the book is on a single country, Latvia, the story related herein is relevant to much of the region, because, indeed, the revolutions of neighboring countries were also marked by the seemingly unrevolutionary zeal for "normality," a marked contrast to the radiant utopias promised to millions across the globe by socialist revolutions. Whereas normality was widely seen across the region as clearly meaning a "not-Soviet" and "not-Communist" state and society, the particular content of this desired "normal" future was murkier and became an object of contestation as Communist states achieved self-determination.

To some, normality entailed the restoration of the social order that existed before states were drawn into the Soviet orbit. To others, the template of normality was not in the past but in the modern West: Western Europe and, to some degree, the United States, represented the desired goal. These two powerful currents both washed together and rushed against each other in politics, debates, and policies across Eastern Europe. The Latvian example, hence, serves to highlight a contest that, although varied in form and content in each individual country, was an important characteristic of Eastern Europe's revolutionary road. The choices for building the future often came down to a contest between new roads and old maps, as states and societies struggled to fill the vessel of "normality" with concrete meaning.

Normality and Transformation

Every epoch produces its own notions and understandings of social change, and the transformation of the East European and post-Soviet space is no exception. In this regard, I suggest that Latvia is a small country with a big story and with theoretical and empirical significance for studies of social change. In Latvia in the middle to late 1980s, a powerful opposition to the Soviet order emerged, based on a widely shared antipathy toward the USSR, a powerful wish for independence, and a desire to return state and society to a state of normality. It was readily apparent that a new order, however, could not be founded on the rejection of the old "abnormal" order, and it was in the wake of the death of this order that the contest over the road to normality was defined. Although many East Europeans broadly agreed about the desirability of fundamental social changes, including, in principle, the institutionalization of democracy and markets, this broad consensus did not mean that they shared the same vision of how these changes were to be realized and how they were to be balanced with other factors like national interests (however defined), social justice, and historical precedents. Radical social change has touched all spheres of social, political, economic, and cultural life in Eastern Europe, though it has been underpinned by the decidedly staid aspiration of normality—this is a central theme of this book. I seek to show how this notion and ambition were implicated in both the unity of the opposition period and the fierce contestation of the post-Communist period.

I hope that this work contributes to the understanding of the transformation of states and societies in Eastern Europe by developing an analytical picture of the multiple and competing logics of change in Latvia in the late Communist and early post-Communist periods. I focus on several particular aspects of social change.

First, I suggest that the notions of "normal" and "normality" can be used to develop greater understanding of the motivations behind and manifestations of transformation in Latvia and, by extension, other societies in Eastern Europe and the post-Soviet space. I offer the theorized concept of normality not as a replacement, but as a supplement to the more widely used explanatory concept of nationalism. Although the concept of nationalism is often associated with changes in this area of the world and is not infrequently used to explain the rise and route of social change, this concept is weakened by its failure to distinguish among different ideas about change, which, while often sharing a common commitment to the "interests of the nation," define those interests in fundamentally different ways. Normality in this context is widely linked (though not always or inevitably) to ideas about the elevation and salvation of the nation, but it retains a flexibility to distinguish between different definitions of "national interest," which otherwise might be conflated, especially where change is explained by factors associated with nationalist sentiment alone. As well, the theorized concept of normality permits the integration of other notions and identities of belonging and difference, which can help to increase the understanding of social change.

Second, I examine the idea that an interesting part of the post-Communist contest between different narratives of transformation has been the battle to define the "natural" order of things in society. That is, part of the process of change has been a struggle between different groups to define and redefine what is socially "natural" and "normal"; ultimately, from a sociological perspective, what comes to be seen as "normal" in any society is socially constructed, and this process of construction is unusually visible in the transformation period. For example, in Chapter 5, on gender and women in the transformation, I outline the process by which a "natural" gender regime (contrasted to the "abnormal" gender regime of the Soviet period) is (re)constructed, and I examine by way of case studies how changes in gender roles and norms are experienced by women in Latvia. Similarly, the political conflict over laws governing citizenship and naturalization in Latvia has been part of a process of debating what a "normal" ethnic or multiethnic society looks like and how it can be realized. In a discussion of post-Communist societies, the sociologist Michael D. Kennedy makes this point:

> The process of identity formation after communism is ironic. Politicians, activists, and analysts emphasize the unprecedented fact of communism's end. At the same time, however, its subjects insist that they want no more "experiments"—they only want what has been proven to succeed. They want to be normal. They wish to be who they "really" are, or who they ought to be. In short, they want to be something inconsistent with the system they recently overturned and the social relations it produced. In this, identity is understood in the most nonsocial of terms: in "natural" terms.[12]

In this book, I examine questions about how the definitions of "who they 'really' are, or who they ought to be" are confronted and contested and how the delegitimation and rejection of the Soviet order open the door to the transformation of the boundaries that define what is "normal" for post-Communist state and society.

Third, this book is a multisited study of the process of social change and "normalization" of state and society in Latvia. Specifically, I look at several important sites of change in post-Communism, including electoral politics, national territories and private property, and gender roles and relations. Whereas at some sites different narratives of normality clash, in others they appear as different but complementary. I show how notions about normality have shaped each site, and, as well, how using normality as a prism through which to look at social change helps point to the bases of conflict and complementarity at each site of transformation.

Reimagining Revolution

Since 1989 and the massive changes that year brought to Eastern Europe, a debate has raged over whether those changes (and those that came later to the Soviet space) constituted a "real" revolution.[13] I suggest that the changes were revolutions, albeit revolutions that redefined rather than reproduced models of modern revolution. Our body of knowledge and theory about revolutions up to the 1980s owed its existence primarily to the great revolutions of the modern era: the French, Russian, and Chinese Revolutions were the foundations of contemporary understandings of the term. But in the Eastern European revolutions of the late 1980s and early 1990s, both the violence and the utopian ideologies inherent in the great revolutions were noticeably absent.

The events in Latvia and neighboring states spanning the middle 1980s to the early 1990s signaled a reinvention of notions of what revolution is and what revolution does. The great revolutions are typically understood to contain a logic of change that embraces a radical break with the past and a progressive rush forward, but there is an alternative and older concept of revolution. This concept derives from the understanding of revolution as a circular movement, like the revolution of a wheel, where the starting point is also the end point. This sense of revolution, although no longer widely associated with the American and French Revolutions, was, to some degree, recognized by revolutionaries of the eighteenth century, who believed they were returning to a "natural" state of freedom and equality of man. In the revolution in Latvia, what emerges is an amalgamation of these two directions of change. Hence, these revolutions combined linearity with circularity, or progress with return. What many of the Eastern European "revolutionaries" sought was not, after all, a radical break with the past, but rather a return to the (pre-Soviet) past. At the same time, many revolutionaries expressed ambitions for progress and modernity that acknowledged the past but did not embrace it in its entirety.

Social Change and Common Sense

Reasonably, we might ask how these imperatives of return and progress, which seem on the surface contradictory, were amalgamated in the anti-

Soviet opposition. I suggest that their amalgamation rested to a large degree on a notion of fundamental change that revolved around the idea and ideal of "normality" and around visions, even if they were not all the same, of a "normal" life. The mobilizational power of this notion was grounded in a belief, widely shared by indigenous populations in Latvia and the other Baltic countries, that the Soviet period was not normal. Not only was the regime illegal and illegitimate, but it was a fundamental deviation from what was perceived to be the normal course of national, state, social, and economic development.

Latvian society, like the societies of other East European states, was powerfully affected by the belief that the Soviet system was both alien and unnatural, because it had been brutally imposed by an outside force and embraced political, social, and cultural traditions widely held to conflict with the national "way of life." Propaganda and the economic, political, social, and environmental projects undertaken in the early decades of Soviet Communism suggest that Soviet revolutionaries *themselves* rejected normality and the bourgeois world it represented.[14] They aspired to a utopia that would surpass normality. Normality was a barrier to achievement rather than a goal, because it represented a world doomed in Marx's theory to failure. In the area of economics, for example, the elevation of the *Stakhanovite*, the shock worker, to icon status perpetuated the idea that extraordinary feats could be "ordinary" in the Soviet Union. Similarly, the lofty goal of surpassing the progress of the capitalist countries in an impossibly short time was hailed as an achievable task.

Environmental analogies to the commitment to clear the hurdles of normality are also telling. One of Josef Stalin's projects, the White Sea–Baltic Sea Canal, focused on the linkage of the two bodies of water through the creation of a passage through the miles of rock and ice between them. The project was considered to be extraordinary not only because its construction, without the help of all but the most elementary technology, seemed a maddening feat, but also because it was given a twenty-month deadline. In reference to the seemingly impossible time frame of the project, Aleksandr Solzhenitsyn quoted the authors of a book on the project as writing: "These are not the tempos of noxious European-American capitalism, these are socialist tempos!"[15] Stephen Hanson, in fact, pointed out that Leninism contained a "promise to overcome ordinary time."[16]

Unlike the Russian Revolution, the anti-Soviet revolution in Eastern Europe was born of opposition to a present dystopia rather than embrace of a future utopia. Nicolae Harsanyi and Michael D. Kennedy highlighted this point with their contention that "as communism helped wipe out alternative socialisms, the dystopia of real existing socialism helped destroy the appeal of utopia itself."[17] Hence, the quality of the Eastern European revolution was antiutopian, as the desired outcome was defined in terms of normality rather than radicalism. In fact, the revolution was itself, in a sense, antirevolutionary, because as late as 1987, the Soviet order continued to be presented in the parlance of revolution: for example, Gorbachev's address on November 2, 1987, was called "October and Perestroika: The Revolution Continues." Whereas revolution in that sense was meant to advance the utopias of Soviet Communism, the antirevolutionary revolution strove toward normality.

The sociologist Ann Swidler defined "common sense" as "the set of assumptions so unselfconscious as to seem a natural, transparent, undeniable part of the structure of the world." She also suggested that there was a "continuum from ideology to tradition to common sense."[18] In Soviet Latvia, however, there was a break between the ideology of Soviet state Communism and the "common sense" about that ideology and state among large segments of the Latvian population. Rather than ideology settling into common sense, it ran up against it. In Soviet Latvia, there was a potent sense that the Soviet order was not normal, that it was illegitimate, illegal, artificially imposed, and contrary to the national "way of life." Though this sentiment could not be publicly articulated until Gorbachev's glasnost opened the doors to freer speech without dangerous penalties, it was put forth in subtle ways before Gorbachev and in more direct language and action after.

There were few political dissidents in Soviet Latvia: the risks of dissent, though they decreased after the death of Stalin, were substantial. Many people voiced their feelings about the Soviet regime in small acts of resistance, retreat into private life, or jokes about the regime shared between close friends, rather than in overt dissent. Folk dancing has long been a part of ethnic Latvian tradition and, since the nineteenth century, part of a tradition of large song festivals. In the Soviet period, Latvian folk dances were mixed with elements of other dance traditions such as ballet. These came to be called, disparagingly, "fake braid dances," a reference to the "authentic" braids associated with Latvian girls and, consequently, with the authentic folk dances of Latvians.

In the sphere of political dissent, the Soviet order was sometimes attacked directly: in a letter written anonymously by twenty-six "Young Communists" in the early 1980s, the writers asserted that Communists "promised nations and individuals freedom, brotherhood, equality, humanity, and full democracy, but in reality there has been only inequality, caprice, and coercion," and "the foundations of the USSR [are]: lying, stealing, drunkenness."[19]

In the period of glasnost, criticism of the Soviet order became more apparent. During the Chautauqua Conference of American and Soviet delegates in Jūrmala, Latvia, in 1986, some Latvians approached delegates from the United States and called out such comments as "We are waiting for freedom, only you can help." Warned by a delegate in one instance of the potential consequences of such outbursts, the speaker responded that "we live in prison anyway."[20]

The Soviet-era changes in Latvia's demographic composition were also part of a larger discourse on the abnormality of the existing situation: in a 1988 letter from the oppositional Latvia's *Latvijas Nacionālā neatkarības kustība* (National Independence Movement, or LNNK) to the Latvian Soviet Socialist Republic (LSSR) Ministers' Cabinet, "central institutions" of the USSR, and other oppositional organizations, the LNNK highlighted the "abnormal" ethnic balance in Latvia, where Latvians were close to falling below 50 percent of the population.[21] The widely shared sense that the Soviet-era mass migrations from other republics had wrought an "abnormal" and dangerous ethnic imbalance became a potent issue in the mobilization against Soviet power. A 1986 letter from the nascent human rights group Helsinki 86 to the United Nations also addressed this issue and more:

> [The state of Latvians] is catastrophic. In the span of a few decades we have become just half of our country's population. In large cities, just a third. . . .Our language is everywhere ignored and laughed at. . . . Our housing is in a catastrophic state. . . . Russians arrive uninvited and shortly receive the best housing. Latvians must live crowded into old housing, in circumstances without dignity. . . . When was there a referendum held in which Latvians gave up their language, their army, [and] their rights to freely interact with all the nations of the world?[22]

The vision of normality that was articulated in the period of opposition was the antithesis of all that was associated with the Soviet regime: instead of oppression, there would be freedom; in place of the Party, there would be parties; instead of the arcane and closed world of Soviet decision making, the public would have a voice, and decision making would be transparent; in the books of history, truth and authenticity would replace lies and omissions; where black soot rose from towering industrial smokestacks, cows would graze in green pastures. These stark dichotomies were articulated as part and parcel of a process of boundary making between the opposition and the Soviet regime against which it stood.

The sociologist William Sewell has suggested that ideological structures exist not in any single actor, but rather in the collectivity, and therefore they contain the contradictions inherent there.[23] Sewell's assertion is relevant to this case because collective action in Eastern Europe was loosely bound around the pursuit of a "normal" state. Normality was defined largely in opposition to the Soviet order and hence could accommodate these contradictions without undermining unity.

The body of "stories" on which the division between the opposition in Latvia and the Soviet regime was based can be imagined as a scheme of opposites, whereby the Soviet order was variously represented by the opposition as (to use some of the local parlance) unnatural, deceptive, uncultured, uncivilized, illegitimate, polluting, murderous, and abnormal. This narrative constructed affinity between Latvians, on the one hand, and a potent estrangement from the Soviet order, on the other. In the period of opposition, this was the defining social boundary, drawn first on the shores of the Daugava in 1986, which enabled mobilization of the population against the Soviet regime. Dainis Īvāns wrote that "the Daugava was like a soul, the murmuring of which only now, in spite of the dams, mud, and pools of stagnation, we began to hear. The Daugava was like a shield. The Daugava became a boundary between US and THEM."[24]

Though the opposition realized an important part of the aspiration for normality with the achievement of full independence in August 1991, much remained undone. The old order was gone, but a new, "normal" one remained to be (re)constructed. In the following section, I elaborate further the idea that the post-Communist period saw the development of a contest between different narratives of change. That is, although there was loose consensus around the notion that social change and "normality" were desirable, there was less agreement about how change should look, what models of change should be followed, and how "normality" was to be defined. I briefly introduce four different narratives of and about change in the early post-Communist period in Latvia.

Ideal Types of Social Change

The ideal type is a methodological device, put forth by the sociologist Max Weber, which facilitates the analysis of historical phenomena. Ideal types are not perfect representations of the phenomena to which they refer, but they highlight particular illuminating aspects of a given phenomenon. For the analysis at hand, I posit four ideal types (see Table 1.1). These types, though born of the "commonsense" invocations and symbols that I iterated

Table 1.1   Narratives of normality in post-Communism

	Revolutionary	Conservative
Progress	Spatial/Modern West	Evolutionary/Immediate Past
Return	Temporal/Distant Past	Reactionary/Immediate Past

earlier, are my conceptual creations: they are devices intended to help clarify the complexities of social change. I use these ideal types to describe narrative positions and groups that embrace these particular narratives. These narratives have been elaborated and elevated in post-Communism and offer different foci, legitimating stories, and prescriptions for the (re)-construction of normality.

The ideal types that I discuss throughout the book all contain stories about the past as well as the present and future. Each offers a sense of Latvia's place in a larger historical and cultural context, and each understands change in terms of this context. Whereas the narratives that dominate and define the periods of opposition and post-Communism are rather different, they share through this period a common orientation toward normality, toward the transformation of a social world perceived to be abnormal in some way.

Spatial normality is the term I use to describe a narrative orientation that takes as its primary model of transformation the modern West.[25] The term *spatial* is intended to represent the location of this narrative's core template of transformation, which is a *place in space:* the West, particularly Western Europe. Notions of normality are tightly bound to the notions of prosperity and security that these modernizers associate with Europe and Europeanness: in a 1996 speech to Parliament, then-Prime Minister Valdis Birkavs, a member of the Latvia's Way party, remarked that "Europe to us is a symbol of the desired feeling of security and standards of welfare." There is no need to construct a revolutionary utopia because the future already exists, and it is, as Jan Gross put it, only an overnight train ride away.[26]

The way to normality is through and to Europe, and the means to get there is to rush into the arms of European institutions: those that seemingly guarantee prosperity (like the European Union) and those that seemingly guarantee security (like the North Atlantic Treaty Organization). Here, economics, particularly the construction of modern capitalism, is a key instrument for achieving normality. This narrative, as well as identifying particular goals, also signals particular dangers in the present and future. Like the temporal narrative (which I describe below), it perceives a potential danger from its Russian neighbor, but unlike that narrative, it also recognizes a danger in the nonintegration of and disharmony with non-Latvians (particularly Russians) in Latvia.

Temporal normality denotes the direction of change typically found among the most nationalistic elements in Latvia. I use this label because this narrative's template of transformation is, in a sense, a *place in time:* the interwar period. In this ideal type, the focus is not on modernization but on restoration and re-creation of the institutions, norms, and values of the interwar period of independence. Change, hence, is a matter of consciously re-creating a social context that was wrought at a previous time by a particular conjuncture of agency and historical circumstance. If prosperity and security are the watchwords of spatial normality, then Latvianness and tradition are the keys to temporal normality. Normality, in other words, is to be found in the past, and that normality is based on the assertion of Latvianness and traditional social organization and authenticity, which were undermined by the Soviet experience.

The temporal ideal type is concerned with economics, though that too is more typically linked to the interests of the primary nation rather than prosperity in a more general sense: there has been some trepidation about full privatization and open markets among some political organizations in this category because of their concern with the well-being of, among others, farmers and pensioners, segments of the population dominated by ethnic Latvians. In terms of the identification of danger in the present and future of Latvia, this narrative posits danger in integration rather than nonintegration of minorities: because the minority population is nearly as large as the Latvian population, the concern is that Latvians rather than non-Latvians will slip into the new cultural and language context. As well, although there is interest in "joining" Europe, there is strong concern about following European prescriptions for change, which are perceived to be unfavorable to the interests of the primary nation.

The spatial and temporal ideal types clearly have different emphases, but they share important characteristics as well. First, they operate on a common assumption that there is a transformation imperative across the fields of politics, economics, and social life. Both narratives highlight the discontinuity of post-Communism with Communism: change is perceived as fundamentally revolutionary rather than evolutionary in that the "remnants" *(atliekas)* of the Communist past are to be discarded in the dustbin of history rather than retained as a basis for transformation.

Second, in post-Communist politics, nationalism is more a matter of degree than a distinct political option. Individual rights and freedoms are clearly present in these visions of democracy, but the principle of individual emancipation does not stand alone. Rather, the state extends civic guarantees of individual rights and liberties, but it is also widely seen as the guarantor of national survival. Hence, the state theoretically exists to ensure group rights, most notably those of the primary nation. This concern has been present in both dominant narratives though, again, to varying degrees.

Third, there is some shared sense of continuity with the interwar state in the temporal and spatial narratives. This is apparent in a number of ways, including the fact that independent Latvia provides a reference point in both: the temporal narrative has spoken for the renewal of the *First Republic of Latvia,* and the spatial narrative has supported the construction of the *Second Republic of Latvia.* I suggest that collective memory as a model *of* normality is shared between the spatial and temporal ideal types. Collective memory as a model *for* normality (that is, for its reconstruction), however, is embraced primarily by the temporal narrative.

Beyond these commonalties, I suggest that the two dominant ideal types are alternatives in a category of "revolutionary" narratives. Both were born of and draw on the revolution that toppled the Soviet regime, and both subscribe to a revolutionary notion that there must be a radical break with the Soviet past.

A third ideal type has been evident in the contest over change as well, though this one can be more accurately characterized as an "evolutionary" narrative. This is so because, rather than embracing a radical break from the Soviet past, this narrative has highlighted an evolutionary transformation of Soviet structures like the socialist economy and citizenship regime.

I label this ideal type *evolutionary.* This term is used to connote a narrative that is important though clearly not dominant in the early post-Communist period. Unlike the temporal ideal type, which asserts continuity with a relatively distant past, the evolutionary ideal type has embraced continuity with the immediate past. The goals of political organizations in this category have been more evolutionary than revolutionary: although these organizations have not rejected change, it has commonly been seen as evolving from recent history rather than turning away from that legacy. The evolutionary quality of this narrative is most apparent in the social and economic fields: it rejects changes in social and political status wrought by a new citizenship structure that privileges citizens of the interwar state and their descendants. Furthermore, this narrative is critical of the changes in economic status that have come with the opening of the markets and the rapid rise of the power of private capital.

The evolutionary ideal type highlights an imperative of preservation in terms of the political power of non-Latvians (through extension of citizenship without conditions to all inhabitants) and economic security of working people (primarily through redistributive economic mechanisms). The evolutionary ideal type posits danger in the nonintegration of Latvia's minorities, though it is less concerned with nonintegration into the common European home; it seeks to strengthen markets and relations in the East at least as much as in the West. In contrast to the ideal-typical spatial and temporal narratives, the evolutionary narrative is nearly invisible outside the political field, largely because of its weakness in that field.

In all these ideal types, there is broad agreement on several points relating to the tasks at hand. First, all recognize an economic imperative and accept some degree of marketization and privatization as necessary for improving the lot and the prospects of the state and population. Second, all accept basic parliamentary democracy as the basis of the post-Communist political process in Latvia, though the extension of franchise and the basis of constitutionality, among other things, are contested.

The final ideal type in the scheme is the *reactionary* narrative, which, although not readily apparent in Latvia in the initial period of post-Communism (which is covered by this work), is visible in some other post-Communist states like Russia and Ukraine. The reactionary ideal type is concerned with the legacy of the immediate past, though it is a preservationist rather than evolutionary narrative. In common with the temporal type, it highlights return, but its proponents (often unreformed Communists or those hit hardest by post-Communism's dislocations) advocate a return to the immediate past. In Russia, this has translated to a call for the restoration of the Soviet Union, its territory and its political, economic, and social structures. In Belarus, there have been political gestures toward reunification with Russia, and in Ukraine, several candidates in the 1999 presidential race made a similar call. Even in non-Slavic areas of the former Soviet Union, nostalgia for the immediate past has a powerful pull. It is worth noting in this study not only because it extends the scheme of ideal types beyond the frontiers of Latvia, but because Latvia, as a former Soviet republic with a large Russian population, is potentially affected by the power and influence of this narrative in neighboring states and among segments of its own population, particularly the large contingent of retired Soviet army officers.

Overview of Chapters

The following chapters are dedicated to the examination of contests over the direction and quality of transformation at different sites of change. The analysis of different sites permits a study of the character and evolution of social change in a comparative manner. This study shows that despite the broad unity in opposition to the Soviet order, the direction of change after the collapse of that order, far from being clear, was contested. More important, the study highlights the fact that no single logic of change dominated the early years of transformation. The different sites of change lend themselves to a comparison that focuses in particular on the degree to which narrative differences are manifested in conflict or complementarity and ways the different definitions of normality shape actions in each field.

In Chapter 2, which focuses on the period of opposition, I highlight the mobilization of ordinary people unsatisfied with the Soviet order and examine the process by which "personal troubles" were translated into "public issues" through the construction of a narrative that became a basis for opposition to the extant order.[27] This portion of the work provides a basis for understanding the development and centrality of notions about normality and highlights the way that these notions operated as critical unifiers as the opposition confronted the Soviet regime. The unity underpinned by the oppositional vision of "normality," as described in later chapters, disintegrates in the very late Communist and early post-Communist periods, and normality becomes a site of contest over social change.

In Chapter 3, I introduce the first site of post-Communist change: electoral politics. The political field is key to this study because it represents the central site from which post-Communist social change has emanated: the character and direction of change have been strongly determined by legislative actions that both preceded and followed the first post-Communist elections of 1993. The actions of the legislature have, as I show, been colored by the different narratives embraced and constructed by political organizations in the Parliament.

In Chapter 4, I focus on national places and spaces and the way in which these have been part of the process of social change. The process of (re)constructing normality is not just a process of changing political and economic structures; it is also a process of transforming—rendering "normal"—the symbolic landscape. The particular dimensions of the transformation of space and place also represent aspects of the process of normalization that evoke different levels of contest and conflict and involve different sets of agents. In this chapter, I take up the particular issues of the changing of street names in the capital city of Riga, the dispute with neighboring Russia over the shared border, and the policy of rural property restitution to prewar owners in Latvia.

The changes in the post-Soviet space include some fundamental alterations in the gender regimes of those countries, a topic I explore in Chapter 5. This field of change offers a picture somewhat different from those of politics and place and space. Although the direction of change in, for example, the political field, is intensely contested, this field has been the site of a marginalization of women that derives from all leading narratives and is scarcely the object of contest, not only because it has generated less public interest than other fields, but also because of a complementarity of narratives not found elsewhere.

The (re)creation of normality in social life has entailed the (re)creation of a gender regime that is profoundly influenced by the emergence of the imperatives of both traditionalization (the reinstitution of pre-Soviet gender norms and roles) and modernization (the institutionalization of modernity in, most prominently, the marketplace). The resulting processes of domestication on the one hand and commodification on the other affect the opportunities and roles available to women in post-Communism, an argument that I elaborate by using case studies of social welfare and prostitution in post-Communist Latvia.

The Road to the Future

The Bearslayer of Pumpurs and Rainis is a hero of epic proportions, whose role is to protect and sacrifice for the nation. He does not, however, do this alone, and, as the Bearslayer declares near the end of *Fire and Night,*

> The life of the nation is by thousands of years longer
> than the short life of even the greatest hero,
> After me there will be others, who will complete the journey.

In late-twentieth-century Latvia, the journey of the nation led away from Soviet Communism, but the road beyond that turn was twisted and uncertain. Answers to the questions of who would complete this journey and where it would lead state and society were not readily apparent in a context where utopia was eschewed in favor of normality and normality was defined with a variety of models. In this work, I follow the maps of and for change drawn by different actors seeking to define Latvia's journey at the dawn of independent statehood. I consider, to the extent possible in a still rapidly changing context, where those roads have led and could still lead.

From Opposition to Independence: Social Movements in Latvia, 1986–1991

Prior to 1987, independent mass demonstrations in the Soviet Socialist Republic of Latvia, indeed, in the entire Union of Soviet Socialist Republics, were unheard of. Not only were they strictly forbidden by Soviet authorities, but the fear wrought by decades of repression seemed to make oppositional collective action very unlikely. Although pockets of resistance and individual dissident efforts dotted the Soviet historical map, the masses were docile, going to the streets only in response to compulsory parades and marches designed to commemorate holidays like May Day and Great October Revolution Day. In 1986, a policy of greater openness in society, glasnost, was initiated by the new General Secretary of the Communist Party of the USSR, Mikhail Gorbachev. Among the changes brought about by glasnost was an increased tolerance by authorities of open expression in society, though this too was limited, as the policy was intended to strengthen rather than weaken the Union. The unprecedented mass social movements that emerged in the era of glasnost combined the legacies of the past and an uncertain course into the region's future, successfully challenging the Soviet state in pursuit of independence and hastening the demise of the world's last great empire.

Much has been written on the social movements of this period, and my intention is not to duplicate the good historical work that has been done. Rather, in this chapter I present an analysis of how the opposition period, which dated from 1986 through summer 1991, was implicated in the construction of a potent narrative boundary between the anti-Soviet opposition and the Soviet regime. I show how oppositional social movements in Latvia helped to instantiate a boundary drawn around notions that labeled as abnormal (or, by the same token, illegitimate, uncultured, uncivilized, unnatural) the Soviet order and represented themselves as the normal (or, again, legitimate, cultured, civilized, natural) alternative to this. This sense continues to color much of the understanding of the period. For example, the editors of a recent Latvian book on the subject wrote in their preface that the "Latvian national [opposition] movement, that led to the renewal of Latvia's statehood, can be understood in the first instance as a *natural* answer to the model of society offered by the Soviet occupation regime"[1] (italics added). The definitions and models of normality were to be contested openly in post-Communism, but the opposition presented a unified front against the Soviet order, sharing a common rejection of the regime, its past, and its practices.

Identity and Solidarity

I first examine the construction of collective identities and solidarity of an oppositional nature under the unfavorable conditions of authoritarianism. In this section I offer a brief look at the situation in Latvia and of Latvians in the mid-1980s, at the dawn of the opposition period. I link the situation at that time to the construction and dissemination of a particular oppositional narrative that found broad resonance in the community and fostered activism, despite the fact that there was no history of mass resistance in the fifty years since Soviet occupation began, and surveillance of the population by security forces intent on rooting out independent action and initiative was still stringent.

Independent action in Latvia before the Gorbachev period was rare. Although a few dissenters, known more often in the West than locally, spoke against the regime and in favor of democracy and independence, their num-

2   Full view of the Freedom Monument with the inscription "For Fatherland and Freedom"

bers were few, and many spent considerable time in prisons or camps in the Russian interior. During the late 1970s, a small independent folklore movement developed in Latvia. It was initiated by a group of individuals concerned that Latvia's cultural heritage was being forgotten. Whereas national song festivals occurred during the Soviet period, they reflected a "Sovietized" culture: songs about the nation or the national past were purged from the programs, the music of other Soviet republics was included, and traditional Latvian folk dances were mixed with elements of ballet. The folklore movement sought to bring back traditional culture in unofficial gatherings and programs.

The activities of the folklorists represented the construction of small autonomous spaces, but they were limited in both participation and scope. In addition, the early 1980s and General Secretary Yuri Andropov's short-lived tenure brought the reassertion of a repressive climate that saw new dissident arrests and harsher punishments for political transgressions. The transition, then, of a politically passive population into a mass movement for change in the mid- to late 1980s represented a fundamental transformation of the public sphere.

An important aspect of the construction of collective identity and initiation of collective action was linked to the formation and dissemination of a narrative that constructed a boundary between, as Dainis Īvāns wrote, US and THEM, with the contention that the Soviet order was, across a broad variety of spheres, abnormal, and that the opposition offered an alternative. The narrative was a story constructed and told at various sites, which I elaborate below. It created connections between sites of discontent to construct a larger story of how the Soviet order represented abnormality, incivility, pollution of land and culture, deception, and so on.

Although the Soviet narrative of history, a story developed to legitimate and support the power of the Soviet regime in Latvia, dominated the public sphere, an alternative narrative was constructed outside the public realm, which relied heavily on the individual memories of Latvians and others, memories that collided with official accounts of history. This alternative narrative of history deviated from the dominant public narrative about socialist progress and prosperity, economic and social justice, and fraternal friendship and equality of the various Soviet nationalities and nations. The alternative narrative appropriated events and rendered them as episodes in a larger story about the abnormality of the Soviet order. It also allowed the marriage of macroevents—such as the occupation of Latvia in 1940 and the mass deportations of civilians to Siberia—and microevents—such as being forced to use the Russian language instead of Latvian for a public transaction or waiting for over a decade to be assigned a family apartment—to form a common story that, although widely known, began to be told in the public sphere only in 1986.

The powerful alternative narrative that emerged in the public sphere around this time also highlighted the issue of national survival and engendered and reinforced what the historian Juris Dreifelds called a " 'now or never' mentality," exemplified by the Latvian writer Jānis Peters's claim that if the opposition were to fail as it did in 1959 (when "national Communists" tried to "Latvianize" the republic's government), then "we will not rise a second time."[2] The telling and retelling of the alternative narrative in the public sphere helped to galvanize anti-Soviet opposition. By allowing the telling of the story, glasnost opened the door for those who identified with the story to mobilize with a reasonable expectation of solidarity, even under conditions that precluded formal organization of opposition sympathizers and activists.

Also important in the mobilization of a hitherto politically passive public was the politicization of identities. This process was an important aspect of public mobilization, which was activated by the iteration of alternative narratives of history and the politicization of the quiescent masses. Below, I briefly consider three dimensions of identity politicization that took place through the vehicles of the cultural sphere, the secondary economy, and Soviet political life.

In the cultural landscape of Soviet Latvia, an emergent politicized collective identity that could transcend loose ethnic ties was forged. A loose ethnic identity was clearly present throughout the Soviet period. As Soviet occupation had not yet seen the passing of the generations that recalled independence and that had a national identity engrained by the experience, a strong Latvian identity was still present in most families with a Latvian background. The use of the Latvian language in the private sphere among friends and family and the private celebration of Latvian holidays like the summer solstice (public celebration was forbidden) underpinned tightly bound small-scale networks and a loose large-scale web of ethnic kin. It was also in the private sphere that dissatisfaction with the regime was expressed, as the Latvian historian Taurens has suggested, through "personal lifestyle [e.g., decorative art, family traditions], political apathy, a retreat in to private life, or alcohol abuse."[3]

Activity in the cultural sphere straddled the line between public and private; it was state regulated, but it provided a vehicle for Latvian cultural traditions like folk dancing (albeit sometimes "diluted" by the Soviets) and for the subtle, between-the-lines expression of grievances by writers, poets, and artists in official publications such as *Literatūra un māksla* (Literature and art). By the early and mid-1980s, small but significant islands of autonomy were appearing in the cultural sphere. Although independent political activity of any kind was still severely circumscribed, the cultural landscape was beginning to shift in the direction of more open expression of grievances. Popular music began to embrace themes that highlighted grievances widely shared by Latvians. The reach of this music was broad, because much of it received public air play. For example, in 1986, a song called *Dzimtā valoda* (Mother tongue; literally, language of birth) by the rock group "Līvi" was hugely popular, in the words of one Latvian, "a national anthem" of the time. The song reflected a shared concern that the Latvian language was losing ground in Latvia and highlighted a primal tie between language and life: "The language of my birth is my mother," went the refrain. That the song spoke to public grievances and against the regime was confirmed when, in early 1987, the Latvian Communist Party Central Committee issued a statement that condemned the song's election as the most popular song of 1986.[4] Together with earlier songs, like Raimonds Pauls's *Vēl ir laiks* (There is still time), a seasonal allegory of Latvians' experience under Soviet occupation that was widely known but was not permitted public play, this music constituted a center that linked like-minded listeners through common experience and a shared grievance frame.

Youth culture, in particular, reflected the turn toward not just increased autonomy, but resistance. Rock music and art were among the most powerful vehicles of identity politicization. The spring Art Days of 1987, for example, provided an official forum for artistic endeavors that made political as well as cultural statements. Students at the Art Academy in Riga organized a "live" artistic exhibit that featured students lying in the academy yard, their heads and torsos covered and caged, their legs jutting out from the cages and propped on wooden boards, a readable metaphor for the stifling of free expression.[5] Rock music too had become both a messenger and symbol of resistance, especially in the wake of a rock concert by the group "Pērkons" in the city of Ogre in 1985. After the concert, several youths demolished the inside of a passenger train. As a result, the Latvian youths received unusually severe sentences: the harshest was three years in a maximum-security work colony. The rock group was subsequently disbanded as well. A punk subculture also appeared in the 1980s, which embraced the slogan "Where German tanks failed, Riga's punks will prevail." The implication was that they would drive the Soviets from Latvia, as the German army had failed to do during the Second World War.

The countries of the Soviet bloc were well known for their extensive secondary economies in which goods and information exchanged hands outside the boundaries of the official and legal command economy. The existence of these secondary markets was relevant not only for acquisition but also for maintaining and establishing personal ties. Steven Pfaff wrote on East Germany that "tightly knit networks nurture collective identities and solidarity, provide informal organization and contacts, and supply information otherwise unavailable to individuals. These networks take on particular importance in Communist societies . . . because in addition to constriction of social and political opportunities, chronic shortages and economic shortfalls make informal relationships the 'key to the provision of many goods and services.' "[6]

I take this notion as the starting point of my second proposition on the politicization of identity, but I qualify and elaborate it below. Notably, although these practical links were the "key to the provision of many goods and services," they may have, but did not necessarily, as Pfaff suggested, "nurture collective identities and solidarities." Rather than building solidarity, the constant need for barter and bribery may have increased feelings of alienation and bitterness and a sense that the situation was, by modern standards, abnormal. After all, the same second-economy mechanism that saw to the provision of a needed garden hose or a desired pair of panty hose also underpinned public officials' demanding gifts for services rendered and inhabitants being forced into the secondary market in search of goods that should have been available in the primary market.

On the other hand, *some* private exchange was solidarity generating, though this often sprang from an exchange of knowledge or information rather than just goods or services, especially where the knowledge was proscribed, as of Latvian history. An example of this is the private book market that sprang up at the Čiekurkalns farmers' market in Riga in 1987. The Latvian author Andris Kolbergs described the market as follows:

> For some reason, [marketers] began to trade in used shoes and clothing. But this wasn't enough for private initiative, and [people] began to bring from their basements and attics hidden pre-war books and magazines for sale. That, which according to documents, would have been taken from the libraries and burned [after Soviet occupation], which should not even have existed [was for sale]. Suddenly, my generation was given back the historical and factual materials whose existence had been denied in the school books. When [the authorities] discovered [the market], it was shut down, but spilled water cannot be gathered up again, and booksellers al-

ready knew one another and agreed upon trades, sales, and purchases among themselves.[7]

In a system where "knowing" outside the boundaries of state-approved teachings was a form of resistance, knowledge links between friends and families and even strangers could generate solidarity. The same mechanism that pitted knowledge against power also politicized the identities of those who sought and held that knowledge, by making "knowing" (for example, Latvian history) a political act.

The third point about the politicization of identities and the generation of social solidarity concerns Latvians' lack of loyalty to the regime and the lack of regime legitimacy among Latvians. In a political autobiography, Eduards Berklavs, a former Communist purged from party and position for "nationalism" in the 1950s, published a letter written in the early 1980s and signed by twenty-six "Young Communist [organization] members and Soviet workers" (though, the letter added, it "would be signed by a hundred million or more Soviet citizens if we were free to gather their signatures"). The letter begins with the assertion that "the foundations of the USSR [are]: lying, stealing, drunkenness" and continues as follows:

> But what can one do if, even with the best of intentions, one cannot find any sphere which is not built on lies and deception; if in the USSR nearly everyone steals who has something to steal, and if everyday by the liquor stores, even hours before they open, there stand tens or even hundreds of people, though there is plenty of alcohol in the shop. This disease is gradually taking over Latvia as well. That is a tragedy, that is the destruction of the nation.
>
> From whence comes this epidemic [of lying]? Where did it start? It started in Moscow, from Lenin himself, from the initiation of the communist party. They promised nations and individuals freedom, brotherhood, equality, humanity and full democracy, but in reality there have been only inequality, caprice, and coercion.[8]

The dearth of loyalty to and legitimacy of the regime can be linked to several aspects of Soviet political life and political order. Notably, there was the clash between history as it was taught, represented, and celebrated by the Soviet regime and history as it existed in the living memory of those who had experienced the interwar period of independence, World War II, and the occupation of Latvia. The history of Latvia's forcible incorporation into the Soviet Union became the story of the fulfillment of the "people's wishes"[9] and the "mandate" of 97.6 percent received in a (compulsory) vote for a new Parliament (from a single Soviet-selected list). Just as narratives that connect and make sense of experiences build collective identities, narratives that run counter to lived experience can undermine collective identity (like a Soviet collective identity) and the legitimacy of the "storyteller" and, possibly, can build links between those whose experiences tell a different "story."

Another aspect of life undermining Soviet legitimacy in Soviet Latvia can be linked to Burawoy and Lukacs's observation about socialist "painting rituals" in Hungary. They wrote: "Precisely because workers have to act out the virtues of socialism, they become conscious of its failings. In painting socialism as just and rational they become critical of its irrationality and injustice. The necessity of an ideology to justify class domination leads to a critique of state socialism for failing to live up to its ideals."[10] This observation highlights how, in forcing the workers of Hungary to participate in rituals proclaiming the system to be just, they were made increasingly conscious of its injustice. Latvia offers a similar case, perhaps one with even more acute contradictions. As in Burawoy and Lukacs's case, claims about the superior level of prosperity and justice highlighted rather than obscured the absence of a genuine level of either in Latvia. Because public criticism of the state was prohibited, private griping about the conditions of daily life became a political act as well.

Finally, public declarations and rituals proclaiming the brotherhood of nations in the Soviet Union were props on the stage of a reality that belied such claims. The political scientist Rasma Kārkliņš noted that in the USSR there was "an active publication campaign depicting the harmony between nations, their unbreakable friendship, and the great achievements brought about by their fraternal union. . . . In contrast to the great mass of propagandistic material, uncensored reports about the quality of ethnic relations [were] scarce."[11] Among the facts that undermined claims of equality and brotherhood among ethnic groups in the USSR were the following: preferential treatment for Russian migrants from other parts of the Soviet Union in receiving new apartments while Latvians waited as long as two decades; diminishing use of the Latvian language in places of work and government business; insults directed by Russians toward those who used Latvian in public places; and a climate of growing hostility between Latvians and Russians.

The last point is especially salient. Just before the time of mass protest action, the ethnic climate had worsened to the point that it was not unusual to see graffiti in public places that read *Kazhdij ubitij latish—odno posazhenoje derevo* (Every dead Latvian—[like] one planted tree; the implied meaning is that the city is improved by planting a tree and, as well, by killing a Latvian) or *Ruskim Riigu, gansam figu* (Riga for Russians, nothing for Latvian fascists).[12] Violence had also grown, but the local militia typically took little action against youthful perpetrators. An important event in this respect was the beating of Latvian high school students by Russian teenagers in April 1987. Kolbergs, who investigated the event, not reported in the official media, wrote the following:

> Riga's High School for the Practical Arts . . . rented the "Ziemeļ-blāzma" hall [for a school dance]. The evening was closed [to out-siders], the dance would have come off fine, but a group of youths had gathered around the hall. As the youths were armed with sticks and other weapons, and as they were shouting "Kill Latvians; kill fascists!" and tried to break into the building, and those that did tried to provoke fights, no one thought that they had peace on their minds, and the militia suggested that the dance end early, and orga-nizers agreed. At that time, some of the [students at the dance] left for home. And then it became clear that the bellicose youths were not just in the hall yard, but that they were well organized, that they were following shouted army-like commands, that groups of youths were stationed throughout surrounding streets and were blocking every route to the bus and train stops. They attacked [the Latvian students] in large groups. . . . Two hundred youths [accord-ing to official estimates] with sticks, metal pipes, belts with heavy buckles, and other weapons jumped on the school kids just because they were Latvian. That this is the only reason was later confirmed by the attackers themselves.[13]

Youths taken into custody at the scene were not prosecuted despite the serious injuries some victims had suffered. This was a notable contrast to the harsh punishment received by the three Latvian youths for demolishing a train car following the 1985 Pērkons concert.

Incidents like this were significant because they increased both resent-ment against the Soviet regime and Russian domination and solidarity in the face of adversity, especially among young people. Several days after the incident at the dance hall, around five hundred Latvian youths held a spontaneous demonstration in the heart of Riga, "possibly intended to show their strength to the militia and their Russian peers." They shouted slogans like "Free, free Latvia" and "Long live Latvia" as they ran through the streets of Riga. As one of the very first public demonstrations of this period, this attracted (unlike the beatings) press attention, and the newspaper *Rīgas balss* (Riga's voice) carried a piece on the "disorders."[14]

Avenues for the politicization of identities and the construction and consolidation of Latvian solidarity against the Soviet regime were open before the mobilization of a large segment of the Latvian population, particularly in the late Soviet period. Cultural ties and initiatives, networks of knowledge exchanges, and the vacuum left by the near-absence of regime legitimacy created fertile soil for the rise of alternative narratives outside the official public sphere.

Opportunity and Resources in the Period of Glasnost

Although the oppositional narrative and identity and solidarity that emerged from alternative stories of history, kinship, and action are central to the story of mass mobilization in Soviet Latvia, it is also important to consider the enormous changes in political life and, consequently, the political opportunity structure, wrought by General Secretary Gorbachev's reforms. Though the policy of glasnost, or greater openness, was limited in that it was intended to strengthen rather than weaken (or destroy) the Union, it provided the medium in which the seed of widespread grievances could be nurtured.

Political opportunity as an analytical construct is multidimensional and broad. For the purposes of this study, I specify four dimensions of this concept. They are separately enumerated, but not mutually exclusive: changes in one can clearly affect others. First, political opportunity may be a product of state structures that permit or proscribe activity in civil society. In the case at hand, the opening of the public sphere after decades of moribund civil society was signaled by the Chautauqua Conference of 1986 and by growing tolerance of independent activity in the civic arena.

Second, governing elites may limit or extend political opportunities beyond civil society to include the institutions of governance themselves. In Latvia, this situation trailed by several years the extension of opportunity in the civic arena and was apparent only in the partly open field of contestation for seats in the Congress of People's Deputies in 1989. Third, political opportunity for opposition forces may be enhanced by weak regime legitimacy and public perceptions of weakness in the regime. In Latvia, the Soviet regime suffered a low degree of political legitimacy, and conformity was founded more on fear than loyalty. The growing perception of regime impotence and the increasing sense that the regime was unwilling or unable to use force against the opposition also underpinned expanded political opportunity in the Baltics.

Fourth, movements may generate their own political opportunities, so that a previous successful collective action can make future collective actions an attractive proposition for potential participants. This proposition appears to be supported by the seemingly exponential increase in protest participants in Latvia from the inception of collective action in 1986 to the end of the protest cycle in 1991.[15]

The Chautauqua Conference, held in September 1986 in Jūrmala, Latvia, is an important historical landmark in any analysis of the development of protest movements in the Baltic states. The Chautauqua Conference brought together private citizens and public officials from the United States and the Soviet Union in a "town hall" meeting. The local audience of Latvians and Russians was largely handpicked and did not speak out critically at the conference, but large crowds gathered outside and sought out participants looking for information. American diplomats commented at the time that "they could not recall another occasion when such a sustained critique of Soviet policies was approved for domestic consumption."[16]

Among the remarks that created a stir was the declaration of the U.S. President's Soviet Affairs Adviser that "the use of force and the absence of freely given consent are the reasons the United States has never recognized and will not recognize the legality of the forcible incorporation of Latvia, Lithuania, and Estonia into the Soviet Union." He also gave a "detailed background of Soviet occupation of Latvia, describing the 1940 elections in occupied Latvia as a 'farce.'" Jack Matlock's remarks on nonrecognition were not directly broadcast by the media, but television news made reference to them without comment. United Press International reported that word of his remarks "spread like wildfire through Riga." Apparently, few Latvians were aware of the U.S. policy of nonrecognition.[17]

Participants from the United States were also provided by the American Latvian Association (ALA) with lapel pins to hand out to people both in and outside the conference; the pins depicted the American flag and the pre-1940 maroon and white Latvian flag joined at the poles. During television coverage of the conference, the pins worn by some delegates were shown up close numerous times for up to ten seconds, though television employees claimed that their purpose was to "show the Latvian people how the Americans were dressed," and "since most Americans were wearing the pins . . . they couldn't be avoided."[18]

Although the Chautauqua Conference in Latvia did not have immediate political ramifications, it helped set the stage for later collective action. The

Latvian historian Ļubova Zīle wrote that "the very fact that such a conference took place, that American representatives were permitted to come to
the USSR, showed that socialist thinking had experienced a sea change."[19]
Several points are of particular importance here. First, the U.S. delegation
fundamentally undermined Soviet claims to legitimacy by reiterating their
support for a policy of not recognizing the incorporation of the Baltic countries into the Soviet Union. Matlock's remark questioned the foundation of
the Soviet presence there and, as such, bolstered Baltic claims about the
illegitimacy of the regime. Second, although some conference delegates and
the local Latvians who sought them out were harassed by authorities, the
conference demonstrated that a new level of openness had been reached and
that even questions about the legitimacy of Soviet power could be broached
(albeit, by outsiders). Third, during the conference, cracks in the mechanism
of state control were apparent. Making a related point, Anthony Oberschall
noted:

> When a state has legitimacy, its agents enforce laws, follow adminis-
> trative rules, and comply with executive orders not only because
> they might be disciplined if they didn't, but because it is morally
> right to do so. If the state is illegitimate, its agents conform to re-
> gime leaders from expediency and fear, just as the population does.
> In a crisis, when the regime weakens and the opposition might
> emerge the winner, the agents of the state lose fear of their superi-
> ors. . . . Communications specialists and cultural gatekeepers start
> reporting news about previous non-persons. Censors pass material
> they would have banned earlier. . . . The police no longer rough up
> demonstrators and fail to make arrests. . . . Corruption is exposed
> once more. Such permissive controls embolden previously fearful
> and silent individuals and groups to speak out. . . . Thus a crescendo
> of criticism and opposition spread in all institutions.[20]

The broad and relatively open television coverage of remarks like those of
the delegate Jack Matlock and the repeated televising of the ALA pin with
the forbidden prewar flag were among the clearest, though not the only,
examples of declining control and subsiding fear.

A second important test of Gorbachev's policy of greater openness came
several months later. On October 14, 1986, Dainis Īvāns and Artūrs Snips
published their article in the newspaper *Literatūra un māksla*, criticizing proposed Soviet plans to build the Daugavpils hydroelectric station. As noted
earlier, the issue was broadly resonant, and the public responded to the

call for stopping the HES. The success of the campaign, unanticipated and unprecedented in Soviet Latvia, had a powerful impact on society: Īvāns wrote that the year of the Daugava campaign "flow[ed] together in a concentrated wave of strength that irreversibly [tore] apart a half-century's erected prisons of prohibition [and] artificially-altered norms and values of post-war Latvia."[21]

Part of the independent activism around the HES issue can be explained by the growth of political opportunities. The Chautauqua Conference had shown that an unprecedented degree of openness was possible in the Gorbachev-era public sphere, but critical comments at the conference had come primarily from visitors to Latvia rather than local residents, and the boundaries of internal openness were still unknown. Clearly, at this time, those who participated in collective action were taking risks, albeit risks that began to show the expansiveness of opportunity and paved the way for later mass protest.

Another important factor in mobilization was information, especially information previously hidden by the state. As a result of Gorbachev's policy of glasnost, information of both historical and contemporary significance that had been hidden or misrepresented by the Soviet state came to light. Speaking about the period of mobilization, Zīle, who also participated in the opposition, described the situation as follows:

> [As a result of the new policy of openness] new information appeared. We learned things we had not known previously. A large amount of information came out in to the open: about deportations, the destructiveness of collectivization, what had happened as a result of Stalinist politics. And all of that made us think, consider, evaluate ourselves, and we began to seek out other people who thought as we did. We began to unite. . . . All the information that came to us, that rained down on us—that was what awakened us, that was the energy. No money was needed, and no one had any [money] in any case.[22]

In this instance, previously concealed information and acquisition of new knowledge about history, politics, and society by ordinary citizens provided a basis for unity, as well as "energy" for mobilization.

Another part of the explanation for the unprecedented independent action around the Daugavpils HES issue is the symbolic power of the river Daugava, invoked by the initiators of the campaign and well known to Latvians from songs like *Daugav' abas malas* (Shores of the Daugava) and the epic of *Lāčplēsis*. The Daugava is widely held to be Latvia's "river of destiny," and the campaign drew from and appealed to this sense.

In considering the role of symbols in collective action, the definition offered by Abner Cohen is useful. He wrote that symbols are "objects, acts, concepts, or linguistic formations that stand *ambiguously* for a multiplicity of disparate meanings, evoke sentiments and emotions, and impel men to action."[23] The Daugava as a symbol was multivocal. It was a potential ecological problem and, as such, could be symbolically linked to existing ecological problems with which the public was familiar, like widespread water pollution. It was also, as framed by the authors of the article, a symbol of Latvia and its historical and cultural heritage. The article used the well-known symbol of the Daugava to convey a powerful new message that tied these two symbolic dimensions together: the destruction of the land of Latvia was the equivalent of the destruction of the Latvian nation.

Notably, after the Soviet occupation, one of the first undertakings of the new regime had been to replace symbols of independent Latvia—the flag, national crest, anthem, and street names, among others—with Soviet symbols. These symbols were to some degree accepted and tolerated by local populations, but they generated little allegiance. Karen Cerulo made a distinction between "normal" and "deviant" national symbols:

> *Normal symbols are those whose syntactic features meet the expectations of their targets.* Normal symbols fall within the parameters of the symbolic grammar typical to the groups targeted by the message; these symbols conform to the target group's rules and conventional modes of expression. In contrast, *deviant symbols display syntactic features that contradict a target group's expectations* . . . deviant symbols distort the symbolic grammar common to the groups represented by the symbols.

Furthermore, "the more normal a symbol's structure, the greater its potential to generate a strong audience connection and response."[24] The Daugava was a symbol that could evoke just such a response, because it resonated with widely shared notions about the land and culture of Latvia and was an effective vehicle for communicating a message about perceived and actual threats to the survival of the nation.

Symbols like the Daugava may be understood as resources for social movement mobilizations. In the near-absence of tangible resources for mobilization (as Zīle noted, there was no money), the Latvian opposition relied on intangible resources to which it had ready access and which conferred legitimacy on its claims and demands.

The anti-Soviet opposition also had very limited access to tangible resources like mediums of mass communication and secure meeting spaces, though Radio Free Europe broadcasts from West Germany disseminated news of collective actions into Latvia. Furthermore, the Soviet state monopolized the public sphere: clubs, newspapers, and unions existed in the Soviet period, but they did not constitute an independent public sphere, as all were linked to and overseen by the state or party. What the opposition initially had to work with was a nascent politicized identity based in ethnicity and culture, a mass of new information that came to light under Gorbachev, and a cultural store of myths, symbols, songs, and stories.

Symbolic reclamation of the nation was a centerpiece of collective action in the early opposition period. Although overt political demands were still risky, and few in the opposition were prepared to ask for full national independence, symbolic demands, like those related to environmental protection, or symbolic deeds, such as commemorating the Stalinist mass deportations of Balts, were important because they laid bare problems widely believed to be symptomatic of a larger problem, the Soviet regime itself.

Through 1986, public activity grew, but it was limited in size. The first informal organization to appear at this time was Helsinki 86, which was organized in Liepāja in July 1986 by Linards Grantiņš, Raimonds Bitenieks, and Mārtiņš Bariss. Helsinki 86 defined itself as a human rights organization dedicated to seeing that rights were recognized in accordance with the Helsinki Act of 1975. They invited others "who would like, in their free time, openly and without compensation, and with their own resources" to join that group. Through 1986, the group remained small, and their activities were, although courageous, predominantly legalistic bids for regime recognition of rights rather than large-scale public activities. For example, in 1986, the group sought state permission to publish a journal, *Auseklis,* to "inform society about the fulfillment of the Helsinki final act on human rights and about hidden or misrepresented historical events." The request was denied by the government. The same year, the group prepared a memo for the General Secretary of the Central Committee of the Communist Party of the USSR, asking for help in "realizing the 69th article of the LSSR Constitution," which (theoretically) granted republics the right to secede from the USSR.[25] In late 1987, the group prepared a general memorandum of goals, which included the following:

The renewal of Latvian language rights . . . ; the de-ideologization
of Latvian national history; the truthful interpretation of historical
events; consistent with the republic's constitution, to emphasize
Latvia's autonomous status within the community of republics; to
reorient Latvia's economy so that it might in the first instance meet
the needs of Latvia's inhabitants; to stop the decline of the ecological situation; to halt the unhealthy immigration process; . . . without
delay; to see to the release of Latvian political prisoners . . . ; to
liquidate the privileges that accrue to those in particular posts or
the [Communist] party; . . . to further active citizenship in the economic, political, and spiritual spheres; to accomplish true local government; [and] to renew the genuine power of the soviets because
it is impossible to view as soviet power the capricious rule of the
Stalinist clique and its copies that were brought into the Baltics in
1940.[26]

Typical of the phase of change when rejection of the "abnormalities" of the
Soviet order defined the opposition, this list of goals focused more on undoing Soviet actions than on the construction of any alternative structure. The
construction of oppositional narratives in terms of this rejection was, in fact,
characteristic of much of the period up until 1991.

In February 1987, the *Vides aizsardzības klubs* (Ecological Protection Club
of Latvia, or VAK) was formed with the goal of "uniting all those who wished
to participate in the protection, rescue, and maintenance of cultural monuments, ecological and human development."[27] The group sought to fight
polluters and those responsible for the destruction of cultural monuments,
even to the point of seeking juridical prosecution. VAK became more active
as information about ecological catastrophes in Latvia came to light, but
although the overtly apolitical topic of environmental pollution was permitted some public airing, public reporting of the actual activities of VAK was
proscribed by the regime. Quoting from the VAK journal, Zīle wrote that
the Latvian news agency Latinform "[prohibited] official mass information
sources from publishing anything about meetings or other VAK activities."[28]
Despite the official muzzle on reporting, people came to meetings and participated in activities in degraded areas like Sloka, home of an All-Union
paper mill; Olaine, where pharmaceuticals were manufactured; and Ventspils, a heavily industrialized port city with a rate of birth defects far above
the national average.

Both Helsinki 86 and VAK drew public attention to important problems
like human rights abuses and environmental pollution, but their actual mem-

bership was tiny, and public participation in 1986 was limited. Throughout 1987, however, the scale and breadth of public action grew as it became clear that social control mechanisms were weak, social and political problems were many, and public mobilization through existing channels was possible.

Much early collective action centered around the symbolic reclamation of time and space. The first large demonstration in the Baltic states took place on June 14, 1987. It was called by Helsinki 86 to mark the anniversary of the mass deportation of Balts to labor camps in 1941. As mass information mediums in the USSR could not be used to broadcast such an invitation, the call went out over Radio Free Europe and by word of mouth. The demonstration was set for 4:00 P.M., when people left work and were on the streets. Thousands of people laid flowers at the Freedom Monument, though Latin-form reported that only a handful of people had appeared. Although not officially permitted, the demonstration took place with a minimum of disturbance. Nevertheless, all three Helsinki 86 organizers were called up in June for military training. When Grantiņš did not appear for his training because of poor health, he was arrested and sentenced to six months' imprisonment.

The next demonstration called by Helsinki 86, however, was provocative because it marked the anniversary of the signing of the Molotov-Ribbentrop Pact, the secret protocols of which had divided part of Eastern Europe, including the Baltics, into spheres of influence between the Soviets and Nazis. The Soviets still denied the existence of the protocols at this time. Before August 23, 1987, Helsinki 86 again made its intentions known to the government in a prepared document. The organization asked for the publication of the secret protocols to the pact and stated its intention to invite people to leave flowers at the Freedom Monument. Fearing police reprisals, the group invited people to come to the monument in small groups throughout the day rather than in a large group, though the state had itself put up obstacles to a large gathering with a sudden street renovation nearby and large public buses parked around the monument area and surrounded by militia. The crowd of people who gathered, however, broke the cordon, and thousands again demonstrated at the monument. Before the anniversary day, the Helsinki 86 organizers were taken to detention, and during the day, hundreds more were arrested.[29]

The calendar demonstrations, at least in their early incarnation, were symbolically rather than overtly political. Marking the mass deportations of June 14, 1941, was a way of symbolically "talking" both about Stalin's crimes (which was permissible) and the deportation of Latvians that continued well after Stalin's passing (which was not). As history was something many Latvians felt had been "taken" from them by the Soviets, the reclamation of historical memory was a significant milestone, which represented a "normalization" of historical events. The importance of the early openness in building the opposition is highlighted in a letter written by Eduards Ber-klavs, a former Communist purged for nationalistic views in the 1950s and an activist in the oppositional Latvia's National Independence Movement (LNNK), to a friend in 1987: "It is of course axiomatic—in order to find the right path out of the woods, we need to know where we are. In order to move along the road of progress . . . it is necessary to have genuine democratic practice and full openness."[30] In a sense, then, the opposition's attempt to locate itself in "authentic" history was a way of establishing its bearings before moving into the next phase of change.

The calendar demonstrations, initially called by Helsinki 86, rapidly gained momentum on their own and, in the absence of any significant tangible mobilizational resources, acted as their own resources for future action. Making a similar point about mobilization in Eastern Germany in 1989, Steven Pfaff wrote: "Prior to November 1989, there were no new large-scale areas of political participation opening up that could give rise to demonstrations other than the protests themselves."[31] This was true in Latvia as well. The next significant date on the Latvian historical calendar was November 18, which marked the anniversary of the official founding of the independent interwar state in 1918. Participants reported that at the August 23 commemoration, many demonstrators departed with the words, "Until November 18."[32]

The state made extensive preparations for the anticipated November 18 demonstration, and the Latvian Communist Party assured Moscow that "timely preventive measures to stop ideological enemies from utilizing the 18 November anniversary of bourgeois Latvia" had been put in place. Zīle also noted that the Komitet gosudarstvennoi bezopasnosti (KGB) may have been responsible for circulating rumors intended to destabilize interethnic equilibrium, rumors that "Latvian nationalists planned on November 18 to settle the score with non-Latvians [in Latvia]." The Latvian Communist Party Central Committee also organized what was called in internal documents a "protest meeting . . . in Riga against the interference of the United States in the internal matters of a sovereign republic." The meeting, held at *Strēlnieku laukums* (Red Riflemen's Square), was attended by 1,500 to 2,000 people, many of them bused to Riga for the occasion. A Latinform press rendering of the meaning of the event, which was closed to anyone without a pass into the square, went as follows: "These revolutionary soldiers carved in granite [the red riflemen] symbolize the Latvian nation's trust in socialist ideas, their preparation to always stand in guard of Soviet power, and the fraternal friendship of Soviet nations."

Fearing bloodshed and reprisals, Helsinki 86 backed off from calling a demonstration, though it invited people to leave flowers at the Freedom Monument and the National Theater (site of the official founding of the interwar state), adding that participants should be "calm and disciplined" and should leave the sites after putting down their flowers.[33] Because the Freedom Monument was ringed by state militia on November 18, protesters commemorated the day by leaving flowers and candles at other historical sites. The interwar flag of Latvia also appeared in various places that day.

The collective actions of 1987, which grew from the initiatives of a small number of mostly working-class dissidents and attracted several thousand participants, opened the door for the entry of cultural elites into opposition and for much larger demonstrations the following year. As Juris Dreifelds has noted, "[The early demonstrations] were certainly a catalyst in the re-awakening of the Latvian intelligentsia, which by the spring of 1988 took on the leading role in articulating Latvian national grievances."[34] It has been suggested that "Latvia's Helsinki group was like an icebreaker that broke open the stream into which the Writers' Union [and other creative unions] could swim, taking with it a notable part of [Latvian inhabitants]."[35] In addition to the entrance of cultural elites into oppositional activities, this year also witnessed a serious and growing dissonance in the political elite, just as the same calendar demonstrations that evoked official Communist Party condemnation in 1987 played host to sympathetic Communist Party officials in 1988.

In March 1988, Latvia's creative unions called a meeting to undertake a dialogue on the consequences of Stalinism in Latvia and the role and responsibility of the creative intelligentsia in dealing with this issue. Dreifelds wrote that the "chairman, Jānis Peters, invited the artistic community to explore the subtler manifestations of Stalinism, which [aimed] to 'prevent independent thinking, forbid an attachment to a nation and a language, and . . . destroy historical memory and cultural heritage.' "[36] Shortly after the meeting, on March 25, the Writers' Union organized a public action at the *Brāļu kapi* (Cemetery of the Brethren) to commemorate the 1949 deportation of over 43,000 people from Latvia. Before the action, the press undertook a broad discussion of the historical event and publicized the upcoming Writers' Union commemoration. In contrast, Helsinki 86's planned demonstration at the Freedom Monument on the same day received no publicity in the official press, despite organizers' notification of their intent to gather.

The state probably permitted and even to a limited extent supported the commemoration at the Cemetery of the Brethren, while suppressing information about and harassing demonstrators at the Helsinki gathering, for two reasons. First, it hoped to split Latvian public sympathies. Second, it had to reassert some control over the direction of public sentiment, shifting it away from Helsinki 86, which embraced radical demands for change, to an officially sanctioned group like the Writers' Union, which, at least up to that point, voiced moderate views. If this was indeed the regime strategy, it achieved only limited success. Whereas the Writers' Union gathering attracted about 25,000 people, the Helsinki 86 demonstration was attended by about 5,000 people, and some people going home from the Writers' Union commemoration also joined those who were at the Freedom Monument for a spontaneous meeting at which the pre-1940 Latvian anthem, long forbidden, was sung.[37]

The continued centrality and power of informal organizations were underscored by the high profile of VAK in 1988. Although Helsinki 86's calendar demonstrations continued to grow in popularity, this year also saw the first large-scale demonstrations organized by VAK. The group's first major action was the April 28, 1988, protest against the building of a metrorail system in the capital city of Riga. VAK and its supporters contended that the metro was both unnecessary and dangerous: the metro would duplicate bus lines already in operation, possibly at the expense of lowering the area's water table and destabilizing the fragile foundations of historical buildings in the 800-year-old city. The public action against the metro project was more overtly political than earlier activities against ecological threats, because it also raised the issue of demographic minoritization in Latvia: the project would have brought thousands of migrant workers to Latvia, further reducing the Latvians' 52 percent majority in the republic. Signs carried by demonstrators declared not only "The metro is not a friend," but also "The metro [is] one more step toward the destruction of the Latvian nation." The metro project was subsequently canceled.

The success of the metro campaign encouraged VAK to organize protests against other ecological problems coming to light. Among the highlighted ecological grievances were the pollution caused by the paper mill at Sloka, the pollution of the Bay of Riga and the Baltic Sea, and the proposed nuclear-power electricity station in western Latvia. It has been suggested that the late Soviet-era environmental movements were but "surrogates" for "real" nationalist movements.[38] The notion, however, that the environmental agenda was just a facade for a "true agenda" is difficult to reconcile with the Baltic context. First, although the Soviet state was clearly less threatened by an environmental agenda than it would have been by an overtly nationalist platform, it did not view environmental activism as "nonthreatening." On the contrary, Zīle wrote that "[VAK's] activities in Latvia were of increasing concern to the Central Committee of the Latvian Communist Party [in 1988]; therefore, under its orders, state apparatuses were directed to undermine the ecological protection actions undertaken by the so-called 'greens'; [these actions] were constantly postponed or disrupted, even 'moved' off to the edge of [Riga] so as to cause less discomfort to party leaders."[39]

Second, and more important, ecological consciousness and concern were rooted in both science and culture, and resistance to dangerous and polluting practices was less a "surrogate" for national resistance than an integral part of it. That is, ecological disasters were a centerpiece of action: they represented genuine problems faced by the state and nation (for instance, untreated waste water from Riga, a city of about 800,000 people, poured into the Bay of Riga daily, and the hyperindustrialized port city of Ventspils had a frighteningly high rate of birth defects). It was often unspoken but widely understood that the solution to these problems lay not in a piecemeal approach to individual disasters, but rather in the reestablishment of a state that would respond to rather than repress Latvian interests. This was clear from Visvaldis Lāms's remarks at the Writers' Congress of 1988: "The [Soviet] bureaucrats are ready to drown the Daugava, they are ready to build Latvia full of factories it does not need, to which workers will be brought from thousands of kilometers away. They are ready to drown this whole nation. . . . They are ready for everything. And while the power of this apparatus is not broken, we can talk [about the problems] all we want [but nothing will change]."[40]

Ecological problems, although clearly a mobilizational issue themselves, were in 1988, as they had been in 1986, a symbol of national problems as well. To suggest that ecological issues were symbols of political issues like national survival, however, is not the same as saying that political intentions were "hiding" behind ecological issues. The destruction of the land was, in the movement discourse, directly linked to the destruction of the Latvian nation because of ecological consequences and because building some of the proposed projects would have brought thousands of non-Latvian workers to Latvia, further contributing to the reduction of the Latvians' bare majority in the republic.

In April 1988, Gunārs Astra, one of the dissidents who had spent a considerable number of years in Soviet prison camps up through February 1988, died. Although it was often the case that Soviet dissidents were better known outside their own countries (as they often made their appeals to the West), Astra had become widely known in Latvia in the short period of glasnost. His funeral in Riga was attended by over 5,000 people. The ceremony was a powerful symbolic ritual marking the passing of one of the few individuals who had spoken for the cause of independence when such a thing was considered by the state to be treasonous. It was the first public gathering at which the national anthem was sung with orchestral accompaniment, and it was the first public display of the still-illegal independence-era Latvian flag, which was draped over Astra's coffin.[41]

Maintaining the momentum generated by the March 25 commemoration at the Cemetery of the Brethren, the Writers' Union in early June organized a meeting that called on other creative unions, including journalists and artists, to participate as well. The chairman Jānis Peters opened the meeting by acknowledging public expectations and anxieties surrounding the well-publicized gathering of the cultural elite, which had already taken tentative steps toward embracing change: "The time of great questions has arrived, [and] on our shoulders, [the shoulders] of the creative elite, lie thousands [of questions of] 'why?' 'how?' 'when?' 'how much longer?' and 'in what way?'" The speeches included one by the journalist and Communist Party member Mavriks Vulfsōns, who declared that, as one who had witnessed and participated in the events of 1940, he could attest to the falsity of the Soviet claim that the USSR had taken power in Latvia in a people's revolution. Rather, he stated, Soviet power was the product of a Soviet military occupation. He wrote in his memoir that "in front of television cameras, I read the secret protocols which Molotov and Ribbentrop had signed—a criminal document which put a seal on the fate of the Baltic states and their peoples for half a century. There was a strict ban on making any mention of the documents, of course, even though the world beyond the Iron Curtain was well aware of them."[42] This was the first open challenge to the legitimacy of Soviet rule made by a prominent political figure in Latvia. Dainis Īvāns suggested that Vulfsōns's challenge to Soviet legitimacy was of profound importance to the opposition: "First, it found the greatest resonance in the wake of the meeting. Second, people's reaction toward the national past symbolized by this fact influenced their ideas about Latvia's future [and] illuminated the gap between those who clearly defended Latvia's interests and [those who were] imperialists."[43]

The resolutions that emerged from the meeting further built on the notion that the past and present practices of the Soviet order were not acceptable and asked for a reevaluation of historical events, including the consequences of the Molotov-Ribbentrop Pact; more stringent controls on in-migration, which was seen as presenting a grave threat to the language, culture, and existence of the nation; and greater status for the Latvian language in the public sphere, where it was crowded out by Russian. There was a strong focus on undoing Soviet practices and considerably less at this point on what would later be done. In this way, an oppositional narrative that highlighted resistance was constructed and expanded without undermining unity and calling forth differences of opinion about what a future order might look like. As well, de facto independence came more rapidly than most had expected—there were good reasons to think that the process of regaining independence would be lengthy—and this is also an important reason that opposition rather than proposition occupied the stage.

On June 14, 1988, VAK organized a protest action that attracted a crowd of over 100,000 and included the appearance of Central Committee Secretary Anatolijs Gorbunōvs. Demonstrators carried placards voicing a variety of grievances and demands: "We want independence for Latvia!" "A free Latvia in a united Europe!" and "The Latvian nation and culture are on the verge of extinction!"[44]

Several significant collective actions followed that summer. Among the most notable was the July folklore festival, Baltica-88, where participants had demanded that the flags of the interwar Baltic states be rehabilitated, and all three flags were flown. Cerulo's suggestion that "normal" national symbols, those that are culturally rooted rather than imposed (as Soviet symbols were), evoke powerful emotional responses is evidenced by many events of this period. For example, on the folk symbol called the *auseklītis* (roughly, morning star—a cross-shaped form), which was widely used by the opposition forces, Dainis Īvāns wrote:

> *Auseklītis* became a common symbol of recognition for Us [*savējie*] and the symbolic idea of the Awakening. It could not be painted on tanks or war planes because it was a symbol of strength that contained within itself good will and practice. It was all about symbols. Of course, a symbol determines the content of action and striving. The *auseklītis* of the flags of the Awakening was woven in naturally and clearly. . . . It was not forced on us, but was born as a symbol of the Lielvārdes belt[45] [and] gave forth its own sense of unity.[46]

In mid-1988, some VAK members split off to form a new group, the Latvian National Independence Movement (LNNK). LNNK was openly nationalistic, and its demands were more politically radical than those of groups since Helsinki 86 had been. As with Helsinki 86, however, opposition was heavily premised on the rejection of the actions and practices of the Soviet regime. For example, in an address to the First Congress of the LNNK in February 1989, Eduards Berklavs offered the following words: "And let us rise in an unending struggle against those who forcefully occupied our fatherland in order to steal our wealth, extinguish our language and culture, pollute our land, and suppress our freedom, [and] destroy us as a nation!"[47] Although the sense that the present order was, as the statement suggests, illegal and illegitimate, bellicose, destructive, genocidal, polluting, and authoritarian unmistakably signaled the desire to transform state and society radically, the statement foresaw the general outlines of a future order, "Latvian" and "free," without filling in the particular content of that order. The opposition iterated and disseminated a potent sense that the Soviet order was fundamentally abnormal: the message was resonant, on the one hand, with the experience of many inhabitants, and unifying, on the other hand, because it was based on opposition rather than proposition. This is not to suggest that there were not points of fundamental contention between, for example, Latvia's Popular Front and the LNNK—there were, particularly on issues of immigration of Soviet citizens from other republics and future citizenship for those immigrants—but rather to highlight that these were far less visible in the oppositional narrative than was unity in opposition to the Soviet order. As a letter from the LNNK to Communist Party members stated, "The time has come to forget arguments, disagreements, and the actions of the past and to go forth in the decisive attack [against the regime]."[48]

LNNK's cooperative endeavors with VAK reflected a new direction of opposition: the groups initiated mass demonstrations aimed at, among others, relegalizing the flag of independent Latvia. Although the "poetic spaces" of the nation had been retaken with the "rescue" of the Daugava, the defeat of the Riga metro, and the reclamation of spaces like the Freedom Monument, at which it had previously been illegal even to place flowers, and "authentic" time had been reclaimed with the commemoration of nationally significant historical dates, the preeminent symbol of the Latvian nation and the Latvian *state* as an independent entity, the flag, had not yet gotten official recognition.

Success came quickly, and on November 4, 1988, the Presidium of the Supreme Soviet of the Latvian SSR passed a resolution, "On the Cultural-Historical Symbols of the Latvian Nation," relegalizing the flag. On November 11, *Lāčplēša diena* (Bearslayer Day), the flag was raised above Riga Castle in an emotional and jubilant ceremony. On November 18, Latvian independence day, the flags of independent Estonia and Lithuania flew in Riga as well. On this day, too, another old symbol was present: the man whose face was replaced by Lenin's and Stalin's in 1940. Kārlis Ulmanis, independent Latvia's last president, appeared on posters carried by demonstrators, suggesting even more powerfully the reclamation of the symbols not just of nation but of state.

Institutionalizing Opposition

Although a number of theoretical approaches in the study of social movements have taken formal organization to be a necessary precursor to mass mobilization, the experiences of the anti-Communist opposition in Eastern Europe suggest that loose networks and informal rather than formal organizations are the units of analysis best suited for these cases. Indeed, much of the literature on anti-Communist mobilizations in Eastern Europe leaves formal organization entirely out of the picture, positing that mobilization was generated by informal sources. This is partly true, but the case at hand suggests that formal organization played an important role in the opposition period, albeit at a phase in the protest cycle not foreseen by the resource mobilization perspective, a dominant theoretical perspective in social movements literature. Rather than serving as a force for mobilization of collective action, formal organization in Latvia operated to unite an already existing field of opposition movements under a shared frame of protest, to broaden the opposition's appeal and scope, and to strengthen the movement to extend its power from the civic arena to institutions of governance.

In Latvia, the opposition was consolidated in the formal organization of the *Latvijas Tautas fronte* (Latvian Popular Front, or LTF). The June 1988 meeting of the creative unions became the foundation for the LTF, established in October 1988. The resolutions that emerged from the meeting were the stimulus for the creation of an organizing committee for a front in June 1988. The group included seventeen prominent intellectuals, clergymen, and human rights activists, with well-known figures such as Dainis Īvāns, who had publicized the Daugavpils HES project in 1986, and Juris Vidiņš, a doctor and spokesperson for Helsinki 86. Dreifelds wrote that, in response to the step, "[Jānis] Peters and the [rest of the] leadership of the creative unions moved quickly to thwart this effort and to put organizational initiative in the hands of individuals less visibly affiliated with protest and opposition groups." Hence, the same program was undertaken, but under the signatures of a more "officially acceptable" group of signatories. As part of this effort, LTF support groups were mobilized at the grassroots level throughout the summer months, and professionals and intellectuals were also recruited for the front.[49]

The LTF founding congress was held in early October. On the eve of the meeting, 150,000 people filled the amphitheater in Riga to rally in support of the LTF. Latvian flags flew in the stands, and an imposing banner showing the Bearslayer over the words "Away with the Occupation" joined smaller signs demanding the rule of law and deploring continued in-migration. The rally also featured the reintroduction of nationalistic songs unsung in public for decades. One hundred thousand copies of a song sheet were printed by the LTF for distribution to those who would have forgotten or did not know the words to songs like "I Will Sing for You, Fatherland," "Our Land," and "God Bless Latvia," the pre-1940 national anthem of Latvia. The public singing of songs as a unity-generating ritual has been little examined, but the sense of empowerment generated by masses singing mutually meaningful songs may be conveyed to some degree by a poem written by J. Kronbergs in 1988. Entitled "The Singing Revolution," the poem describes how a drop of water hits a rock and rolls off, but many drops of water hit a rock and change its shape.[50]

Among those who spoke at the congress were Dainis Īvāns, the Latvian Communist Party First Secretary Anatolijs Gorbunōvs, the poet Māra Zālīte, and the writer Jānis Peters. Many of the remarks, like those of Peters, highlighted the importance of national sovereignty but continued to frame aspirations in terms of socialism, asking for "national solidarity and a truly socialistic society, . . . national self-determination and an association of free sovereign states." Peters rejected the notion of a "Soviet nationality" as abnormal, likening it to a "zoological experiment" comparable to the bizarre experiments of the Stalin-era scientist Lysenko.[51]

The LTF congress highlighted the themes of democracy, sovereignty, and "true socialism," though the precise content of those terms remained elusive. The "invitation" issued earlier by the founders of the LTF had iterated a number of goals that included the realization of "sovereignty" and "rights and freedoms" as laid out by the Soviet Constitution and United Nations Declaration on Human Rights, the renewal of societal morals and values, and the protection of the environment for the healthy development of the nation. The invitation further stated: "We believe that the leadership of the republic and party that have governed up to this point has, in all these spheres, brought us to a point of crisis. With outdated, undemocratic methods of governance, this situation cannot be resolved. It is necessary for the whole nation to take action within a context of socialist pluralism. The creative activity of the nation needs to be united with competent diagnoses of the situation and the construction of alternatives."[52] At the congress itself, many of the resolutions passed mirrored the basic foci of the creative unions at the June meeting: there were calls for greater protection of the environment, limits on in-migration, and publication of the secret protocols to the Molotov-Ribbentrop Pact. As was typical in the opposition period, the goals that focused on undoing what had been done by the Soviets, such as reversing polluting practices or representing history with greater accuracy, were relatively concrete. Goals related to the long term were, again, abstract, iterated in a language of "democracy" and "rights" that was, perhaps with intent, vague. At the first LTF congress, none of the resolutions demanded full independence. This step was to come at the second congress in 1989.

The LTF mobilized a larger portion of society than had previously participated in opposition. In part, this may be attributed to its creation of a resonant master frame. According to David Snow and Robert Benford, master frames "provide the interpretive medium through which collective actors associated with different movements within a cycle assign blame for the problem they are attempting to ameliorate."[53] In the case of the LTF, blame was assigned less directly than by implication. Even in 1988, directly taking on the Soviet government carried risks. The LTF highlighted widely shared problems like ecological destruction and economic shortages and widely shared concerns like the declining use of the Latvian language in official contexts, but it was broadly understood that the culprit behind these misfortunes was the Soviet state, its institutions, and policies.

The potency of a master frame can vary, among other things, on the basis of its "empirical credibility, experiential commensurability, and ideational centrality or narrative fidelity." In this case, the basic frame of the LTF resonated with the widely shared notion that things in state and society were not as they should be, and its potency emerged, in part, from its acknowledgment that improvement, for a wide variety of identities and interests, required fundamental change.

The master frame that emerged from the LTF congress had to synthesize the two dominant streams of opposition in Latvia. The first and more radical stream was represented by organizations like Helsinki 86, the Ecological Protection Club (VAK), and the Latvian National Independence Movement (LNNK). These organizations took a determined stance in favor of independence even early in the opposition period. To the extent that they embraced perestroika, they did so with the view that it was a short stop on the road to full independence. The second stream, represented by the cultural elite and embodied by the creative unions, took a more moderate stance on changes, shying away from demands for full independence and favoring a program that highlighted economic sovereignty and political autonomy in a federated structure.

The master frame hence had to be broad enough to encompass both moderate and radical interests. What emerged was not a political program, but rather a frame that tapped into a spectrum of grievances. In the mid-1980s, the situation in Latvia looked grim from a variety of perspectives: cultural elites had limited freedom to write and create; consumers lacked goods, and goods lacked quality; young Latvians in Riga feared a growing threat from Russian gangs; farmers lamented the poor condition of agriculture; many Latvians were alarmed by the prospect of linguistic and demographic minoritization; and Latvia's inhabitants faced the prospect of old environmental threats as well as new ones. The LTF frame resonated across a wide spectrum because it articulated a sense that something had to change, and there was reason to hope that change would come.

Despite the cautious approach to speaking out for full independence, most participants saw the best hope for change in a free Latvia. In his opening speech at the LTF congress, Jānis Peters called the development of popular movements for change in the Baltics an "irreversible reality." He added that the Baltic nations "are unified in their movement toward a true socialist society, toward national self-determination, and sovereignty within an association of free states. Only formation of a state where the rule of law is practiced can guarantee achievement of these goals, a state where arbitrariness is replaced by legality, and bureaucratic caprice [is eliminated]."[54] If, in 1988, many speakers danced around the fire of the word *independence*, but did not dare to go near it, by 1989, the term had made its way from the agenda of radicals to the speeches and publications of moderates.

Finally, in terms of articulational scope, the LTF program highlighted what Snow and Benford have termed an "elaborated master frame."[55] This designates a frame "organized in terms of a wide range of ideas," and Snow and Benford suggested that "being more syntactically flexible and lexically universalistic than the restricted frame, the elaborated master frame allows for numerous aggrieved groups to tap it and elaborate their grievances in terms of its basic problem-solving schema."[56] As noted earlier, the "problem-solving schema" was based more on opposition than proposition. The frame was strategically inclusive and, in contrast to some earlier groups, sought to expand its appeal to include non-Latvians who were opposed to the Soviet system.

Although many of the dominant themes and addresses at the congress were iterated in nationalist language that highlighted issues particular to Latvians in Latvia, the LTF made the first overt effort of the opposition period to reach out to Latvia's minority populations. The congress did more than unite existing formal and informal organizations representing Latvian interests; it also undertook the task of strategically expanding the scope of the movement by appealing to the minority populations, who made up about 48 percent of the total population and included non-Latvians who shared Latvians' concern about issues like shortages and the lack of basic civic freedoms.

The regime's general weakness and low level of legitimacy among many Russians as well as Latvians was a resource for the opposition. The schematic strategically employed by the LTF was one of "us versus them," where the movement identity relied in part on defining itself against the symbols and structure of the Soviet state, rather than highlighting an exclusive movement identity. The pre-LTF opposition had been founded on an exclusive national identity, but the LTF changed direction in that it sought to define more people into than out of the movement. The success of the strategy in bringing non-Latvians into the anti-Soviet opposition was most apparent in the March 1990 referendum on Latvian independence, in which a majority of both Latvians and non-Latvians voted for the establishment of an independent state.

In Latvia, a master frame that could tap a wide range of grievances was important, but arguably not sufficient for mobilizing a massive movement. Also critical for transforming grievances into action was the presence of prominent members of the cultural elite in the front. There had been broad admiration for the initiative and courage of Helsinki 86's working-class members, but Helsinki 86 had never gathered a large membership base; the number of demonstrators it attracted at its meetings, although they numbered in the thousands, was far fewer than the number attracted by the LTF. Helsinki 86 was an "unofficial" group and had no links to elites who might provide a degree of protection. The LTF was, in contrast, officially registered and openly supported by prominent cultural figures like Jānis Peters and Māra Zālīte, who were trusted by the public and whose presence in the front signaled that the risk of opposition was diminishing. The leadership of Helsinki 86 had been variously beaten, arrested, and, in some cases, exiled from the country, but the leadership of the LTF remained comfortably ensconced in their positions and suffered no real repercussions for their opposition.

More than 1,000 delegates representing over 100,000 people participated in the first LTF congress. Just under one-third of the delegates were members of the Communist Party, and 10 to 12 percent were minorities. The congress also elected a Governing Council of one hundred representatives, which in turn selected a thirteen-member board headed by Dainis Īvāns.[57] Opposition was thus institutionalized in a sitting board and bureaucratized in a slew of task-oriented committees committed to realizing the goals passed from early Helsinki and other informal group initiatives to the creative unions to the LTF.

The founding of the LTF was significant for the fact that it united radical and moderate forces in the opposition, but it was notable as well for the forces it split. In its acceptance and integration of Communist reformers like Anatolijs Gorbunōvs and supporters in the Russian-speaking community, it created an irreparable division in the Latvian Communist Party and a rift in the Russian community, part of which was made up of hard-liners who took a determined stance against liberalization. Within several months of the LTF congress, the hard-liners formed their own countermovement, the International Front, discussed in the following section.

Although it had been formally founded earlier, the Latvian National Independence Movement held its first congress in February 1989. The LNNK embraced a stance of cooperation with the LTF and its political initiatives, noting that "under the current circumstances, we need to work with the LTF—the largest, strongest organization that is also best able to cooperate with state institutions," but it took a more radical stand on the issue of separation from the USSR and focused most visibly on the need for full political independence to normalize the ethnic situation in Latvia:

> No organization that existed before the LNNK had a clear political goal, none had put forth as their task the return of the state to the Latvian nation. Therefore, among us, a small Latvian patriot group, there arose a desire to create a broad national patriotic organization. We worked to help the nation see its precarious situation: Latvians in their own homeland were, for the first time in their 4000 year history, a minority because genocide had been unleashed against the core nations—Latvians and Livs. LNNK, as the first broad political organization in society, put forth an unconditional demand and action program for the liquidation of occupation and colonization in Latvia.[58]

This move prefigured the contest that came in a later period between national patriotic groups like the LNNK and more moderate groups like the LTF and its political progeny. At this point, however, oppositional status permitted differences to be largely submerged. Dainis Īvāns pondered this point in his book on the opposition period, writing that "the political regrouping of the year 1988 was a genuine attempt to begin a newly harmonious and ethical time. Outside powers had broken and divided us in order to destroy us. The fight against this fate—it called us into a single line."[59]

Despite the creation of a formal and bureaucratic social movement structure in the form of the LTF, popular activity continued to occupy a prominent place in opposition to the regime. Frequent demonstrations drew public and state (and, increasingly, Western media) attention to a broad spectrum of issues. Demonstrations commemorating Latvian historical events like the March 25 deportations continued, and new issues, like the killing of civilians in Georgia SSR by the Soviet army and the protests against the military drafting of Latvians, also spurred collective action. Fall 1989 saw a mass rally against the policy of recruiting workers from other republics to Union enterprises in Latvia, the public raising of the pre-1940 Latvian flag over Riga Castle, and the commemoration of interwar Latvia's independence day, which was attended by over 500,000 of the republic's 2.6 million people.[60]

Zīle wrote that the "LTF, the LNNK, [and] other groups born of the awakening [the period of opposition] understood that meetings and demonstrations would not bring Latvia sovereignty, that concrete work was needed."[61] The LTF, which united oppositional organizations against the Soviet regime, sought to expand its influence beyond civil society to the structures of governance. Hence the LTF undertook a campaign to elect sympathetic candidates to the newly created Congress of People's Deputies. Although prevented from officially registering as an independent party, the LTF underwrote informational and support efforts on behalf of some candidates in the March 1989 elections. The election results yielded a bounty for reformers: the majority of candidates were affiliated with the LTF program, and the LTF estimated that fully 75 percent of the new deputies were reform-minded.[62]

This electoral victory underscores the importance of formal organization in the Latvian period of opposition. Although initial public mobilization was not initiated by formal social movement organizations, as has often been the case in the West, a formal organization (the LTF) helped sustain, expand, and organize (in this case, for electoral challenges) an already existing, albeit informal, protest movement. Notably, the experience of the opposition period for the Soviet republics like the Baltics differs from that for most East Bloc states like Czechoslovakia and East Germany, where mass mobilization was overwhelmingly short-lived and informal because the goal of overthrowing Communists was rapidly achieved.

By 1989, the rebirth of civil society was apparent in many sectors. The LTF was the dominant and unifying force in independent political life, but other groups continued to spring up for a variety of civic and political pur-

poses. Older organizations like pre-1940 political parties such as the Social
Democrats reappeared, as did international organizations like the Red Cross
and the Boy Scouts. Mothers of young men of draft age founded a League
of Women, which sought to protect draftees from abuses in the Soviet army
and put forth a plan for alternative military service. A nascent free press
was also apparent, as a multitude of new newspapers, magazines, and other
publications emerged.

The international context was also changing rapidly and radically. The
people's uprisings in Eastern Europe and the subsequent opening of the East
Bloc in autumn 1989 were encouraging, especially to those in the Baltics who
sought full separation from the USSR. Gorbachev's policy of noninterfer-
ence in the internal matters of former Soviet satellites was viewed as a positive sign. That same autumn, the LTF accepted a new platform that outlined
a course toward full independence for Latvia.

Early 1990 saw some fundamental changes at the highest levels of the
Latvian SSR's government. In January 1990, the Supreme Soviet of the Latvian Soviet Socialist Republic accepted a revision of the Constitution that
gave the Communist Party the same status as any other social organization
in society and gave citizens the right to form political parties and create new
independent organizations. At the same time, the Supreme Soviet took up
the question of the "State flag, hymn, and crest," which addressed the issue
of renewing the pre-1940 symbols that, although legal, did not have official
status. The question was hotly debated and created an unusual coalition of
opponents to the renewal of prewar symbols. Most opposition deputies stood
firmly behind acceptance of the symbols, while official conservative Communists and those affiliated with the Citizens' Committee, a radical nationalist group, lined up together against the action, the latter rejecting the move
because it objected to the use of free Latvia's symbols in occupied Latvia
and saw renewal as debasement. The issue was resolved in favor of renewal
in February.[63] To some degree, this issue illustrated a dissonance between
radical and moderate factions in opposition, which was not readily apparent
elsewhere. The clash over the appropriate place for prewar models and symbols became in the post-Communist period, however, an issue in political
and social life.

In February, the Latvian Supreme Soviet accepted by a majority vote a
declaration that Latvia's incorporation into the USSR was illegal from the
beginning, and, furthermore, that it was necessary to undertake steps toward
making Latvia an independent state. Economic decentralization also occupied an important place in public debate as the Baltic countries pushed to
take full control of their own economies.

On March 18, 1990, elections to the Latvian Supreme Soviet were held, and, again, LTF-supported candidates participated. Although one could argue that LTF and other reformist forces already had strong links with and allies in the Latvian SSR government, the program of the LTF was directed at gaining elected power rather than co-opting the inner circles of a government in which people had little confidence. The elections (and later runoff votes) gave the LTF a strong voice in the Supreme Soviet: fully 131 of 201 seats were taken by candidates that had expressed support for the LTF platform. Conservative Communists won 58 seats.[64]

Less than two months later, on May 4, 1990, the Latvian SSR Supreme Soviet, following the lead of Estonia and Lithuania, voted on a measure to renew the Republic of Latvia, setting forth a period of transition and asking for the creation of a committee in Moscow to negotiate the transition. With a mass of people gathered outside the Supreme Soviet building and a loudspeaker calling out the results vote by vote, the progressive forces won the ballot with 138 votes. The deputies of the conservative Communist faction walked out of the chamber. Zīle evaluated the significance of the vote as follows: "In this way, the USSR lost its power in Latvia, and with that henceforth all state governance was handed over to the Parliament: the Latvian Supreme Soviet was then the highest state power in Latvia." An April 1990 opinion poll of 24,600 inhabitants of Latvia determined that fully 92 percent of Latvians and 45 percent of non-Latvians favored the action of the Supreme Soviet.[65]

With the declaration of sovereignty, the Supreme Soviet of Latvia created a situation in which political jurisdiction in the territory of the republic was claimed by two governing bodies, one seated in Riga and the other in Moscow. Over the next year and a half, this unusual political situation brought new tension, as well as the first use of weapons in the opposition period.

Communists and Countermovements

In the East Bloc, the confrontation between civil society and the state was characterized by a struggle between forces for democracy and the Communist state. In the case of the Baltics, however, the field of struggle was crowded with a multitude of conflicting interests. There republic-level communist parties and proindependence forces were in conflict not only with one another, but also with the central Communist government in Moscow and local pro-Soviet movements. By the late 1980s, progressive and conservative wings of local communist parties were in conflict with each other as well.

In Latvia, the major pro-Soviet movement in civil society was the International Front (henceforth, Interfront). The Interfront's process of mobilization differed from that of the Popular Front. The LTF, as noted earlier, followed a pattern where public mobilization was drawn around shared narratives of resistance and informal groups that emerged before the creation of a formal movement structure in the Popular Front. The diverse interests of the "informals," as they were called, were represented in the new structure in an elected committee made up of representatives of different groups. The Interfront, on the other hand, proceeded from a formal basis: the formation of a social movement preceded and directed mobilization. The Interfront was founded at a January 1989 congress on the initiative of a handful of Russians, most of them professionals or managers. It has also been suggested that the Interfront was not fully the product of local initiative: for instance, the former U.S. ambassador to the Soviet Union, Jack F. Matlock, wrote in his memoir of the period:

> Bureaucrats in the economic ministries [in Moscow] who considered the enterprises they had built in the Baltic their private property fanned anti-Baltic sentiments with the active help of the KGB, conservative apparatchiks in the Communist Party, and military officers. They began organizing opposition groups in the Baltic states that they could manipulate, in the hope that this would counter the Baltic drive for independence.
>
> Their principal method was to create organizations, largely of ethnic Russians, called "International Fronts" . . . which would organize demonstrations or strikes to protest moves by the national organizations.[66]

Initially, the Interfront was made up of two wings. One was a progressive wing that supported Gorbachev's liberalization. This wing advocated change but was not comfortable in the Popular Front, where it felt unwelcome, mostly because many members did not speak Latvian or did not speak it well. The other wing was conservative, made up of hard-liners who looked askance at changes they saw as threatening to the Soviet order. The Interfront rapidly evolved into an essentially defensive movement and hence could not accommodate those Russians who, although wary of full Baltic independence, also saw a need for reform of Soviet economic and governing structures and an expansion of civil society.[67] The leadership and constituency that remained after progressive forces were marginalized were influenced by and participated in the construction of a narrative that was hostile to the ideas and initiatives of both the Popular Front and Gorbachev.

The historical narrative embraced by those who supported the conservative program of the Interfront differed in important respects from that of the Latvian opposition. The historical narrative patched together (and, in some instances, misrepresented) particular pieces of history and ignored events elevated in the Latvian narrative. The centerpiece of the narrative was not that the USSR *occupied* Latvia in 1940, but that the Soviet army (whose veterans made up a significant proportion of supporters) *liberated* Latvia from German fascism (Germany occupied Latvia from 1941 to 1944) and indigenous bourgeois nationalism. Furthermore, the anti-independence narrative iterated the notions that Latvia was a historical territory of Russia and that the period of independence in Latvia was a historical anomaly.

An interesting illustration of the disjuncture between the historical narratives of anti-Soviet and pro-Soviet forces is the following: in 1940, boxcars were dispatched from the USSR to Latvia bearing the stenciled inscription "Bread for Starving Latvian People." Photographs of the cars entered Soviet history as evidence of the USSR helping hungry Balts with food. Latvians, meanwhile, take this "history" to be a ruse, as Balts, who enjoyed a higher living standard than most of the Soviet Union's inhabitants, were not starving in 1940. The boxcars, say Baltic historians, arrived empty and were used to take the fruits of Soviet plunder *back* to the USSR.[68]

Unlike the Popular Front, which had supporters and activists in the Russian community, the Interfront had very few Latvian supporters. In another sense, however, the Interfront was less a Russian movement than a Soviet one: it used Soviet symbols and highlighted the preservation of the Soviet state system. Furthermore, rather than being founded on popular support, the Interfront was largely propped up by its association with still-powerful Soviet structures like the Communist Party, official trade unions, and management of state enterprises. These institutions also afforded hard-liners in the Interfront some protection in undertaking actions that appeared to have the intent of provoking confrontations with Popular Front supporters. A series of small explosions, including blasts at a Riga army garrison command building in December 1990, were believed by the reformist Latvian government to be the work of pro-Soviet loyalists intent on destabilizing the political situation in Latvia. Hard-liners had reason to believe that they could benefit from an eruption of disorder in the republic: they hoped that in such an instance the authorities in Moscow would impose presidential rule.

Some issues that affected a large number of Russians, such as the passage of a language law declaring Latvian the state language in May 1989, served to increase non-Latvian support for the Interfront, but they never became broad-based movements. Anatol Lieven has suggested two possible reasons for this: first, workers in republic-level enterprises (many of whom were Russian) may have feared retaliatory dismissal from their jobs, and, second, workers generally saw managers and Soviet trade-union officials as lacking credibility. The workers were well aware of the relatively advantaged positions of these officials who owned dachas and cars and shopped at hard-currency stores to which ordinary Russian workers never had access.[69] Furthermore, Tatiana Kukarina and Vladimir Tikhomirov, themselves former supporters of the Interfront, wrote that the authoritarian tendencies of the leadership and the overbureaucratization of the movement drove many members away.[70]

Although the Interfront assumed a threatening posture toward the pro-independence forces, it proved to be a rather impotent force. One of the most visible Interfront demonstrations took place on January 15, 1991, just two days after the killings of Lithuanian civilians by the Soviet army in Vilnius. Under threat of military force, pro-independence forces turned Riga's streets into barricades, seeking to protect the buildings that housed the free press and reform-minded Parliament. In this atmosphere of siege, the Interfront called a meeting at the Army Sports Club stadium in Riga and announced to the 8,000 to 10,000 participants that the *Vislatvijas glābšanas komiteja* (Salvation Committee of Latvia) was assuming executive power in the republic until new elections for the Latvian Supreme Soviet were held.[71] No realization of the committee's declaration took place, however, and by the end of January a tense equilibrium had returned to Riga.

The anti-independence movements in the Baltics collapsed soon after institutions such as the Communist Party and official trade unions, which provided support and supporters, lost their influence. As well, some members of the leadership of these movements (especially those associated with the military, the Interior Ministry, and the KGB) left for Russia after the failed coup of August 1991.

Opposition and State Power

After the Baltic Supreme Soviets turned their backs on Moscow in spring 1990, the republic- and federal-level governments were locked in an intractable impasse. At the same time, the Baltic republics expanded their autonomy with economic and political initiatives, and Gorbachev, increasingly under pressure from conservative forces in his party, held fast against independence. Rumors of an imminent coup in Moscow circulated in the Baltics, but the newly elected legislatures continued their work. To the irritation of the Soviet army command, the Latvian Supreme Soviet voted to prohibit soldiers stationed in Latvia from voting in elections and instructed municipalities to halt supplies and social services to Soviet army bases. By late 1990, representatives of the army in the Baltics asked the Congress of People's Deputies to impose presidential rule in the Baltic republics.

Early 1991 was characterized by a standoff between the newly elected Parliament of the self-declared Republic of Latvia and the Soviet military and other conservative forces. Although the confrontation was primarily between state institutions at this point, collective action remained an important part of the opposition effort. The quality of collective action, however, had changed. Whereas previously it had been expressive and oppositional, it was now defensive: collective action was a response to the needs of the newly elected Supreme Soviet and an effort to protect that which had already been achieved on the path to independence.

The problems of January 1991 began on the second day of the year, when the special forces of the USSR Interior Ministry, the OMON, took the Press Building in Riga, halting publication of most newspapers. On January 8, the Latvian Supreme Soviet took the step of declaring illegal the basing of Soviet soldiers on Latvian territory, and the next day the White House issued a statement criticizing Soviet intentions to bring new military forces into the Baltic countries. On the tenth, the League of Women organized a protest against the drafting of young men from the Baltics into the Soviet army, and on the eleventh, the LTF organized a mass rally in support of the legally elected Supreme Soviet and against military interference in the Baltics.[72]

The January 13 early morning attack by Soviet forces on the Lithuanian television tower, which left fourteen civilians dead, reverberated across Latvia, and in Riga 500,000 people gathered to protest the use of Soviet military force in Lithuania. The LTF also invited Latvians to protect the Supreme Soviet, Ministers' Cabinet, various communications and press buildings, and bridges in Riga, a call that resulted in the construction of barricades, constantly manned by thousands of unarmed Latvians throughout the day and night, until January 27. It is estimated that 700,000 people participated in the construction and guarding of the barricades during that time.[73] Plakans suggested that "Latvians knew that their barricades and patrols offered no realistic obstacle if the Soviet army chose to act with all the means at its disposal. Rather, they symbolized the will to resist, an element, some said, that had been missing in 1940 when the Soviet armed forces moved into

Latvia without any noticeable resistance from the Ulmanis government or the general population."[74]

During the *barikāžu laiks* (time of the barricades), there were a number of attacks by OMON forces in Latvia, including an attack on the Riga Police Academy and assaults on people guarding the Brasas and Mangaļu bridges in Riga. The most serious attack occurred on the night of January 20, when OMON besieged the Interior Ministry building in Riga, killing four people, mortally wounding a fifth, and injuring nine others. The killings, although drawing condemnation from the Baltic governments and the West, did not result in punishment by the Soviet military or government. As well, several mysterious explosions in Riga that spring and some attacks on Latvian-Lithuanian border control posts were attributed to OMON, a small contingent of which remained in the Baltics.

Throughout spring and summer 1991, the impasse between the Baltic governments and the Soviet regime continued. After the barricades, however, the confrontation became more institutional, and protest moved from the streets to the ballot box. In early March, Latvia held a referendum on independence: of the 87.5 percent of the population that participated, 73.8 percent voted in favor of independence. Several weeks later, an All-Union referendum on the preservation of the USSR took place. Although Latvia refused to participate at an official level, it permitted those who wished to vote, including Soviet troops stationed in Latvia, to do so: 501,280 did, and of those, 95 percent supported the Soviet Union.[75]

In early August, Soviet President Gorbachev invited the Soviet republics to reconsider their stance toward membership in the USSR and to prepare to sign the Union treaty on August 20. In response, the chairman of the Latvian Supreme Soviet, Andrejs Krastiņš, stated that Latvia would not sign the treaty because the Latvian nation had expressed its desire for full autonomy in the March elections and referendum.[76]

The treaty meeting foreseen by Gorbachev did not take place as scheduled. On August 19, 1991, a national salvation committee formed by conservative forces in the USSR staged a coup. In Latvia, OMON forces occupied a number of state and media buildings over the next two days, though they did not take the Supreme Soviet. Hence, the Supreme Soviet continued to work, passing, on August 21, a law on Latvia's status as an independent state and declaring invalid an earlier resolution on gradual movement toward independent statehood. That same day, the foreign minister of the Russian Republic, Andrei Kozyrev, echoing the sentiments of Russian President Yeltsin, invited the nations of the world to recognize Baltic independence; on August 24, President Yeltsin, on behalf of the Russian Federation, signed a declaration recognizing the Baltics as free states. By mid-September, Latvia had been globally recognized, and at the end of September, Latvia took its seat in the United Nations as an independent state, bringing to an end fifty-one years of occupation and nearly five years of collective action in pursuit of this goal.

Conclusion

On the eastern side of the Freedom Monument, on each side of the steps that lead up onto a small terrace at the base of the obelisk, two groups of marchers are forever gathered. On the left side, a procession entitled by the sculptor Kārlis Zale the "Song festival march" advances toward the "Soldiers' march," which proceeds from the right side of the monument. This gathering around the Freedom Monument is, in many ways, not unlike the gatherings at the monument that took place fifty-five years after it was raised. The demonstrations of the mid- and late 1980s, many of which took place at this site, combined elements of battle and elements of song; in the local parlance, this was the "singing revolution." The civility of the battle against the Soviet order was not, however, the only element of change that suggested a reimagination of revolution in the Soviet space. Missing were many of the aspects of "modern revolutions," including the centrality of utopia in the narrative of resistance.

Throughout the oppositional narrative constructed in Latvia ran an anti-utopian ambition for normality and for the fundamental transformation of an order that was widely regarded as illegitimate, uncivilized, uncultured, and undemocratic to its foundations. The elaborated master frame of opposition embraced a spectrum of notions that foresaw a need for social change in "Latvians' interests" or "Latvia's interests," without elaborating those notions far beyond the unifying idea that the Soviet order was contrary to these interests. In this chapter, I have sought to examine the process through which common ideas from the private sphere were transformed into a public narrative that had the power to mobilize a significant proportion of the population for collective action against the Soviet order. This narrative joined macroevents in Latvia's history, like the Soviet occupation of 1940, and microevents of quotidian life in occupied Latvia in a story that was broadly resonant.

The narrative of opposition and its construction and dissemination in Latvian society, which have been the foci of this chapter, are of particular interest because this narrative was powerfully implicated in the post-Communist (re)construction of state and society that followed the de facto achievement of independence. As I suggested earlier, although the shape of the post-Communist order was not inscribed in the revolution that swept the Soviet regime out of Latvia, the notion that state and society were not normal even after independence set the stage for the next phase of transformation, in which the models of normality would be defined and contested.

Normalizing Politics and Politicizing Normality

The Freedom Monument in downtown Riga is composed of a variety of figures carved in stone, from the marchers at the base to the towering figure of a woman at the peak of the obelisk. Each set of figures *(tēli)* tells a story about the nation and its myths and history. On the south and north sides of the monument, just above the steps leading into the eastside terrace, are two carvings that point to powerful notions that have shaped and continue to shape the life of the nation. On the south side is a carving of Vaidelots, adopted father of the Bearslayer of Pumpurs's epic. Vaidelots is a "symbol of national wisdom" and a powerful guardian of national values. He is also, in a sense, a prophet: "After centuries will the nation awaken And reconquer its freedom, / Remembering the noteworthy works of its grandfathers."[1] Vaidelots's words point to the potent notion that the way to the future lies in the wisdom and works of the past. That belief is alive and powerful in Latvia today.

On the other side of the monument, closer to the base, is another carving that tells a different story, a historical tale of the uprising against tsarist power in 1905. The group of figures shows workers moving toward an enemy on horseback. Vaidelotis Apsītis, author of a book on the monument, illustrated this group of figures with the following quotation: "Let us go forth, brothers, quickly, quickly! The future belongs to us!"[2] This story on the monument's wall is underpinned by an imperative of forward movement. In contrast to the staid figure of Vaidelots, the figures in "1905" are in rapid motion; they are agents of a revolutionary moment, the objective of which is to look ahead and seize the future. This notion, too, has had and continues to have powerful sway in Latvia.

The revolution in Latvia in the late 1980s and early 1990s was conceived in a marriage of the imperatives of return and progress, and the contradictions inherent in this reimagined revolution became most clearly apparent at the

3   Vaidelots, adopted father of the Bearslayer, represented on the Freedom Monument

site of post-Communist politics, as Latvia's population began to define and construct a new order. Among the most central objects of contest were the power to legislate and the right of suffrage: that is, early post-Communist politics in Latvia focused on elections and on the composition of the electorate. Elections played a dual role in the (re)construction of normality in the political field because democratic elections themselves signaled a step toward democracy and away from the single-party authoritarianism of the Soviet period. As well, elections were a vehicle of transformation in a context where the (re)construction of a normal state and society was widely seen as being within the domain of governing institutions. Legislative power represented the most visible and probably the most effective site from which to define and determine the path to the future. In this sense, Latvia was like its post-Communist neighbors.

Latvia's experience, however, differs from that of most neighboring states (Estonia being the obvious exception) in that the normalization of politics also involved a fierce contest over the composition of the electorate: in states where the titular population was a strong majority, the issue was far less contentious. In Latvia, the organization of the first post-Communist elections required the provisional resolution of the problem of the electorate, which turned on the issue of who would be defined in and who would be defined out of the body of the voting citizenry. This contest was woven into the electoral contest and postelection legislative debate.

In this chapter, I take up these central issues in the (re)construction of normality in the political field in the early post-Communist period. I seek to pull out guiding notions of change that were part of the founding elections contest. First, I further elaborate the narratives described and discussed in the introductory chapter, by using the first post-Communist elections in Latvia as a point of departure. I discuss how these narrative categories are more illuminating than conventional political categories like left and right or civic and national. I also examine semiotic and substantive aspects of political organizations' campaigns for seats in the Parliament, focusing on campaign posters and election platforms.

In the second part of the chapter, I examine the struggle around the definition of the electorate, using the preelection debate and postelection conflict over the citizenship law as prisms through which to view the early political landscape. I argue that the contest over citizenship was, to an important degree, a contest over the (re)construction of boundaries in society and that the battle over the electorate was, in this sense, as important as the struggle for victory in the elections.

Elections and Transformation

The 1990 election of deputies to the *Augstākā Padome* (Supreme Soviet)[3] of Latvia signaled an important moment in the opposition campaign. At that point, political contestants were still defined primarily in terms of their support or rejection of the Soviet order in Latvia and, together with this, their position on autonomy or independence for Latvia. Thus, although the competitive balloting represented a step toward dissolution of the Soviet order, it could not be construed as a strong step toward the establishment of a stable democratic party system because, with the exception of the Communist Party of Latvia (which, in any case, was in serious disarray by this time), there were neither genuine parties competing nor identifiable political programs that went far beyond abstract prescriptions for change like "democratic rule."

The 1993 elections to the Fifth Saeima (Parliament) of Latvia represented Latvia's "founding elections," the first open and freely contested political race in fifty-two years. At this point, the party system was nascent: of twenty-three political organizations[4] participating in the election, only five were actually political parties. The rest were electoral coalitions, held together by varying degrees of common interest, ambition, and opportunism; loosely bound individuals and interests had yet to coalesce into stable party formations. Furthermore, although policy platforms were iterated by participants, many were vague: on some subjects of importance, like monetary reform and trade policy, some organizations were entirely silent. Nonetheless, the elections represented an important moment in defining problems of and notions about change in post-Communism. On founding elections, the political scientists Guillermo O'Donnell and Phillipe Schmitter wrote:

> [In founding elections] voters will have relatively little experience choosing among candidates. Party identification will probably be weak and candidate images unclear, especially when the period of unrepresentative governance has been lengthy. . . . The ebullience of newly liberalized society is likely to produce big swings in enthusiasm and mood in the face of unprecedented and rapidly occurring events. One can therefore expect a good deal of "tactical voting." Some will wish to vote for candidates and parties that most decisively reject the previous regime, while others will prefer those which seem to offer the best bulwark against such a radical rejection.

This jockeying around may be quite disconnected from longer-term class, sectoral, ethnic, and other interests.[5]

The first post-Communist elections in Latvia mirrored this phenomenon. That is to say that, in a political environment where contestants were many (see Table 3.1) and often did not offer clear policy outlines, voting was informed by general notions about change and by personalities in the contest. This election and its voting patterns represented the start of the development of a competitive, democratic multiparty political environment rather than its achievement.

Beyond highlighting the spectrum of options for post-Communist change that were available, the balloting resulted in the election of eight political organizations to the Saeima and the passage of a host of new and important legislation that would realize some of the visions of change embraced by competitors in the elections (see Table 3.2). The elections represented the culmination of one process—the quest to end the monopoly of a single party

Table 3.1   Parties and coalitions competing in the fifth Saeima elections in 1993

Pretkomunistu apvienība (Anti-Communist Union, or PA)
Konservatīvie un zemnieki (Conservatives and Farmers, or KZ)
Saimniecisko rosības līga (Economic Activists' League, or SRL)
Līdztiesība (Equal Rights)
Demokrātiskā centra partija (Democratic Center Party, or DCP)
Tēvzemei un brīvībai (For Fatherland and Freedom, or TB)
Zaļais saraksts (Green Party, or ZS)
Saskaņa Latvijai, atdzimšana tautsaimniecībai (Harmony for Latvia, Rebirth for the Economy, or SLAT)
Neatkarīgo savienība (Independents' Union, or NS)
Latvijas Kristīgo demokrātu savienība (Latvia's Christian Democratic Union, or KDS)
Latvijas Demokrātiskā darba partija (Latvia's Democratic Work Party, or LDDP)
Latvijas Zemnieku savienība (Latvia's Farmers' Union, or LZS)
Latvijas Liberālā partija (Latvia's Liberal Party, or LLP)
Latvijas laime (Latvia's Luck, or LL)
Latvijas Nacionālā neatkarības kustība (Latvia's National Independence Movement, or LNNK)
Latvijas Tautas fronte (Latvia's Popular Front, or LTF)
Latvijas Sociāldemokrātiskā strādnieku partija (Latvia's Social Democratic Workers' Party, or LSDSP)
Latvijas Vienības partija (Latvia's Unity Party, or LVP)
Latvijas ceļš (Latvia's Way, or LC)
Liberālā alianse (Liberal Alliance, or LA)
Mūsu zeme (Our Land, or MZ)
Republikas platforma (Republic's Platform, or RP)
Krievu nacionālais demokrātiskais saraksts (Russian National Democratic List, or KNDS)

Table 3.2   Number of seats held by winners in the first post-Communist elections
(total of 100 seats)

Latvia's Way—37
Latvia's National Independence Movement—16
Harmony for Latvia, Rebirth for the Economy—12
Latvia's Farmers' Union—11
Equal Rights—7
Christian Democratic Union—6
For Fatherland and Freedom—6
Democratic Center Party—5

in the governance of the state—and the initiation of another—the attempt to consciously (re)construct a "normal" state and society from within the political field.

Narratives and Imperatives of Transformation

In this section, I return to the narratives discussed in the introductory chapter. I suggest that the theorization and application of these ideal-typical narratives to the political field can help to illuminate the contest about change that was taking place in the early post-Communist period. Some political organizations, as the section on posters and platforms shows, exhibited characteristics of more than one ideal type. However imperfect, I suggest that the categories I term "spatial," "temporal," and "evolutionary" highlight important aspects of the contests in various fields of change that dichotomous Western terms like "left" and "right" or "civic" and "national" miss.

At the time that the elections took place, the electoral options offered to potential voters were often neatly categorized in terms of the Western spectrum of right and left by politicians and media both in and outside Latvia. Consider that the Western political spectrum of right and left is frequently applied in the analysis or identification of economic and social policies. Without explanation, a politically aware American, for example, intuitively understands that a politician whose inclinations are described as "right wing" is likely to support, among other things, conservative social policies and laissez-faire economics. A politician labeled as "left wing" is likely to support liberal social policies, redistributive economic politics, and educational and cultural egalitarianism. Similarly, left-wingers are thought to be "progressive," while right-wingers are considered "conservative."

Among the political organizations popularly identified as "right wing" during these elections were For Fatherland and Freedom, Our Land, the

Anti-Communist Union, and the Latvian National Independence Movement. All advocated a regulated market and an extensive social welfare structure. Latvia's National Independence Movement advocated protectionist trading policies, but supported full privatization and an essentially free market. All of these political organizations supported the continuation of socialized medicine and child and invalid allowances in Latvia. The designated "left wing" included political organizations such as Latvia's Democratic Work Party, Latvia's Social Democratic Workers' Party, the Equal Rights Coalition, and Harmony for Latvia, Rebirth for the Economy. Economically, Latvia's Democratic Work Party supported protectionism, limited privatization, and a planned market. Harmony's proposed economic program resembled those of Latvia's Democratic Work Party and Latvia's Social Democratic Workers' Party, except for its support of free trade. The Equal Rights Coalition also favored a planned market, but did not share the negative attitude toward privatization. Again, all organizations advocated state-supported medical and social services.

The native Latvian press, most notably Latvia's largest and most widely read daily, *Diena,* made an effort throughout the preelection campaign to introduce the Western political spectrum of right and left into Latvian political life. For example, in the month before the elections, *Diena* published six left-to-right numerical evaluations of various aspects of contenders' economic programs (privatization, market philosophy, social welfare and taxes, state regulation of the economy, trade, and monetary policy). The graphs and explanations, which appeared on the second page of a newspaper with a total circulation (in Latvian and Russian) of nearly 100,000, were clearly intended to have an impact on voters. The product of *Diena's* effort, however, was more confusing than helpful. For Fatherland and Freedom, a "far right" coalition, was on the left in three of five indicators (and on one other had no published program). Conversely, the Latvian Social Democratic Workers' Party, a "left" political organization, appeared right of center on four of six indicators. As well, Latvia's Liberal Party, another "left" organization, was to the right on five of five indicators. Of the twenty-three competing groups, all of which were rated on privatization, the "right-wing" Anti-Communist Union was the second furthest to the left. Only a handful of groups, including the Latvian Democratic Workers' Party (left), Harmony for Latvia (left), and Latvia's Way (right), lived up to their popular labels on all or all but one indicator.[6] The classifications were not, one may reasonably presume, intended to mislead, but the terms failed to paint an accurate portrait of the politics and programs embraced by contending parties and coalitions.

The categories of "civic" and "national" have also been invoked to describe the dominant notions and narratives of transformation in Eastern Europe. Although they are more resonant than designations like left and right, they are weakened by assumptions inherent in the terms. On the one hand, a civic (or liberal) doctrine of state is presumed to be based on individual rights and freedoms that inhere in membership in the polity. Collective rights fit into this position as rights and protections for minority populations. On the other hand, a nationalist doctrine of state is founded on notions of collective rights for the core nation and obligations to the national community. Whereas the dominant spatial and temporal narratives reflect, to some degree, the civic and national principles, respectively, even the former are colored by a concern for collective national rights that stems from worry about the demographic situation of Latvians in Latvia and the sense that the Soviet regime weakened the cultural, linguistic, and economic standing of Latvians. Both narratives revolve, in part, around notions of rectifying national problems wrought by the regime.

If the spatial narrative fits awkwardly into the civic category, so too does the evolutionary narrative. The latter iterates a language of ethnic and class equality and multiculturalism in politics and society, but it is problematic to label it as "civic" because some of its proponents tend to see "equality" in terms of the Soviet definition, when it meant, for example, the elevation of the Russian language as the dominant means of communication for all of the "equal" nations of the Soviet Union. There were and are individuals who embrace the notions commonly associated with a category like "civic," but sorting political organizations and platforms into categories of civic and national fails to capture the particularities and peculiarities of the post-Communist political moment.

The narratives of spatial and temporal transformation of the early post-Communist period iterated different notions about the path Latvia ought to follow to reach the coveted state of normality, though both shared as a critical point of departure the notion that the period of Soviet occupation was illegitimate, illegal, and abnormal. Furthermore, there was a shared assumption that even after independence, neither the state nor society was "normal." In other words, Communism's economic, social, and political remnants were perceived to linger even after its fall. A campaign leaflet disseminated by supporters of Latvia's Christian Democratic Union declared, for instance, that "Latvia has regained its independence, but it is still necessary to restore full freedom, [and] spiritual and material wealth." Latvia's Unity Party also suggested that "Latvia's independence has been formally restored, but the consequences of occupation have not been eliminated." The party pamphlet further asserted that "Latvia's Unity Party supports the united efforts of patriotic forces to renew the fundamental worth of state and nation." This latter point, reiterated in the campaign literature of numerous parties and coalitions, implied that a state of normality was something that needed to be consciously (re)created.

Notably, both dominant visions of normality also referenced similar sociopolitical bases. That is, one of the outstanding common denominators of the spatial and temporal narratives was their elevation of an essentially parliamentary, democratic, and capitalist order as the antithesis of Communism, and therefore a "natural" alternative to it. The alternatives varied most clearly around the models of normality and prosperity they elevated, the positions they held on questions of nation, and the degree to which free markets were to be balanced by welfare-state provisions. In the political field, the evolutionary narrative, although not dominant, also played a visible role. This narrative shared with the other two a basic commitment to a democratic, parliamentary state, but did not hearken back to the legacy of the independent interwar Latvian state, nor was the Soviet order labeled as fundamentally deviant. This narrative proceeded, instead, from the legacies of that period, though certainly not all were perceived as positive.

As noted earlier, the powerful narrative of temporal normality took as its template of change the independent interwar Latvian state. This path of change was a national and nationalist road, paved with the imperative of protecting and retaining the norms and symbols and institutions of the First Republic. Here, that which was foreign, whether Eastern or Western, was potentially suspect. The East (Russia), on the one hand, was reviled for its centuries-long subjugation of the Latvian people and continued threats to Latvia's sovereignty. The West, while not viewed as a danger, was taken as basically untrustworthy: part of this notion derived from the failure of the West to act when Russia occupied and then reoccupied Latvia in 1940 and 1944, and part arose from the perceived Western sympathy for Russian interests and the "special relationship" that the West had cultivated with Russia since the end of the Cold War. The position that some Western European organizations like the European Community took in favor of a broadly inclusive citizenship law in the early 1990s further reinforced this distrust. This was reflected in, for example, the campaign platform of the Sovereign Union, which promised "not to allow the interference of other countries in Latvia's internal matters and to stop the negative influence of the International Monetary Fund on Latvia's economics."[7] The hesitance of the West to accept the

Baltic states into the North Atlantic Treaty Organization (NATO) was also explained in some political quarters as Western pandering to Russia, which vehemently opposed Baltic membership in the military alliance until fall 2001. Semantically, the temporal narrative linked directly with the past, iterating the goal of restoring the First Republic of Latvia. The campaign literature of the coalition For Fatherland and Freedom, for example, designated its platform a "program for the renewal of the Latvian Republic proclaimed on November 18, 1918." The assertion that the post-Communist state was not a *successor to* but rather a *continuation of* the interwar state appeared in a multitude of platforms. Metaphorically, normality appeared in the campaign in many guises, but most prevalent in the temporal narrative were order and Latvianness. The elevation of these goals appeared in the advertisements of coalitions like Latvia's National Independence Movement, which declared its commitment to "an ordered and Latvian Latvia." The elevation of order, more popular in the temporal category than elsewhere, may have appeared as a prescription for what was popularly known in Latvia as the *juku laiki* (time of disorder). In this category, nostalgia for a strong leader, like Kārlis Ulmanis, who assumed full political power in Latvia after dissolving the Parliament in 1934, may also have been a factor in the elevation of order as a post-Communist value.

The platforms embraced by political organizations in this category were typically socially conservative and economically protectionist. They also placed a premium on Latvian ethnicity and the ethnic composition of the body of the citizenry. Citizenship was viewed as an instrument of economic and political closure, which would institutionally guarantee the survival and dominance of the primary nation. Citizenship was potentially a tool, then, for reconstructing the demographic composition of interwar Latvia politically where doing so physically was impossible. Some of the political organizations in this category also iterated programs highlighting what came to be called the 3D formula: decolonization, de-Bolshevization, deoccupation. This formula posited that even after independence, Latvia was not free because "colonists" (Soviet-era migrants) still resided there, former Communists were still in power, and the Soviet army was still present on the territory (it decamped in 1994).

The spatial narrative of transformation, by contrast, located normality outside the historically specific experience of interwar independence. In the election, political organizations in this category did not locate their template of change in the past, though many clearly referenced interwar history and some highlighted the construction of a Second Republic of Latvia, a legatee (not a copy) of the First Republic (1918–40). The elevation of Europe as a representative of modernity and security and prosperity was one of the defining features of this narrative. Latvia considered itself part of Europe before the Soviet Communist occupation of 1940. Even today, the fact that Latvia's living standards in the 1930s approached those of Scandinavia is common knowledge and a source of pride, in part because it suggests that Latvia was "really" European. A candidate from Latvia's Way, Andrejs Pantelejevs, suggested during the campaign: "We do not seek any new utopias . . . we are working with the goal that Latvians too deserve those times that other nations are now experiencing." Unlike the temporal narrative, the spatial narrative highlighted progress rather than return and modern rather than traditional norms and practices in economics and politics. Notions about the importance of Latvianness appeared in the symbols and platforms of some political organizations in the first elections, but they typically shared rather than dominated the stage.

In the elections, the spatial narrative focused on *construction* rather than *restoration* of a normal state, economy, and society. Although the legacy of the national past received attention in some posters and pronouncements, the practical political platforms were oriented toward progress, modernity, integration, and marketization. They highlighted market reforms and participation in European political and economic structures like the Council of Europe (CE) and the European Union. In these platforms, there was also less emphasis on controversial issues like the extension or denial of citizenship to Soviet-era immigrants: most platforms iterated ideals of individual rights and freedoms for all and some form of naturalization and integration for noncitizens.

The evolutionary narrative, the weakest of the three narratives in the political field, combined notions of change with notions of continuity and foresaw the progressive evolution rather than rejection of particular features of the Soviet legacy. In the elections, political organizations in this category embraced change in the sense that they, like all other groups, accepted a democratic and parliamentary order as a norm and institution in the post-Communist state: this point was never in dispute in the first post-Communist election campaign. But whereas the other narratives embraced a common notion that the Soviet period was not normal and that its institutions, symbols, norms, and practices were inappropriate in the Latvian context, this narrative reflected an imperative of evolution rather than revolution in the transformation of structures and society. It highlighted social and economic continuity with the recent past in that it sought to minimize the changes in social and economic status wrought by new citizenship criteria and the competitive market of post-Communism.

The interwar state of Latvia played no real role in the evolutionary narrative. Notably, every organization in the spatial and temporal category accepted the renewal of interwar Latvia's constitution, which had taken place shortly after independence, but neither of the two groups in the evolutionary category did, and the Russian National Democratic Party specifically advocated "the acceptance of a new democratic constitution for the Republic of Latvia."[8] Furthermore, both political organizations rejected the use of the interwar body of the citizenry as a baseline for the establishment of a post-Communist citizenry, and both advocated the automatic granting of citizenship in the Republic of Latvia to all who resided there at the time that the Supreme Council of Latvia voted for independence—May 4, 1990.

I iterate these narratives separately, but I do not intend them to be mutually exclusive, because they are interpretations rather than fixed categories. Pictures of parties and coalitions competing for seats in the Parliament can be visualized as a continuum. As the following section shows, both the platforms and visual images of parties and coalitions suggest a distribution across that continuum. The categories, however, are based on the strongest symbolic and political tendencies of political organizations and hence offer an illuminating reflection of the streams of change that contested and defined the first post-Communist elections in Latvia. The purpose of the following section is to look at the political dimensions of normalization by using the posters and platforms of these elections as a prism.

The Representation of Politics: Campaign Posters of the First Post-Communist Elections

Although the first post-Communist elections took place nearly two years after the formal reestablishment of independence in Latvia, they marked an important point of change. First, many in Latvia, including strongly nationalist political organizations like the November 18 Union and the Conservative Party, did not accept the legitimacy of the Supreme Council, which was elected while Latvia was still a de facto part of the Soviet Union, but continued to serve until 1993. Even some political organizations, like Latvia's Farmers' Union and Latvia's Christian Democratic Union, which embraced less extreme perspectives on the authority of the Supreme Council, backed the postponement of legislation on, for example, the citizenship question, until a legislature elected in independent Latvia was seated. Hence, with the election of a new Parliament, important issues that had simmered on the back burner in the Supreme Council period made their way into the halls of Parliament.

Second, elections signaled the formal and symbolic reestablishment of the electoral order of interwar Latvia; the elections were referred to as the "Fifth Saeima elections," a rhetorical device that linked them across a divide of fifty-nine years with the Fourth Saeima, elected in 1931 and illegally dismissed in May 1934 by the then-prime minister Kārlis Ulmanis. Furthermore, the constituency method used in the 1990 Supreme Council election was dropped in favor of the proportional party-list method that had been used in interwar Latvia. The primary distinctions of these elections from those of the interwar period were the voting-age minimum, lowered from twenty-one to eighteen years, and the establishment of a requirement that parties or coalitions win no less than 4 percent of the total vote to take seats in the Saeima. The latter change presumably represented a desire to avoid the interwar experience of a Saeima populated by dozens of different parties: in the 1931 Saeima, twenty-seven parties or coalitions were represented.

Imperatives and notions of continuity underpinned the way that the elections were structured, including the composition of the electorate itself, which leads to the third point. Although formal citizenship legislation was postponed until after the Fifth Saeima elections, the issue was provisionally resolved with the establishment of a baseline of citizenship rooted in the interwar period. That is, citizenship and its consequent voting rights were automatically extended to anyone (regardless of ethnicity) who had been a citizen at the time that Latvia was occupied by the Soviet Union and to direct descendants of any such person, regardless of his or her present citizenship or place of residence.

Fourth, the elections represented a new field of play for contestants seeking to establish the dominant path of change that Latvia would pursue in the post-Communist period. In the election campaign, notions of continuity and return ran up against notions of modernization and progress. As well, both were challenged by minority-dominated political organizations representing social and economic (though not political) continuity with the socialist experience. As the slogan of one electoral coalition declared, this was "the time to decide what Latvia will be like." The answer was not, by any means, clear.

Envisioning Change: Symbols and Politics

In this section, I examine the campaign materials of contestants for parliamentary power in post-Communist Latvia. In particular, I highlight campaign posters because they were an important part of the electoral contest. The posters and the images they presented to the public were important in that they both reflected and, potentially, helped to structure notions about the path of change Latvia should take. The duration of the campaign was short, and there were numerous contestants, many of whom were new. Clearly, the voting public's familiarity with the platforms of the twenty-three contenders could not be comprehensive. No one with whom I spoke at that time had read all or even most of the platforms. Everyone had, however, seen the campaign posters. Posters were, at that time, one of the pre-eminent vehicles for disseminating information on competing parties and coalitions. Television advertising was expensive, a luxury only a few organizations could afford. Even paid newspaper advertisements were not purchased by every competing party and coalition. All contenders, however, could and did afford campaign posters, and a fence in downtown Riga where dozens of posters were displayed became a daily gathering place for people wishing to discuss, debate, and argue about parties and politics in the weeks and days before the elections.

The campaign posters referenced a system of meanings embedded in national history and culture and popular political culture, albeit for competing purposes. Although few posters contained programmatic statements, notions about transformation and the desired direction of change could often be read off the symbols used and the contexts in which they appeared. I follow the historian Lisa Tickner, who has written on the images of the suffrage campaign in Britain, in suggesting that "the imagery . . . was not a footnote or an illustration to the 'real' political history going on elsewhere, but an integral part of the fabric of social conflict with its own contradictions and ironies and its own power to shape through, focus debates, and stimulate action."[9] The posters did not just reflect formed political ideologies or beliefs, but contributed to the further imagination and expansion of those notions in an environment in which political contestation was a relatively new phenomenon and few parties or coalitions had well-known or well-articulated platforms.

Political campaign posters, in such a dynamic conception, also fall into the category of cultural productions, which "are composed of shared cultural symbols which are used to mediate between what is already widely known or understood and the articulation of something new. They are rhetorical devices meant to persuade." The sociologist Sonya Rose added that cultural productions

> offer their intended audience interpretations of events and experiences that may become a stimulus for political action. These inter-

4   A demonstrator expresses his party preference near the wall of campaign
     posters in downtown Riga

pretations are particular constructions which cast the events within a limited and limiting perspective. The constructions repress, negate, or remain silent about alternative views. When these interpretations are built into public policies, they directly constrain people's lives. . . . They call upon previously formed subjectivities and work on commonsense understandings to generate solidarity and consent. They appeal to particular aspects of people's experiences and connect these experiences to facets of their identities.[10]

Consistent with Rose's conception, these political posters offered particular interpretations of change that appealed to people's experiences and beliefs, as well as tried to shape them.

Rose's definition of cultural productions also noted the significance of the source of cultural productions: "When [cultural productions] are articulated by members of Parliament or heads of state, owners of significant business enterprises, leaders of unions and organizers of strikes and protest movements, or clergymen, they assume greater significance and wider currency than alternative interpretations offered by those who lack public prominence."[11] In considering power, however, one must consider not just the power of the *source* of a cultural production but the power of the *symbols* used therein. The importance of this point is highlighted by Karen Cerulo in her distinction between "normal" and "deviant" national symbols. The latter may be used by elites in cultural productions, but Cerulo argued that "because of their inconsistencies to the settings from which they emerge, deviant national symbols never come to be fully embraced by the national populations they represent. As such, deviant symbols lack the motivational power of their normative counterparts." By contrast, normal symbols are "highly predictable, and this predictability generates comfort, making the symbols 'approachable'—easy for an audience to receive, process, and accept. As such, normal symbols increase potential for audience attachment and enhance the likelihood of effective communication."[12]

Within the boundaries drawn around "normal" symbols is what Ann Swidler termed the cultural "tool kit." From this kit, actors can fashion a wide variety of cultural productions that remain within the bounds of the normal but convey different messages. Swidler's work is useful in considering the symbolic representation of competing visions of transformation in this election. Swidler wrote that "all real cultures contain diverse, often conflicting symbols, rituals, stories, and guides to action. . . . A culture is not a unified system that pushes action in a consistent direction. Rather, it is more like a 'tool kit' or repertoire from which actors select differing pieces for constructing lines of action."[13] It is possible, then, to recognize that the representations of normality emerging from the dominant competing narratives of change were "authentic" (or as Cerulo might say, "normal") cultural productions, as they drew from the same "tool kit," albeit, toward different political ends.

Important as well is the idea that different "lines of action" need not necessarily be represented by "conflicting symbols," because symbols can be polyvalent, conveying several meanings simultaneously, and multivocal, expressing multiple layers of meaning. The "pieces" of culture used in the political field to represent and (re)construct normality were taken from the same "tool box," which endowed them with legitimacy and recognizability among voters in Latvia. My examination of the campaign posters highlights how different notions about post-Communist change were conveyed through visual symbols that accessed a common bank of cultural signs and symbols, but used them to convey competing ideas about the (re)construction of the post-Communist state.

Posters, Politics, and Post-Communist Normality

Political organizations embracing notions of change that reflected the temporal narrative of transformation used symbols that elevated a "blood and soil" link. Many posters in this category stressed traditional symbols like the oak tree (which is a nationalist symbol in numerous European cultures) or bucolic images of rural Latvia. The tie between blood and soil is linked to the notion that the distinctive qualities of the Latvian nation (and others) are grounded and founded in the local rural culture, which, because of its isolation from cosmopolitan urban centers, remains untainted by outside influences. The metaphor of national purity is thus, logically, located in the countryside and the traditions of rural life.

The understanding of the images in the posters of these parties and coalitions is a contingent one. As is the case with visual allegory, meaning "is not inherent in the image but depends on the competence of the viewer. Only viewers conversant with the association between an image and an idea or conception will appreciate the complexity of the meaning."[14] It is useful to consider why the link between image and idea, in this case, traditional symbols and a temporal vision of post-Communist normality in Latvia, was "readable" in the posters. The broad use of nature symbols in the posters of organizations embracing visions of temporal normality was grounded in a number of historical and cultural bases.

First, nature and reverence of nature are very prominent in Latvian folk stories, songs, poems, and the traditional four-line poems called *dainas*. The centrality of nature in the *dainas* is especially important because they represent a tangible link to Latvia's ancient past, as they are part of a preliterary national culture put to paper only in the nineteenth century. The collective "knowing" that natural symbols like the oak are linked to a distant (if somewhat mythologized) national past is largely attributable to the broad public consumption of Latvian folk culture.

Second, before the Soviet occupation of 1940, Latvia had a predominantly agricultural economy that relied on exports of goods like butter, bacon, and timber for its outside earnings. It was only after its incorporation into the Soviet Union and Stalin's aggressive drive for industrialization that Latvia became a heavily industrial economy. Hence, symbols reminiscent of a natural, agricultural lifestyle were a point of contrast between prewar Latvia and Soviet (as well as post-Communist) Latvia.

The association with tradition and history helped to create legitimacy for political organizations evoking these symbols, and the political, economic, and social claims they made in the public sphere, and on the campaign posters that presented examples of blood and soil imagery. A broadly distributed *Latvijas Nacionālā neatkarības kustība* (Latvia's National Independence Movement, or LNNK) poster depicted a majestic oak gently lit by the sun and contained the slogan "The Nation, the Land, the State."[15] The combination of these three elements in the slogan signaled the notion that the (re)creation of normal social, political, and economic life was broadly seen as the domain of the state rather than, as was the case in the late 1980s, civil society. Whereas civil societies in Eastern Europe proclaimed liberation from the constraints of the state, post-Communist societies like Latvia have again married the fate of the nation and land to the state. In an LNNK newspaper article on the coalition's stance on the citizenship question, a member of the coalition wrote that the "current situation in Latvia is abnormal, because the consequences of occupation and colonization have not been liquidated." The means of liquidating these consequences, which included the demographic situation of Latvians in Latvia, was envisaged as being in the hands of the state, which would take steps to address the issue through, among others, citizenship legislation.[16]

The oak foregrounded in the poster shown is a polyvalent symbol representing strength, national unity, and cultural endurance. These notions were reflected as well in the LNNK platform that promoted a "Latvian Latvia" and highlighted the centrality of culture to the nation ("[Culture] is the wellspring of our Latvian way of life, humane relations, and cultural values,"

5 Poster of the *Latvijas Nacionālā neatkarības kustība* (Latvia's National Independence Movement) coalition

asserted a published advertisement). Cultural works were envisioned as "standing in the way of influences dangerous to our identity, whether they originate in the West or the East." The primary keeper and material guardian of this protective and unifying culture was put forth as the state. The message conveyed by the LNNK was, in sum, one of commitment to tradition and nation and elevation of a state-centered order to ensure the well-being of both. The slogan and the coalition logo both used maroon and white, the colors of the Latvian flag, again reiterating a potent commitment to the nation.

Some of the coalitions in this category were less well financed, which was reflected in the quality and quantity of their posters. One such coalition, *Mūsu zeme* (Our Land, or MZ), displayed only modest letter-size posters, but its leanings were evident. The MZ posters centered a physical representation of Latvia that featured a Latvian flag within the borders. Behind the foregrounded picture, a bright sun rose over the land. The name of the coalition was also symbolic: that Latvia is "Our Land" summed up the core notion embraced by MZ, which promised voters "[a] Latvian Latvia, a national state, in which Latvians constitute a stable majority of Latvia's citizenry."[17] Another of the smaller and materially limited coalitions was the *Pretkomunistu apvienība* (Anti-Communist Union, or PA), which featured no particular symbolism in its posters. Rather it highlighted the name in larger letters and gave a brief programmatic statement in very small letters. The name, however, carried a message. The PA represented one of the most ardent nationalist organizations fielding candidates, and it stood on the notion that, even after the formal reestablishment of independence, Latvia was not free because Soviet-era immigrants remained in Latvia and former Communists like the Supreme Council Presidium chairman Anatolijs Gorbunōvs remained in government. The PA highlighted the 3D formula[18] of decolonization, deoccupation, and de-Bolshevization and promised voters "in the shortest time possible, to free Latvia from communist overlordship."

Some of the posters of the *Konservatīvie un zemnieki* (Conservatives and Farmers, or KZ) also featured trees in a field beneath the slogan "God, Nature, Work," which affirmed the coalition's commitment to values widely perceived to be opposite to those elevated in the Soviet period. Religion was, depending on the era, either frowned on or actively persecuted; nature was victimized by the vagaries of a state and economy driven by the relentless pursuit of construction and production; and the values of work were disabled by a system that rewarded obedience and complacency rather than creativity and ambition. A second KZ poster reiterated a part of the coalition's message. By centering a ramshackle country grain-threshing hut beneath the message "The Latvian must become the keeper of his own land!" the coalition implied that work had been a forgotten value in the Soviet era. The message was that although traditional Latvian smallholdings would have been neatly kept, the state-owned collective farms engendered an indifference toward and diminishment of interest in the upkeep of the farm (the hut is surrounded by overgrown grass) and the maintenance of farm equipment (tools are not put away, but simply propped up against the hut). The scene implied that agriculture, a site of both Latvian tradition and economic sustenance, was damaged by the Soviet experience. KZ's visual platform was strongly linked to its enumerated platform, which prioritized support for small farm holdings and elevated them as the foundation of post-Communist Latvian agriculture.

The appeal of this poster might have been generational as well. Because Latvia had a predominantly rural population before the Soviet occupation, many older people, even those now in urban areas, would have remembered grain-threshing huts and other particulars of rural life; such images would resonate with their knowledge and experience. Posters like those of the KZ

6 Poster of the *Konservatīvie un zemnieki* (Conservatives and Farmers) coalition

also offered a strong contrast to those of, for example, the *Liberālā alianse* (Liberal Alliance, or LA). The LA poster featured bright colors and the face of a young child. The message on the poster was also somewhat less staid than KZ's "God, Work, Nature." The LA poster declared, "Let's think, let's act, let's sing."

The most prominent of a small group of extreme nationalist organizations, *Tēvzemei un brīvībai* (For Fatherland and Freedom, or TB), did not use blood and soil symbolism in its posters, but its name, which is also the inscription carved on the base of the Freedom Monument in Riga, was an indirect visual allegory referring viewers to the monument. The monument, built during the interwar period of independence, is a powerful national symbol, a fact of which the Soviet government was also cognizant when it prohibited even the laying of flowers at the site. As a product of the independent First Republic, the monument clearly has important links to the inter-

7   Posters of the *Liberālā alianse* (Liberal Alliance) surround a Conservatives and Farmers poster

war period, but significantly its design also features visual tributes to older Latvian history and mythology, with its carvings of soldiers marching to battle and figures like the mythical Bearslayer. Thus, the organization's selection of the monument's inscription as its name suggested the centrality of the nation and its past in the coalition's platform.

In addition to this, TB posters featured the coalition's adopted symbol, Laima's cross, a folk design from the *Lielvārdes josta* (Lielvārdes belt). Folk wisdom suggests that the history of the Latvian nation is written in symbols on the belt, which is traditionally worn with the Lielvārdes regional folk costume. The cross represents good fortune, long life, fertility, and health. Although the contrast was not explicitly made, these could be interpreted as metaphors of normality, where the opposite was a Communist period characterized by misfortune, illness, and death. Symbolically, the Laima's cross references the nation as opposed to the individual. The reference to long life was relevant in the campaign in another way as well. In the campaign literature of numerous parties and coalitions appeared the assertion that their election would guarantee the "survival" of the Latvian nation, perceived to be threatened by its bare majority in the country. In this spirit, TB's published program promised "a state with the rule of law for the survival of the Latvian nation."

In contrast to most of the other posters, TB's material also included an extensive programmatic statement, located above the assurance "On our and your list: there are no former Communist Party members, there are no Supreme Council deputies, there are no former or current [state] ministers." The coalition's claim was thus notable for its negative view of political experience. Some of the other parties and coalitions highlighted their experienced candidates, but TB deliberately highlighted its lack of experience in any government associated with the Soviet period, asserting that the Gorbunōvs-Godmanis administration, which was in power in Latvia at that time, had "brought the state to the brink of catastrophe." TB's suspicion of the political elite was further highlighted by its campaign promise to "form a parliamentary commission to investigate the correspondence of the activities of the current administration to the interests of the Latvian state and its citizens." The platform also iterated a suspicion of Europe, the "destination" of so many other political organizations. For Fatherland and Freedom advocated movement toward Europe, but framed this in terms of a "step-by-step integration into Europe, without threatening the interests of the Latvian nation." The notion of Europe as presenting a threat to Latvians' interests was in part a reaction to the initiatives of European organizations like Orga-

8   Poster of the *Tēvzemei un brīvībai* (For Fatherland and Freedom) coalition

nization for Security and Cooperation in Europe to prod Latvia to accept (quickly) an inclusive citizenship law, which would not have fit with the "decolonization" promise of TB.

Groups like *Latvijas Zemnieku savienība* (Latvia's Farmers' Union, or LZS) and *Latvijas Kristīgo demokrātu savienība* (Latvia's Christian Democratic Union, or KDS), which at least rhetorically tended toward the restorationist end of the spectrum, also incorporated traditional symbols in their posters. Although they supported a far less extreme vision of restoration, they embraced distinctly nationalistic themes, as the posters suggest. They represented a location between restorationism and modernization, however, as both platforms exhibited progressive notions as well.

The posters of LZS stressed the importance of agriculture and rural life, but relegated the scene to the background. Rather, the centerpiece of its most visible poster was a black and white portrait of independent interwar Latvia's last president, Kārlis Ulmanis. The irony that Ulmanis abolished all parties, including his own (the interwar LZS), in his 1934 assumption of dictatorial state powers was apparently less significant than his standing in society as a virtual cult figure, especially for older Latvians, many of whom recall the period of Ulmanis's dictatorship with fondness. Whereas Ulmanis has come to be strongly associated with what is broadly considered to be a bright period in Latvia's history, his actions in office, including the dismissal of the democratically elected Saeima, the arrest of some opposition leaders, and the nationalization of a number of non-Latvian-owned businesses, suggest that his contributions to Latvia's interwar success were mixed.[19] The power of the poster was, thus, rooted in its elevation of Ulmanis the national myth rather than Ulmanis the man.

On the LZS poster, the ghostly bicolor countenance of Ulmanis is a stark contrast to the colors that appear behind him. In the background is a picture of well-tended fields, presumably those of a private rather than state farm because they show neat rows of a variety of crops. Beyond the field are the yellow and orange hues of the sun. However, above the colors of day are the ominous colors of night, indicators of a threat on the horizon. The threat suggested by darkness on the horizon, still somewhat distant judging from the fact that the fields were illuminated by daylight, is arguably both historical and actual. Historically, Ulmanis's tenure as president-dictator and Latvia's period of independence were cut short by the Soviet occupation of 1940. In the post-Communist period, Latvia's newly independent government continued, for reasons ranging from Russia's refusal to acknowledge the illegality of the occupation to the emergence of a neoimperialist ideology in Moscow, to fear for its safety and sovereignty. The poster thus sug-

LATVIJAS ZEMNIEKU SAVIENIBA ĪBA

Par Latviju, nacionālu, daiļu un spēcigu!

9   Poster of *Latvijas Zemnieku savienība* (Latvia's Farmers' Union)

gested the possibility of a bright national future not unlike the popularly constructed radiant past, while reminding the cognizant viewer of the once and future threat to the daylight of independence.

Both the foreground and background images in the poster suggest restorationist and traditionalist leanings. The party itself was a restored institution: in a July 1990 party conference, participants "decided to reinstate the party on the same basis as its original foundation."[20] In terms of the imagery, Ulmanis represented the positive experiences of the interwar period despite his political shortcomings. The published campaign material of this organization also reflected these notions in its declaration "in favor of the renewal of a genuinely independent and democratic first Republic of Latvia." Reflecting the statist policies of interwar Latvia, as well as the interests of the economically besieged farmers of post-Communist Latvia, the LZS also took a cautious line on opening the market. The LZS embraced greater protection for farmers, arguing in its platform that the "strength of the state is founded on agriculture, which alone can ensure the survival of the Latvian nation, [and] the state's economic independence and self-reliance."

There was a distance, however, between the extreme restorationists like For Fatherland and Freedom and the LZS for several reasons. First, the LZS, although it highlighted a "Latvian Latvia," also left open the door for the political integration of non-Latvians through a naturalization process, though this too was based on historical example: "Relying on the Latvian nation's historical experience, the Farmers' Union is convinced that Latvia will never be a two or more community state, [and] that all nationalities living here will with time be fully integrated." Second, the LZS iterated the importance of European integration and membership in political, economic, and military organizations of the West. Whereas For Fatherland and Freedom, for example, also advocated participation in (some) European structures in principle, the attitude toward them was more suspicious and tentative. Even the LNNK represented a more tentative commitment to Europe, noting in one advertisement that "Latvia belongs to Europe, but on [its own] conditions." The LZS, though, stood for "Latvia's real integration into Europe's political and economic circle" and "active politics" in organizations like NATO.

The most prominent poster of Latvia's Christian Democratic Union recalled the theme of the natural world and suggested a connection to the "Latvianness" embodied by rural tradition. Indeed, the KDS also highlighted in its program the centrality of the nation. The poster, however, focused more on sky than earth. It showed a recently seeded field in the foreground, with a cluster of trees typical in Latvian agricultural areas in the distance, but a greater portion of the poster was occupied by a vivid blue sky and clusters of clouds. The interpretation of Christian values embraced by the KDS also put it on the fence between the restorationism embodied by, for example, For Fatherland and Freedom, and the more progressive notions of change found in the programs of, for example, the Democratic Center Party or Latvia's Way. The KDS held some strongly nationalist views (one of its published ads declared that "the sovereign power of the Latvian state belongs to the Latvian nation"), but it also preached a doctrine of basic tolerance that precluded categorical exclusion of others. Hence it promised that "every person will have the right to declare for Latvian citizenship." Furthermore, although one published platform embraced a "social market foundation—private property and private initiative," a newspaper ad qualified this with the assertion that "neither communism nor pure capitalism are acceptable to a Christian." Together with the poster's slogan, "It is time to renew basic values," the vast sky and the relatively small earth suggested the omniscience of a higher power and deference to the wisdom of Christianity and its "basic values." The statement that values were to be renewed also alluded to a notion that Christian values were not of consequence in the atheistic Soviet state, but that they were present before that, presumably in the independent interwar state.

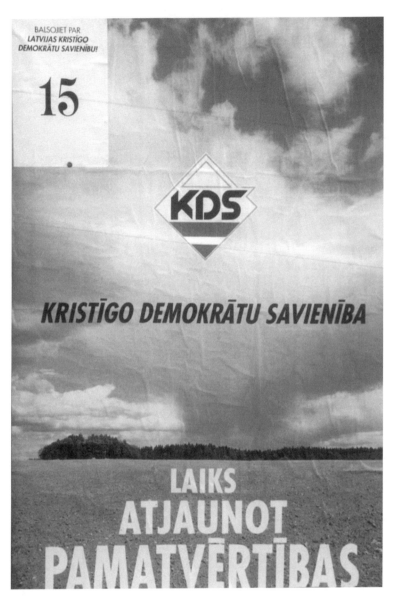

10   Poster of *Latvijas Kristīgo demokrātu savienība* (Latvia's Christian
      Democratic Union)

Although the poster of the *Republikas platforma* (Republic's Platform, or RP) centered a representation of the natural world, the platform put forth a position that favored modernization over restoration. The symbol chosen by RP, a stork, was also less representative of restorationist notions than, for example, agricultural scenes or the oak tree. The stork symbolizes luck, and, Latvians believe, when the bird nests around one's home, it is a sign of good fortune. Hence, the representation was linked more to individual than collective good fortune: in the RP program, the potential for that luck seemed to reside in the individualistic marketplace, because it declared: "A nation can be free, if it has a free and modern economic system!" Above the head of the stork were the words, "Today the time has come to decide what Latvia will be like." The Latvia that RP envisioned recognized the interwar experience, but did not take it as a model in its particulars. The coalition suggested: "A democratic parliamentary republic is renewable respecting the principles of the 1922 Constitution. That can be complemented by norms that respect modern ideas about the distribution of power and human rights."[21]

Latvijas Tautas fronte (Latvia's Popular Front, or LTF), the leader of the opposition in the late Soviet period, recalled in its posters the period of its greatest power. One of the posters featured a photo of a demonstration from that period, which showed a sea of Latvian flags and masses of anti-Soviet demonstrators. The LTF, hence, situated itself in recent history, elevating its own achievements in the opposition period. As one published advertisement stated, "You know these people well and know what they have done for the good of Latvia's independence." Its main slogan and platform, however, distanced it from a number of the positions taken by the LTF during the opposition period. The campaign slogan *Esi saimnieks savā zemē!* (Be the master of your own land!), with its nationalistic overtones, conveyed some of this distance, because although the LTF had worked in earnest to make the opposition organization broadly inclusive and enjoyed a significant degree of support among progressive Russians, the post-Communist LTF appealed particularly to Latvians. This was apparent in the party's position on the issue of citizenship as well, which foresaw "the right to become a citizen of Latvia, based on quotas, for those who have integrated into a Latvian environment" and promised "the humane realization of decolonization, the support of voluntary repatriation."[22] Hence, whereas the poster recalled the progressive and transformatory imperatives that the opposition-era LTF had embraced, the slogan stepped away from the broadly inclusive appeal on which the LTF had stood when, for example, it supported candidates for the 1990 elections to the Supreme Soviet of Latvia.

Groups with distinct leanings toward modernization and a European

11   Poster of the *Republikas platforma* (Republic's Platform) coalition

template of transformation, like *Latvijas ceļš* (Latvia's Way, or LC) and the *Demokrātiskā centra partija* (Democratic Center Party, or DCP), typically combined traditional and modern symbols, suggesting an amalgamation of the imperatives of tradition and progress. These posters did not evoke Europe per se, but they presented images that evoked modernity, particularly in contrast to those of the temporal ideal type. Some of the posters also deviated from the characteristically Latvian color palate of neutrals and used bright colors, though some also kept to the "normal" range of colors and the colors of the Latvian flag.

The Democratic Center Party offered a poster with graphics depicting a maroon and white ribbon entering one end of a dark labyrinth and emerging from the other intact. The allusion could be read as either historical or contemporary. Historically, the white and maroon ribbon could be read as the Latvian nation and the drab labyrinth as the Soviet period. The interpretation might thus be that the nation has successfully steered its way through the labyrinth and is now free to pursue its own road. Unlike that of the temporal normalization posters, the implication was that the road to the future was linear rather than circular: the ribbon's path did not lead back to the point of entry, the interwar period, but rather away from it. With respect to contemporary politics, the symbolism could suggest that the labyrinth, well known from mythology, was the period of transition, with its accompanying problems and obstacles, through which the DCP, presumably represented by the ribbon, would guide Latvia's state and society. The reflection of this notion in the DCP's political platform was its heavy focus on economic crisis, for which it put forth an "anticrisis economic program." The program pragmatically identified particular roots of crisis, like slow privatization, and put forth specific recommendations for each. Both the poster and platform conveyed a sense of pragmatism and modernity.

The political advertisements of *Latvijas ceļš* (Latvia's Way, or LC) were more prominent than those of any other party because this was by far the best-financed coalition.[23] The LC posters integrated the coalition's name, visible in advertisements not only in written form but also in the form of a modern bicolor logo, with Latvian folk designs taken from fragments of a well-known historical artifact, the Lielvārdes belt. The modern appearance of the logo, which appeared between two belt fragments on one of LC's posters, implied that while the LC offered continuity with the national road of the past, as represented by the belt, it was modern in its outlook. The coalition unified not only notions about continuity and change, but also a wide assortment of politicians with diverse political backgrounds, including the former first secretary of the Communist Party of Latvia and the sitting

12   Posters of the *Demokrātiskā centra partija* (Democratic Center Party)

chairman of the Presidium of the Supreme Council Anatolijs Gorbunōvs, the former president of the World Federation of Free Latvians and émigré Gunārs Meierovics, and semiprominent figures from the opposition period. One of the slogans of the coalition highlighted this unexpected diversity and put forth a message about the pragmatic programmatic direction of the organization: "Only those who can unify themselves can unify others." The coalition took a strong stance in favor of economic and political progress, declaring that Latvia was at a "crossroads" and that "the blossoming of the nation and state is possible only by bravely going down the road of reform."[24] As in the case of the DCP, representations and rhetoric of nation appeared in the campaign but did not define it. Rather, the visual representation of a road ahead in the DCP poster and the rhetorical symbolism of a way forward conveyed by the name and slogans of LC suggested that, for these political organizations, the national past was an important memory but not a destination. Other political organizations further distanced themselves from the national past. Some of these, like the *Liberālā alianse* (Liberal Alliance, or LA) and *Saskaņa Latvijai, atdzimšana tautsaimniecībai* (Harmony for Latvia, Rebirth for the Economy, or SLAT), highlighted young people or children in posters that did not feature colors or designs typically associated with traditional Latvian folk art. On the one hand, these representations suggested a grounding in the present and a programmatic path into the future rather than the past. On the other hand, the economic strategy for realizing such a future was quite different. The LA based its politics on a stringent definition of individual freedom, which was its "main goal." It also embraced as the "party's strategic goal, the priority of the individual over the state's interests."[25] The LA went further than any of the other political organizations in its assertion of the primacy of the free market and individual initiative, taking this as the cornerstone of its modernization program.[26] SLAT embraced a "rational balance between the past and present" and suggested that "harmony between the citizenry and ethnicities" was the "prerequisite of social and economic reform and the foundation of Latvia's independence."[27] Furthermore, its stance on the market foresaw greater regulation of the market and more extensive protection of individuals from the market.

Arguably, only LA, SLAT, and one other group, *Latvijas laime* (Latvia's Luck, or LL), made any overt political appeal to young voters. LL (which had earlier gone by the name Fools' Party) featured mostly young celebrities rather than politicians. It was considered by many older voters to be an elaborate joke, an impression that the organization seemed to cultivate with its bizarre political posters that carried slogans like "A place for every fool in the Saeima" and "We will steal less than others." Though quite a few young people expressed vocal support for Latvia's Luck and wore LL T-shirts, the group received far below the 4 percent of the vote required to win seats in the Parliament.

One of SLAT's posters featured five happy young people on a plain white background beneath the slogan "It is your choice! Youth choose harmony." The slogan was a play on words, as the word "harmony" represented both itself and the first word of the coalition's name. The poster's potential appeal may have been more broadly based than that of many of its competitors. Whereas most other posters and parties targeted Latvian audiences, SLAT also sought to appeal to non-Latvian voters, who made up approximately 20 percent of the electorate at that time. The name "Harmony for Latvia" highlighted the party's concern with ethnic harmony and cooperation, and

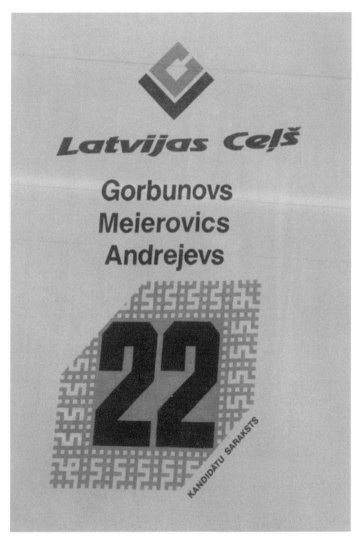

13   Banner of the *Latvijas ceļš* (Latvia's Way) coalition

14   Three posters of the *Saskaņa Latvijai, atdzimšana tautsaimniecībai*
(Harmony for Latvia, Rebirth for the Economy) coalition

its program embraced a policy on citizenship that would have expanded the body of the citizenry to include Soviet-era migrants more rapidly than those of most other political organizations. The platform foresaw automatic Latvian citizenship for people born in Latvia or married to a citizen of Latvia and naturalization based on stated desire, ten-year residency, and Latvian language knowledge at the conversational level. The poster as well had no specifically ethnic colors or characteristics and seemed to disconnect its models from any particular ethnic identity, presenting them only as a group of presumably prosperous (they are all relatively well dressed) and contented young people.

By posting its message exclusively in Latvian, however, the coalition was suggesting that although it elevated the notion of ethnic and class harmony, it also focused on Latvians as its primary constituency and did not wish to alienate potential Latvian voters by appearing to be a "Russian party," something that would not have endeared the party to the many voters who still saw a strong association between "Russian" and "Soviet."

In the election, *Latvijas Sociāldemokrātiskā strādnieku partija* (Latvia's Social Democratic Workers' Party, or LSDSP) and *Latvijas Demokrātiskā darba partija* (Latvia's Democratic Work Party, or LDDP) shared the characteristics typical of the spatial category in terms of their approach to national and citizenship issues, but embraced economic practices that opted for capitalist markets with broad social welfare guarantees and protections, which was termed by some a *sociālais tirgus* (social market) approach. The LDDP's most visible poster was one featuring only a stark and serious portrait of the politician Juris Bojārs, looking eerily like Lenin with his bald pate and bearded frown. Bojārs had been barred from standing for elections after the Supreme Council passed a resolution legally banning any present or former foreign intelligence agents from taking seats in the Saeima (Bojārs had been a colonel in the Soviet KGB and was hence excluded from participation), but he continued to represent the LDDP as its leading, albeit unelectable, politician. The appeal or lack of appeal of Bojārs as the centerpiece of the poster is difficult to gauge, though the appeal the party would have had for Latvians may have been compromised by the association of Bojārs with the widely despised KGB. The LDDP structured its economic program along socialistic lines in the sense that it embraced a high degree of state participation in the economy and a strong welfare state that included free education and medical services. The LDDP was also one of a few political organizations that directly appealed to older people, promising to fulfill the "resolutions of the First Congress of Latvia's Federation of Pensioners." Because of Latvia's top-heavy demographic composition, especially in the ethnic Latvian popula-

15   Poster of the *Neatkarīgo savienība* (Independents' Union) above a *Latvijas laime* (Latvia's Luck) poster with the words "First Promise: We will steal less than others."

tion, this appeal made political sense, because this segment of the population was not only vulnerable to market forces, but also numerically significant.

The spectrum of economic positions in the category of political organizations leaning toward a spatial vision of post-Communist normality was aptly represented by the contrast of two posters pasted a short distance from each other on a fence in downtown Riga. A large Latvia's Social Democratic Workers' Party poster was tacked over a pair of smaller *Saimnieciskās rosības līga* (Economic Activists' League, or SRL) posters. On the former, the banner read as follows: "Professional education; normal, dignified wages." The latter read: "Hard-working people—wealthy people; wealthy people will build a wealthy Latvia." These two slogans represented a growing dialogue about the nature of Latvia's new capitalism, which was to become more significant later on. The former supported greater regulation (guaranteeing normal, dignified wages to workers), while the latter offered a businessperson's advocacy of a free, presumably competitive forum for the acquisition of wealth. This dialogue also prefigured what was to be a theme in Latvia's second national elections in 1995. The trend, also seen in, for example, Poland and Hungary, appeared to be that first elections were, on the whole, a referendum on historical interpretations and broadly conceived paths to the future, whereas second elections were more strongly influenced by the achievements and pain of economic transition.

After considering some of the important contrasts among posters and programs of political organizations in the spatial and temporal categories, it is important to highlight the point that they also shared some fundamental similarities. First, the narratives of these political organizations were based on a common assumption that there was a transformation imperative that touched, to varying degrees, politics, social life, and economics. Both the temporal and spatial narratives elevated a common revolutionary notion of discontinuity with the Soviet period and the (re)creation of state and society in a fundamentally different mold. Second, the primary nation was a primary actor (if not always *the* primary actor) in both narratives and all programs. All programs assumed a degree of continuity with the interwar past in that the body of the citizenry of that period was the baseline from which any further expansion of that body would evolve. Furthermore, all claimed to serve national interests, though the definition of those interests and the notions about how these interests could be realized were different.

The similarities that temporal and spatial narratives of change shared in the political field distinguished them from the third narrative, which was present, though clearly not dominant, in the first post-Communist elections. Two of the coalitions contending for places in the Parliament espoused an

16   Poster of *Latvijas Demokrātiskā darba partija* (Latvia's Democratic
Work Party)

17   Posters of *Latvijas Sociāldemokrātiskā strādnieku partija* (Latvia's Social Democratic Workers' Party) above two *Saimnieciskās rosības līga* (Economic Activists' League) posters

evolutionary narrative of change that included a degree of social and economic continuity with the Soviet order. These political organizations did not link up with the independent Latvian past, though they did not politically link up with the Soviet past either. The political rejection of the Soviet order, however, did not translate into wholesale rejection of the Soviet social and economic order. It highlighted social and economic continuity, rejecting changes in status wrought by a new structure of citizenship and capitalist markets that impoverished as well as enriched. In the embrace of economic continuity, these organizations shared similarities with the LDDP and LSDSP. No less notably, these groups shared commonalties with political organizations inclined toward restorationism like Our Land and For Fatherland and Freedom, which also embraced a strong state in the marketplace, though the latter based its embrace of this stance on the statism of the interwar period and the perceived need to protect vulnerable segments of the ethnic Latvian population, like farmers and older people, from the vagaries of a competitive free market.

The most visible of the two political organizations in this group was *Līdztiesība* (Equal Rights). Unlike those of other contenders, the Equal Rights posters spoke to potential voters in both Latvian and Russian, a fact that would, in the minds of many voters, have labeled it a "Russian" (or Soviet) coalition. One of the posters depicted four small figures chiseling around Latvia's borders. The central image used neither visual allegory nor color symbolism. Rather, the abstract allusions in many other posters were replaced by the concrete representation of a theme of national division. A prosaic promise to unify the country followed beneath: "They divided Latvia; into citizens and noncitizens; into rich and poor; into Latvians and non-Latvians; We will unify Latvia!" The unidentified "they" of the slogan were nationalists whose agendas included the desire to re-create Latvia's favorable interwar demographic situation politically by permanently disenfranchising Soviet-era immigrants. The coalition's favorable attitude toward the retention of socialist economic policies was suggested by the line decrying the division of rich and poor in Latvia. The theme of unity was also reiterated by the presence of a small cluster of stars at the top of the poster. The stars were clearly modeled on those held up by the female figure atop the Latvian Freedom Monument. Traditionally, they represent the unity of Latvia's regions. In this context, however, they were detached from their "normal" meaning and represented a different unity.

Political platforms, together with campaign posters, are useful for both identifying the political spectrum that defined the first post-Communist elections and locating political organizations on that spectrum. In the follow-

Viņi saskaldīja Latviju

pilsoņos un nepilsoņos,
bagātajos un nabagajos,
latviešos un nelatviešos.

Mēs apvienosim Latviju!

Они раскололи Латвию

на граждан и неграждан,
на богатых и бедных,
на латышей и нелатышей.

Мы объединим Латвию!

18   Poster of the *Līdztiesība* (Equal Rights) coalition

ing section of the chapter, I again invoke the spectrum of narratives to follow the debate about citizenship legislation that took place before the elections and then to follow the winners of seats in Parliament (eight of the twenty-three political organizations were successful in the election), who represented all points on the political spectrum, through the passage of a citizenship law.

Making Citizens

In this section, I examine the debate and legislation on the issue of citizenship and naturalization policy in the Fifth Saeima. I use this case as a prism through which to look at the way that the narratives of transformation informed and influenced parliamentary politics. I chose citizenship as a case study in this chapter because it was a topic of great salience and debate in Latvia. Two of the reasons that control over citizenship was seen as a way of controlling Latvia's destiny are related to the position of Latvians in Latvia. First, Latvia is a country of just 2.6 million people. Words used by the Western press to describe it include designations like "little," "mini," and "tiny" (though both its population and land mass are far from the smallest in Europe). Internally as well, Latvia adheres to a self-definition that derives from its relatively small geographical size and (Latvian) population. In the early post-Communist period, this was manifested in a kind of small nation realpolitik: in the words of one Latvian journalist, "If we want to be in Europe, we have to play by the rules that are set forth for us."[28] This "small nation complex" was closely intertwined with the second reason I cite: Latvia's post-Communist demographic situation. Although the territory of Latvia has historically been multicultural rather than homogenous, the demographic situation in which Latvians found themselves after the fall of Communism was unprecedented in the modern history of that territory: the share of Latvians in the population declined from about 75 percent in 1935 to just 52 percent in 1989. (Since then, the proportion has grown to just over 57 percent, according to the 2000 census.) During this same period, the share of Russians in the total population rose from about 10 percent in the interwar period to 34 percent in the post-Communist period. (In 2000, the proportion of Russians decreased to about 29.5 percent.)[29]

In this context, both the opposition period and the early post-Communist period saw broad expressions of fears about national extinction. The concern extended beyond the sense that ethnic Latvians would become a minority in the territory of Latvia and encompassed as well the belief that Latvian culture and language were under increasing threat. The politics of small nationhood thus permeated the debate about citizenship in the form of disagreement over what constituted "Latvia's interest." Political organizations in the spatial category highlighted Latvia's interest in joining Europe for reasons of security and welfare, but organizations in the temporal category elevated Latvia's interest in reconstructing a fundamentally "Latvian Latvia," where Europe represented a relative rather than an absolute value. The evolutionary narrative around this point was somewhat less visible as it did not specifically concern itself with the fate of the Latvian *nation*, focusing rather on the post-Communist construction of a multicultural Latvian *state*.

The third reason that the legislation of a citizenship regime in post-Communist Latvia was of central importance has to do with the institutionalization of the relationship between the independent interwar Latvian state and the post-Communist state. Rogers Brubaker made the point that in constituting citizenries, states must determine, first, how an initial body of citizenry is to be established and, second, how the "continuous recruitment" of the citizenry is to be instituted. In Latvian politics, the answer to both of these questions was informed by the different narratives present in the political field. The initial body of the citizenry in both the temporal and spatial narratives was that of the interwar First Republic of Latvia, which, according to both Latvian politicians and international law (under which the occupation was not recognized), had never de jure ceased to exist.

Brubaker distinguished between what he called a "new-state model" and a "restored-state model." In the former, the "task of a new state is to define an initial body of citizens; this is usually done in a territorially inclusive fashion." In the latter, the "task of the restored state is to confirm the status of an already existing citizenry and to restore citizenship and statehood to real effectiveness."[30] In terms of establishing the baseline of the citizenry, both temporal and spatial models called on the "restored-state model," though the temporal narrative saw this in terms of continuity whereas the spatial model saw it in terms of succession (to the interwar state). In contrast, the evolutionary narrative looked to the "new-state model," seeking legislation to assure that persons in residence at the declaration of Latvia's independence (May 4, 1990) would legitimately be entitled to membership in the core citizenry.

In terms of "continuous recruitment" of the citizenry, the similarity between the stance of temporal and spatial categories dissolved into sharp differences. In deciding how "continuous recruitment" is to be structured, said Brubaker, a state designates "what rules should govern the continuous and automatic replenishment of the citizenry through the ascriptive assignment of citizenship, usually at birth." Brubaker noted that in most European states, the replenishment of the citizenry is usually based on the principle of *jus sanguinis;* that is, citizenship is conferred through descent.[31] In Latvia, however, because the baseline community of citizens was narrow, encompassing under 70 percent of the total population of the country, this principle would have left the country with a substantial proportion of noncitizens. Political organizations in the temporal category supported a "recruitment" law consistent with this principle: they sought to limit, as much as possible, the citizenship community to interwar citizens and their descendants. Provisions were made by some organizations for naturalization, but, under their proposals, the vast majority of the citizenry would have derived from the *jus sanguinis* principle.

On the other hand, organizations in the spatial category largely supported a *jus sanguinis* principle combined with a greater or lesser degree of naturalization that would create a citizenry composed of both descendants and naturalized persons. The battle over citizenship most visible in the Supreme Council and Fifth Saeima was a battle over this particular aspect of creating the community of citizens.

An already complex issue, the citizenship question was further complicated by the relationship of post-Communist claims about citizenship to the interwar Citizenship Law of 1919. The 1919 law, discussed more extensively further on, followed a model much like the one elaborated by Brubaker as the prototypical European model; that is, *constitution of the citizenry on the basis of territorial residence* and *replenishment of the citizenry primarily on the basis of descent.* Interestingly, some restorationist politicians, as well as some supporting continuity from the Soviet period, called on the law to be reinstituted. For example, Mikhail Gavrilov of the Democratic Initiative Center Party, which supported automatic extension of citizenship to all residents, commented in an interview: "All the time we hear talk about renewing the former—the first—republic. However, talking about the independence declared in 1918, the democratic citizenship law passed at that time is rejected."[32] This sentiment was echoed in a statement by Jānis Straume of the November 18 Union, an organization (later merged into the electoral coalition For Fatherland and Freedom) that supported a highly exclusionary policy: "Is a new citizenship law even necessary? The political program of the November 18 Union is based on the stringent realization of the principle of legal state restoration in the renewal of the Republic of Latvia. From this perspective, LR's 1919 law on citizenship has never been legally abolished, and, while Latvia's occupation has not been ended, there are no institutions that would have the right to abolish, change, or supplement that law."[33]

Although these politicians of fundamentally different narrative visions embraced the same practical renewal of the interwar law, their reading of the context for reinstitution of that law was not the same. Gavrilov's interpretation of renewal meant the reinstitution of the law as it had been applied to Latvia as a *new state* (as per Brubaker's models); in this instance, it would have defined the baseline citizenship community as the body of residents in the state at its legal conception and continued based on *jus sanguinis* from there. Straume, on the other hand, interpreted renewal of the law in term of the *restored state*, in which case the applicable principle was only that of *jus sanguinis*, or citizenship through descent. Hence, the narrative embraced by these individuals and their organizations informed the way that the 1919 law was practically interpreted.

The remainder of this section is divided into several parts. First, because historical notions have played a powerful structuring role in the transformation of Latvia, I look at the way that citizenship was constructed, construed, and realized in independent interwar Latvia and the Soviet Union. Second, I follow the debate about citizenship from the late period of the Supreme Council, which was elected in 1990 in a semifree election that included all citizens of Soviet Latvia, to the period of the Fifth Saeima, elected in 1993 by citizens of the interwar state and their descendants, during which the first full citizenship law of post-Communist Latvia was written and accepted.

Constituting a Civic Community in a National State: The Interwar Experience

Though interwar Latvia appears in the temporal narrative of transformation as a specifically Latvian state, it was in fact far from homogenous in its ethnic composition. In 1920, ethnic Latvians made up about 72.7 percent of the total population. Their proportion rose to 75.5 percent in 1935. In 1935, during the last census of the interwar republic, Russians represented about 10.6 percent of the population, followed in size by Jews, who were 4.8 percent of the population, and Germans, who represented 3.2 percent of inhabitants.[34] A comprehensive count for the last years of the republic is unavailable as the 1940 census was interrupted by war and occupation, but it is reasonable to conclude that the change in the Latvian proportion would have been insubstantial: the emigration of most of the German population to Germany in the fall of 1939 was balanced by the immigration of Jews escaping Hitler's Third Reich.[35]

In interwar Latvia, the citizenship community was grafted onto the heterogeneous ethnic community; in other words, membership in the body of the citizenry was independent of ascribed characteristics like ethnicity. The citizenship law passed on August 23, 1919, established a foundational body of citizens based on legal residence in the territory of the new Latvian state:

> I. As a Latvian citizen shall be considered every subject of former Russia, irrespective of nationality and creed, who lives on Latvian territory, hails from districts forming the territory of Latvia, or who belonged already to such districts, in accordance with the Russian law, prior to August 1, 1914, and has up to the day of the promulgation of the present law acquired no other citizenship.
>
> II. Citizens who temporarily reside outside Latvia, but otherwise answer the conditions mentioned in Article I, shall not lose the claim to Latvian citizenship, if within one year from the day this law was promulgated, they return to Latvia, or register themselves as Latvian citizens.

The citizenship community was to be "replenished" based on descent, but for those who did not meet the conditions for citizenship stipulated above, the law provided for naturalization with certain conditions:

> IV. Subjects of foreign countries may be admitted to Latvian citizenship, if they have lived on Latvian territory five years without interruption. . . .
>
> V. In consideration of special services rendered to the State of Latvia, foreign subjects mentioned in Article IV may, having applied to the Minister of the Interior, acquire the rights of Latvian citizenship without a previous permanent sojourn of five years in Latvia, by special resolution of the National Council of Latvia.

Under the citizenship law, women derived citizenship from their husbands and children from their parents. If a male Latvian citizen married a woman citizen of another state, she took on his Latvian citizenship. On the other hand, if a woman holding Latvian citizenship married a man holding the citizenship of another state, she took on his foreign citizenship. A Latvian woman could regain citizenship if she was divorced from her foreign spouse. Dual citizenship was not recognized.[36]

The peace treaty between Latvia and Russia, signed in August 1920 and recognized as the basis of Latvian and Russian relations at that time, also contained provisions that reiterated earlier principles. According to Article 8 of the treaty:

> Persons residing, on the day of the ratification of the Treaty within the frontiers of Latvia, and likewise refugees residing in Russia who were unregistered, or whose parents were registered, before August 1st, 1914, in urban, rural or corporate societies, in the territory now forming the State of Latvia, are recognized as Latvian citizens.
>
> Persons of the same category residing at the moment of ratification of this present Treaty within the frontiers of Russia, with the exception of the refugees above-mentioned, are recognized as Russian subjects.
>
> Nevertheless, any person of the age of 18 years and above, residing in Latvian territory, has the right during one year, dating from the day of the ratification of the present Treaty, to declare that he does not desire to retain his Latvian nationality and to opt in favour of Russia. . . .
>
> Likewise, Russian citizens can, under the terms of the second paragraph of this clause, during the same period of time and under the same conditions, opt for the status of Latvian citizens.[37]

Under the repatriation provisions of the 1920 treaty, about 400,000 people returned to Latvia to claim citizenship rights.[38]

Some additions to the citizenship regime were introduced in a 1927 law. Among others, the law stipulated that persons sentenced for major crimes were not eligible for citizenship under most conditions. It also provided for a woman's right to keep her Latvian citizenship if she married a stateless man and for him to take on her citizenship.[39] The fundamental principles iterated in the earlier law, however, remained in place.

Political rights were inscribed in the Constitution of 1922, which held that "supreme power is wielded by the people, i.e., the totality of citizens of both sexes who have reached the age of 21." Article 2 also provided for the election of a Parliament of one hundred members by the citizenry for a term of three years "by direct, secret, universal, and proportional vote."[40] Both Latvian and minority parties were represented in all four Parliaments elected during the interwar period. A freely functioning press and provisions for universal education also attached to the general rights of the people. Individual rights were supplemented by collective rights, which protected the political and cultural interests of minority communities constituting about one-quarter of the population. In this spirit, the state provided for educational autonomy by creating minority councils that oversaw ethnic schools teaching in the minority language (Latvian was offered as a subject). The state also undertook to subsidize all manner of cultural endeavors of both the majority and minorities. Minority languages could be and were used broadly in both official and unofficial forums, and a strong minority press existed alongside the Latvian press.

Although the Constitution was not formally abrogated (though provisions on parliamentary powers were suspended) and the legal citizenship regime remained unaltered, the 1934 coup d'état in which President Kārlis Ulmanis took power into his own hands transformed the political, economic, and social landscape of Latvia. Ulmanis embraced a nationalist program of a "strong and Latvian Latvia," which affected minority as well as Latvian populations in several significant ways. First, after 1934, minorities were still permitted to organize their own schools, but Ulmanis decreed that all Latvian children, including those with one Latvian parent, must attend Latvian schools.[41] This "Latvianization" policy in education had a particularly profound effect on Latgalians in Latvia.[42] The Latgalian language is very similar to Latvian, but many Latgalians claim that it is a separate language, rather than a dialect of Latvian (as many Latvians believe). During the Ulmanis period, the use of Latgalian in schools and for official business was limited, and, although it could legally be used in the cultural sphere, the use of the "middle dialect" (Latvian) was "suggested" by the state.[43] Catholicism, the religion practiced by most Latgalians, was also marginalized by the Ulmanis regime, which elevated Lutheranism, the religion of most Latvians. The process of "Lutheranization" saw the replacement of school catechisms with Lutheran teachings and the increased building of Lutheran churches in the Latgalian region, as well as rhetorical attacks on the Catholic Church.[44] Second, the official status of the Latvian language was elevated; in the parliamentary period, the German and Russian languages were permitted in state and commercial business along with Latvian, but a new law declared that only Latvian could be written and spoken in these spheres, except where more than 50 percent of the population was non-Latvian.[45] Third, within days of taking power, Ulmanis muzzled an array of non-Latvian as well as Latvian newspapers, limiting the freedom as well as the ethnic spectrum of press available. Fourth, politicians of all political stripes were pushed aside and, in some cases, jailed, albeit, for short periods. Competitive politics at the national level ceased to exist. Fifth, the German- and Jewish-dominated private business sector was affected by the economic politics of Ulmanis, who sought to bring factories and firms under state control and "into the hands of Latvians."[46]

The record of the interwar period with respect to citizenship rights is mixed. On the one hand, political citizenship rights were extended to all who inhabited the territory of Latvia after 1914, and civic rights were enshrined in the Constitution. A strong welfare state also ensured a degree of social rights based on citizenship.[47] On the other hand, the postcoup Ulmanis government transformed the regime of rights in policy and practice. The utility of political rights was undermined by the suspension of constitutional provisions that underpinned the power of the elected legislature. Furthermore, civic rights were undermined by, for example, restrictions on the freedom of the press. Notably as well, provisions for individual rights for all combined with collective rights for minority populations were subordinated to a potent nationalistic notion of collective rights intended to ensure the protection, power, and prosperity of the primary nation.

The precedents and models that can be retrieved from this period are multiple. The realization of citizenship and democracy changed across this period from a multicultural interpretation and manifestation to an exclusive ethnically circumscribed regime and from legislative democracy to presidential rule. Even the citizenship law itself, as I noted earlier, lends itself to different understandings. History appears in post-Communist politics, then, as interpretation: it is integrated into different and often competing narratives that tie together pieces of history that are consistent with the stories they tell about the past and about change and normality.

Soviet Citizenship: Equality and Authoritarianism

The 1940 occupation of Latvia was shortly followed by "elections," in which a new legislature for the Soviet republic of Latvia was selected. These (mock) elections took place on July 14 and 15, and, according to official Soviet information on the balloting, fully 97.6 percent of Soviet Latvian voters participated and overwhelmingly confirmed the single-party (the *komunistiskā darba tautas bloks* or Communist Working People's Bloc) slate of candidates.[48] Up to the 1989 elections for the Congress of People's Deputies, when the Communist Party's monopoly on power was challenged, Soviet voters participated in elections that featured a single party and few, if any, choices in terms of individual candidates. Furthermore, voters in the Soviet context were, to a greater or lesser degree, required to vote, and a stamp in one's passport confirmed that one had fulfilled one's duty as a Soviet citizen. All Soviet citizens shared the vote;[49] however, the population of Soviet citizens who could participate as candidates was circumscribed on the basis of membership in the Communist Party, and in Latvia in 1990 under 7 percent of the population belonged to the Communist Party. Of this segment of the population, Latvians constituted under 40 percent.[50] Civic rights were enshrined in the Soviet Union, though the exercise of many of those rights and the construction of an independent civil society around them were prohibited in practice. Those who sought to practice rights like the right of association were, with various degrees of severity, punished by the security apparatuses of the state.

The Soviet order, in theory, provided for full and equal citizenship. In practice, it offered equal status, but citizenship status was delinked from the realization of citizenship rights by the state's monopolization of power and the public sphere. This was evident in, for example, the circumscribed provision of civic rights: the 1977 Constitution offered freedoms of "speech, press, assembly, meetings, street processions, and demonstrations," albeit only "in accordance with the interests of the working people and for the purpose of strengthening and developing the socialist system."[51] In this authoritarian context, "Citizenship [became] a matter of holding a passport, obeying national laws, cheering for the country's team, and, occasionally, voting in choreographed elections or plebiscites."[52]

Social citizenship rights played a more prominent role in the Soviet Union, as they were, to a greater degree than other forms of citizenship, intimately intertwined with the ideology of state itself. The socialist state, as the ostensible product and servant of the working class, elevated the pursuit of social and economic equality, a principle reflected in the Soviet Constitutions. For example, the 1977 Constitution conferred on Soviet citizens largely social and economic rights like the right to housing, medical care, education, and material security in the event of illness or disability, though benefit levels were not specified.[53]

The Soviet Union elevated individual rights and equality in theory, but, to a large degree, undermined them in practice. Collective rights too presented a mixed picture. On the one hand, the practice of collective rights of minority nations inhered in the structure of the Soviet order itself.[54] Thus the administrative structuring of the Soviet Union into fifteen *national* republics meant that the titular population of those republics was entitled to educational instruction in their own language, that (some) local cultural initiatives like theater productions and folk dance groups were supported by the state, and that, to a greater or lesser degree, (loyal) indigenous Communist elites enjoyed access to power in their own republic. Publication of books and periodicals in the local language was also extensive.

These rights of nations, on the other hand, had particular qualities and limitations. First, most did not apply to all minority nationalities: only titular populations of Soviet republics were granted many of these rights. For example, the right to an education in one's own language through the first university degree was conferred only on Russians and titular populations of republics. Smaller nations in those republics were subordinated to either the titular population's or the Russian structures of education and administration. In Latvia, although the Latgalian population had suffered some ill effects during the Ulmanis period, their lot worsened considerably under the Soviet regime. At this time, the Latgalian language was barred from official life, and the Latgalian language courses that had been offered as a subject (though not the language of school instruction) under Ulmanis were entirely deleted from the curriculum. A handful of newspapers and a journal in Latgalian continued to be published until the early 1950s, but in 1956, the Education Ministry of the Latvian SSR handed down a directive calling for a "regime of unified linguistic development" and declaring illegal the use of the Latgalian language in public and private life.[55]

This treatment of nontitular minorities was not irrelevant to (non-Latgalian) Latvians either. As noted earlier, the ethnic Latvian population of the republic was slipping, and, by the 1980s, some Latvians had begun to fear that if the titular population fell below 50 percent, a point it was approaching as the 1986 census registered a 52 percent share of the population, republic status and the accompanying privileges like education in the national language could be lost. This fear was, arguably, a factor in the mobilization of the population for independence from the Soviet Union as well.

Second, the rights of nations and nationalities in the Soviet order inhered in a bureaucratic structure rather than a cultural context. The "value" of any nation (and its language and culture) was not absolute, but relative to political needs and considerations of the particular period. The latitude given to populations to speak the local language and practice the local culture was dependent on political factors. With respect to the language issue, Graham Smith wrote that in the Khrushchev period, "reforms favored Russian as a medium of instruction in native schools while exempting Russians from learning local languages. This paved the way for the promotion of Russian language teaching, with particularly negative effects for the languages of the more minor, non-union republic-based nationalities." Khrushchev also argued at that point that the national republics were "losing their former significance."[56]

Third, permitting national difference to exist through the granting of collective minority nation rights was also a political instrument in the tradition of *divide et imperia*. The center was strengthened through the "[deliberate exaggeration of] differences among its minorities."[57] The pitting of non-

Russian nationalities against one another was, according to some, particularly acute in the Soviet army where Russian dominance in a multiethnic context had to be ensured. At the same time, however, a policy of *sblizheniye* (drawing together)[58] was also pursued, which ensured the dominance of the Russian language as the common means of communication in public life. This was consistent with more general Soviet notions about the homogenization of society, a principle enshrined even in the 1977 Constitution, the nineteenth article of which asserts that the "Soviet state promotes the intensification of the social homogeneity of society."[59]

In the Soviet period, citizenship conferred a degree of formal political, economic, and social equality, but the quality of equality was determined not through representative institutions or independent civil society, but rather by the state itself, which exercised a high degree of control in the public sphere. Soviet citizenship divorced membership from power in the polity but did offer minimum conditions for the realization of economic and social needs. The Soviet citizenship regime was powerful as a shadow case in the debate over post-Communist citizenship. The "equality" of the institution of Soviet citizenship informed, on the one hand, political organizations in the evolutionary category in the sense that they, to varying degrees, supported a successor state (to the Soviet Union) principle that would have transferred the "equality" of social and economic status, to which they were accustomed, to the new state. On the other hand, the Soviet citizenship experience also existed in the background of temporal and spatial narratives of change in the sense that it defined the opposite pole of "normal" citizenship. Because political power did not inhere in citizenship, ethnic Latvians largely did not exercise control over the political conditions of their existence, which resulted in the massive changes in the demographic position of Latvians in Latvia. Fundamental changes in the citizenship regime, from the restoration of the core body of the citizenry to the variously stringent attempts to control the expansion of that body, were widely understood to be "correctives" to the damage and distortion caused by the political powerlessness inherent in Soviet citizenship and in the Soviet "equality" that had privileged ethnic Russians in terms of housing, jobs, language, and power.

Contesting Boundaries: The Politics of Citizenship in Early Post-Communism

In an opinion piece published in late 1990, on the debate about how citizenship was to be structured in Latvia, a commentator for the first large independent paper to appear in this period wrote:

[In the USSR] We were not citizens. In that circumstance, we could not be citizens. At best we were subjects, that is, subjected to the power of the Leader: Stalin, Khrushchev, Brezhnev.

A citizen can appear in a democratic state with the rule of law, where the state and individuals are equal before the law, where the state and person are joined in a relationship of trust, assuming rights and taking on mutual responsibilities. Consciously and with free will, rather than by force.

The author of this piece also raised the issue of collective rights of nations, which he claimed were part of a democratic citizenship regime: "The rights of the nation to life are not less than those of the individual, because [the nation] is constituted by many individual persons, who have been formed by language, traditions, culture, worldview—all that which, through the centuries, has become interwoven with the particular geography, climate, economic order, historical events. . . . In a democratic state, no government can ignore the right of the nation to live in its own Fatherland."

Indeed, in the late Communist and early post-Communist periods in Latvia, the debate over citizenship revolved around conflicting notions of how citizenship and the body of citizenry were to be defined in post-Communism and raised a number of important questions: What were the rights of nations and what were the rights of individuals in the new context? What were the boundaries of collective rights of both the majority and minorities in the state? Were these boundaries appropriately inscribed by contemporary norms? Were they appropriately inscribed by history? Below I examine more closely the debate about citizenship in Latvia, beginning with the period of the Supreme Council and continuing through the passage of a citizenship law in 1994. The debate reflects a spectrum of conflicting notions about the way that citizenship as an institution inheres in the process of (re)constructing state and society in Latvia.

The controversy about how citizenship should be structured began in earnest in the late Communist period and continued into the post-Communist period. The issue was first pursued in the Supreme Council, which was elected in 1990, and it heated up as the campaign for seats in the Fifth Saeima got under way in late winter and spring 1993. Several issues defined the debate. First, there was fundamental disagreement among political organizations both inside and outside the Supreme Council, which would continue to govern until the Fifth Saeima was elected, as to whether that body could legitimately pass legislation on citizenship. Some politicians, like the Supreme Council chairman Anatolijs Gorbunōvs and politicians from political organizations like Latvia's Democratic Workers' Party and the Democratic Center Party, maintained that a law should be passed by the Supreme Council. Mikhail Gavrilov of the Russian-dominated Democratic Initiative Center Party argued that the "current parliament has managed to declare Latvia's independence, therefore it is its obligation to accept a citizenship law."[60] Others disputed this point, contending that only a post-Communist Parliament elected by citizens of independent Latvia in an independent Latvia could legitimately resolve the citizenship question. The fact that the Parliament had been elected in the Soviet period and by all Soviet citizens in residence in Latvia (including members of the Soviet army stationed there) in 1990 underpinned the objections: Arvīds Ulme of the Green Party declared that the Supreme Council, "which was elected by citizens from another state [Soviet Union] living in Latvia, as well as representatives of the Soviet army, does not have the right to make decisions about citizenship criteria." Valdis Šteins of the Conservative Party (which later merged into the electoral coalition Conservatives and Farmers) argued: "The AP [Supreme Council] is an authority that was elected in an imperial period under imperial rules. Now, in independent Latvia, it becomes illegal."[61] Some political organizations like Latvia's Popular Front hoped for a public referendum on the question, the results of which would provide a basis for the passage of a law in the Fifth Saeima. The issue was resolved when the Supreme Council chose to renew the interwar body of the citizenry as the legal basis of the post-Communist citizenry, but opted out of passing a law on the extension of citizenship beyond those boundaries.

Second, there was disagreement on what residency requirement a citizenship law would impose. The notion of a period of residency, however, was more symbolic than substantive, because the vast majority of residents met *any* proposed residency requirement. It was estimated that 93 percent met a sixteen-year requirement, 97 percent met a ten-year requirement, and 99 percent met a five-year requirement.[62] As such, the length of the residency requirement, although some political organizations offered suggestions, was little contested in the election campaign. Rather, what was contested was whether a residency requirement was applicable at all. On the one hand, political organizations embracing the evolutionary narrative, like the Russian National Democratic List and the Equal Rights coalition, by definition rejected a residency requirement of any length, because they advocated the formation of a core citizenship based on residence in Latvia on the day that Latvia declared the beginning of a transition to independence—May 4, 1990. On the other hand, the notion that posting a minimum length of residency was misguided in itself emerged from political organizations that embraced restorationist notions of change. For example, Jānis Straume of the political organization November 18 Union (later part of For Fatherland and Freedom) asserted that because the residency requirement was met by nearly all "colonists"

> this requirement . . . foresees the mass naturalization of immigrants, which will in the near term have dire consequences for the Latvian nation, beginning with the loss of political power . . . and the re-peated return of [the country] in to the Russian empire, which in a short time would lead to our full destruction. The first and most important criterion for the granting of citizenship in every demo-cratic state is legal entry [into that state]. . . . That is fully relevant to Latvia. . . . No person who arrived in Latvia during the occupa-tion did that with the permission of the Latvian Republic. . . . As such, all of these persons can be seen as illegal entrants on to Lat-via's territory.[63]

In the electoral campaign, For Fatherland and Freedom, the Anti-Commu-nist League, and Latvia's Unity Party rejected naturalization of Soviet-era migrants and hence rejected any particular term of residence in Latvia as legitimate criteria for citizenship.

Third, the debate over including quotas for naturalization in a citizenship law sparked disagreement. Some political organizations, like Latvia's National Independence Movement, supported quotas that defined and divided the citizenry in terms of ethnic membership: hence, Latvia's National Independence Movement's plan supported the maintenance of the primary nation at no less than 75 percent of the citizenry (which, notably, was approximately the proportion constituted by Latvians in the general population in the interwar period). Many, like the Democratic Center Party and the Liberal Alliance, did not include quotas, and some, like Latvia's Popular Front, advocated unspecified quotas for the naturalization of Soviet-era immigrants. Harmony for Latvia, Rebirth for the Economy spoke out in favor of quotas for those who had immigrated after May 4, 1990. Others, like Uldis Bērziņš of Latvia's Social Democratic Workers' Party, argued: "Talking about quotas as a barrier . . . that seems to me absurd, even immoral. Does it hold, then, that we 'permit' entry into the citizenry a certain number of disloyal strang-ers? We don't need those at all! Granting citizenship means something else: we gain, we admit into the Latvian 'political nation' people of other histori-cal backgrounds who are prepared to work for this land and nation and state with their hearts and blood."[64]

Fourth, among politicians and political organizations that favored naturalization of some kind, there was broad agreement that sworn loyalty to the state and knowledge of the Latvian language would be prerequisites. Some organizations also suggested knowledge of Latvian history and culture, while others did not; but this point did not evoke notable contestation. The issue of language created some fissures, albeit rather small ones. The more nationalist organizations advocated a higher level of knowledge: Romualds Ražuks of Latvia's Popular Front argued that it was not enough "to have minimal language knowledge, [rather] it needs to be appropriate for [one's] job and place in society."[65] Harmony for Latvia, Rebirth for the Economy, on the other hand, suggested that knowledge at a "conversational level" be required.

Political organizations competing in the Fifth Saeima elections also differed in terms of the centrality of the citizenship question to their platforms. The citizenship question was salient in platforms of organizations favoring restoration of the interwar state and reconstruction of a specifically "Latvian Latvia." These organizations also tended to have weaker and more vague economic programs that, in some cases, stretched little beyond advocating the protection of Latvians from the vagaries of the market, increasing the share of capital in Latvian hands, and supporting Latvian-dominated farming. Similarly, the citizenship question prominently figured in the platforms of the two organizations in the evolutionary category. The published platform of the Russian National Democratic List, for example, focused almost exclusively on promises to protect and expand citizenship, Russian-language education, public use of Russian, and Russian cultural institutions. Organizations embracing the spatial narrative included, as noted earlier, proposals for citizenship regimes in their programs, but offered them as a part of larger packages that focused on economic issues like unemployment and privatization, which, polls showed, were also of great interest to voters.[66] The citizenship issue was peripheral rather than central, as these organizations sought to distinguish themselves in terms of economic offerings rather than their stance on questions of nationhood and belonging.

Making Citizenship Law in the Fifth Saeima

In July 1994, the Fifth Saeima passed a bill that defined the boundaries of the citizenry and the conditions of naturalization for those who remained outside those legislated boundaries. On August 11, 1994, the Latvian president Guntis Ulmanis signed that bill into law. Over a year had passed since the Parliament was seated and nearly three years since Latvia had achieved full independence. The bill, considered both inside and outside Latvia to be highly important, not least because it would affect the status of the 27 percent of Latvia's inhabitants without citizenship at that time, had traveled a long and rocky political road.

The Saeima was elected in June 1993 and seated in July of that year. By midautumn, several draft laws had appeared in Parliament. The first one to be submitted was the proposal by the highly nationalist political organization, For Fatherland and Freedom (TB), which had six deputies in the Saeima. The proposal rejected the initiation of any naturalization policy before the Russian army, which still had officers and soldiers on bases in Latvia, was fully demobilized from the territory. Even after the army's departure, TB's proposal foresaw only minimal expansion of the body of the citizenry beyond the renewed prewar citizenship community and direct descendants. TB specifically proscribed the granting of citizenship rights to residents who had moved to Latvia between July 1, 1940, and July 1, 1992, when the law On the Entry and Residence of Foreign Citizens and Stateless Persons was adopted. Exceptions were to be made for Latvian-speaking spouses of citizens.[67]

Latvia's National Independence Movement (LNNK) offered a draft law in early September. Its sixteen deputies differed from TB in that they foresaw a naturalization process for Soviet-era immigrants, which TB barred, but they imposed stringent conditions for naturalization. Naturalization was to take place based on a quota principle, whereby the annual quota would not exceed 10 percent of the natural growth of citizens the previous year. In a country that had low to negative growth through the 1990s,[68] any naturalization would thus be negligible; as one of the LNNK deputies noted, "In 1992, . . . the population growth in Latvia was negative. Therefore, if naturalization started this year, there would be no quota at all." The LNNK also proposed that naturalization be delayed until 1997, when five years would have passed since the passage of the law On Entry and Residence of Foreign Citizens and Stateless Persons. Furthermore, whereas the draft law would have barred dual citizenship generally, it offered an exception for those who had fled Latvia during the Communist period and taken up residence in other states. Finally, it would have made language knowledge a prerequisite of naturalization.[69]

The first governing coalition, which was constituted by the thirty-seven deputies representing Latvia's Way (LC) and the eleven representatives of Latvia's Farmers' Union (LZS), offered the third draft law to appear. Like the previous proposals, this draft law foresaw a confirmation of the pre-1940 citizenry and descendants as the baseline of the post-Communist citizenship community. Like the LNNK, it embraced quotas, though specified them vaguely, suggesting that they "would be determined each year by assessing the demographic and economic situation in the country." Quotas, however, would not be applied to relatives and spouses of Latvians permanently living in Latvia, to spouses of citizens who had been married at least five years, and to those who had "performed services of special merit to the country." Under this system, according to the LC faction chair Andrejs Pantelejevs, around 300,000 people could be naturalized in "the next few years." The ruling coalition proposal also stipulated that would-be citizens must be ten-year residents of Latvia, know the Latvian language at a conversational level (except those over sixty-five years of age), swear an oath of loyalty to the state, and have a legal source of income. Citizenship was to be fully proscribed for all Soviet-era immigrants who were former Soviet army officers or employees of foreign (including Soviet) security services. Though it too offered its draft law only in the fall after the election, the ruling coalition expressed concern about getting a law passed because, as the LC faction chair noted, the law would be the main criterion for Latvia's acceptance into the Council of Europe (CE).[70] The principles of citizenship and naturalization proposed by the twelve deputies from Harmony for Latvia, Rebirth for the Economy closely resembled those of the ruling coalition.

Latvia's Christian Democratic Union (KDS), with six deputies in Parliament, prepared a draft law as well, though it contained fewer specific provisions. It called for the organization of a referendum to formulate the principles on which a citizenship and naturalization law would be drafted. The proposal specified, as had the offering by TB, that naturalization could not begin, in any case, until the Russian troops remaining in Latvia had left. Unlike the other proposals described, the KDS draft law entirely rejected quotas, suggesting that naturalization must take place based on individual cases.

All but one of the eight political organizations in Parliament embraced the notion that the interwar citizenship community should be confirmed as the core of the post-Communist community, though their prescriptions for expanding that community (or not) varied considerably. The single political organization to reject that notion was the Equal Rights coalition, which supported the extension of citizenship to all permanent inhabitants who had entered the country before May 4, 1990. Equal Rights opposed quotas and, as well, rejected any form of dual citizenship, including dual citizenship for the approximately 12,000 residents of Latvia who had at that point accepted Russian citizenship.[71]

Beyond considering a host of possibilities regarding citizenship and naturalization legislation, in fall 1993, the Parliament also entertained some proposals about the cancellation of a treaty that had been signed between Latvia and Russia (represented by Anatolijs Gorbunōvs and Boris Yeltsin,[72] respectively) in January 1991, during the attempted hard-line coup. The treaty, which was ratified by the Supreme Council the day after it was signed, stated that Latvia would grant Latvian citizenship to all permanent residents of Latvia and allowed for dual citizenship (that is, dual Russian-Latvian citizenship). Though the treaty was never actually ratified by the Russian Parliament, nationalist political organizations were eager to cancel it anyway, arguing that Latvia had not been fully independent at the time the treaty was signed. In principle, the ruling coalition also supported cancellation.[73] Arguably, canceling the treaty would have made sense to political organizations wanting to clear the political table before passing legislation that considerably differed from what was stipulated by Gorbunōvs, representing the Supreme Soviet in 1991. Interestingly, the 1991 treaty's basic citizenship tenets bore similarities to the 1920 peace treaty signed between Latvia and Russia, which also held that all those in permanent residence in Latvia would be eligible for citizenship in the new state.

In November 1993, the Parliament voted on five draft citizenship laws, including proposals of the ruling coalition (Latvia's Way and Latvia's Farmers' Union), Latvia's National Independence Movement, For Fatherland and Freedom, Harmony for Latvia, Rebirth for the Economy, and Equal Rights. On November 25, the proposal supported by the ruling coalition was adopted with fifty-three out of one hundred votes. After approval on the first reading, the law was to be sent to the CE and the Council on Security and Cooperation in Europe (CSCE) for appraisal. The adopted law was not supported by nationalist organizations that sought to preserve the interwar citizenship community as the basis of the new polity, and, in the days before the vote, the *nacionālie spēki* (Association of Latvia's National Forces) was formed, uniting Latvia's National Independence Movement, For Fatherland and Freedom, and Latvia's Christian Democratic Union, as well as groups in civil society such as the Green Party, the National Soldiers' Association, the Union Party, the Immigration Council, and the Politically Repressed Persons' Association, among others. The Association of National Forces promoted the adoption of the For Fatherland and Freedom and Latvia's National Independence Movement proposals by the Parliament and lobbied the public against the winning proposal.

The reaction of the CSCE to the proposal was mixed. Although the CSCE representative Max Van der Stoel suggested that language knowledge was an acceptable priority and prerequisite, the quota principle was rejected as being too vague. Van der Stoel argued that under the adopted quota regime, resident aliens would have trouble judging their chances for ever being naturalized.[74] The CE supported provisions dealing with language knowledge, knowledge of the Constitution, the oath of loyalty, and the need for a legal source of income, but it also rejected the notion of quotas, and in March 1994, Latvia's Way opted to remove from quotas the draft law. Instead, noncitizens were to acquire eligibility for naturalization based on their membership in particular categories, for example, the number of years residents had been living in Latvia.[75] Pressure for changing the law was also coming from another external source at that point: in late March, a "citizenship commission" in Russia iterated an official policy that sought not only to ensure citizenship for ethnic Russians in their post-Soviet countries of residence (including Latvia), but also to stress the principle of dual citizenship for these residents. The commission's proposals also offered a different view on language from that iterated in the Latvian law, putting forth the notion that Russian should be "the language of inter-ethnic communication in the entire information space of the former Soviet Union."[76]

The removal by Latvia's Way of the quota principle from the law that had passed the Saeima in its first reading caused a crisis in the ruling coalition, and by May the possibility of a split had arisen. The crisis stemmed from the Farmers' Union's hesitance to accept Latvia's Way's removal of quotas from the law according to the recommendations of the CSCE and European Union. The LZS asserted that removal of the quota principle was contrary to its electoral program, which had foreseen such quotas. LC, at this point, also raised the possibility of seeking votes from other parliamentary factions, with the exception of For Fatherland and Freedom and Equal Rights, which held views far afield of those expressed by LC.[77] The crisis was, however, averted by some compromises, including the promise of LC to support the LZS's proposed increase of the import tariff (to protect Latvian agriculture), despite LC's concern that a tariff increase was not consistent with international norms and could slow the conclusion of a free market pact with the European Union.[78]

LC was eager to move the bill through as quickly as possible, because, as the coalition chair noted, Latvia hoped to be accepted into the CE as soon as the coming fall. In this push toward Europe were two driving forces: on the one hand, the desire for European security; on the other hand, the desire for a "European" standard of living. Holding out against this push were the *nacionālie spēki* (national forces) now nominally united on this issue, who assumed an uncompromising stance in favor of a "Latvian Latvia" and what one newspaper called the "active noncitizens and left-oriented citizens," who supported the full extension of citizenship to all in the immediate term and official status for the Russian language in Latvia.[79]

On June 9, 1994, the bill On Citizenship passed a second reading and, on June 21, a third reading. As a compromise variant, it again contained quotas. Under the law, the other provisions of which remained essentially unchanged, naturalization could begin immediately for Latvians returning to Latvia, people who had graduated from a Latvian high school (including non-Latvians), and those who had been married to a Latvian citizen for at least ten years. Beyond that, naturalization could begin from the first day of 1996 and would be open to noncitizens from sixteen to twenty years of age who had been born in Latvia. Beginning in the year 2000, the rest of the noncitizen population could be naturalized under a principle that foresaw an annual quota of 0.10 percent of the total number of Latvian citizens of the previous year, a total that, according to the newspaper *Diena*, would have been about 1,976 persons per year. The second variant also received harsh reviews from external sources. On the one hand, the CSCE expressed disappointment that quotas had turned up again in the law, and the CE suggested that Latvia would not be offered membership until the restrictive quotas were dropped;[80] on the other hand, Russia threatened to hold up Russian-Latvian economic agreements and to revoke the temporarily granted Most Favored Nation status extended to Latvia.[81]

In spite of the fact that the law was sponsored by the ruling coalition, representatives of Latvia's Way continued to speak out against quotas: Prime Minister Valdis Birkavs, a member of LC, suggested that "with quotas, we are sending signals to the world that we do not want to be in Europe, but in the CIS [Commonwealth of Independent States]."[82] Indeed, the suggestion that the choice before Latvia was one of a road to the CIS or to Europe reappeared as a prominent theme at this point: on successive days, Latvia's largest newspaper, *Diena,* carried commentaries with the headlines "Running from Europe, we will run into Russia" and "CE or CIS—Latvia has no other choices."[83] The former account commented as follows:

> The law, that is, the order, under which a state accepts into the citizenry its noncitizens is the internal matter of each state, no one, ostensibly, denies that. But only "ostensibly." Because with this law ... the Council of Europe links Latvia's acceptance into or rejection from the Council. And, despite the fact that the CE is a body with a greater symbolic than practical meaning, without membership in that there is no possibility for membership in the European Union *(Eiropas savienība).* Therefore, this law will determine whether Latvia will get into Europe or will remain a potential Russian base in the Baltics, between Estonia and Lithuania, which are already coun-

cil members because they have laws that satisfy the leaders of Europe and—noting, of course, how else but with that—a third interested party—the mother of most noncitizens, Russia.[84]

The core of the pro-European stance was based on a scenario that Latvia's acceptance into the CE at that time and not later was critical. The reasoning was explained in the commentary by *Diena's* deputy editor: "Why is it important for Latvia to join the CE soon? Because sometime in 1995 Russia will join the CE and, with that, will acquire veto power over the acceptance of new states. H. P. Furer [head of the CE's Department of Political Issues] believes that Russia could be accepted as soon as next spring. With that [if Latvia is not already accepted] Latvia's politics will come under Russia's influence."[85] The fear was that if Russia joined before rather than at the same time as or later than Latvia, it would have the power to dictate the conditions under which Latvia could be admitted.

On June 27, *Diena* published a commentary that reiterated the choice before the Parliament in terms of Europe or Russia: "In this situation we have two alternatives—democratic Europe or imperialistic Russia. The survival of the nation—about which so much has been said—can be guaranteed only by the former."[86] That day as well, President Guntis Ulmanis vetoed the law, stating that he could not sign the law because he felt that with the law Latvia was "isolating itself from the other countries of the world and would thus remain alone with its problems." He argued that the Parliament needed to revise Article 14, which set out quotas, warning that under the current restrictions Latvia could become home to a massive number of Russian citizens if stateless persons in residence in Latvia opted for the citizenship offered to them by Russia.[87]

The notion that Latvia had to change its laws to join Europe was rejected by nationalist factions concerned about the maintenance of a Latvian Latvia and the survival of the nation. The issue was framed by political organizations like For Fatherland and Freedom and Latvia's National Independence Movement, not as Europe versus Russia, but rather as Latvia versus Russia or a Latvian Latvia versus a Russian Latvia. In the debate on the postveto version of the law, one LNNK deputy exclaimed: "It will be integration into Russia with such a law, and it is childish to think it will be anything else." Some deputies also chided Europe for its "meddling in Latvia's internal affairs."[88] Europe and even the United States had at this point become something of a lightning rod for the frustration of nationalist organizations, as the national forces spoke out against the intervention of the West in Latvia's internal affairs, even picketing the U.S. embassy in Riga.[89]

A new law, which abandoned the quotas rejected by European structures and Russia, was passed in the Parliament on July 22, by a vote of fifty-eight to twenty-one, with four abstentions. The law stipulated that citizenship could be granted over a period of years to legal residents who met the following criteria:

• Having been permanent residents of Latvia for five years, counting from May 4, 1990, or from the date a permanent residence permit was granted;
• Having command of the Latvian language;
• Knowing the basic tenets of Latvia's Constitution;
• Knowing the national anthem of Latvia and Latvia's history;
• Swearing an oath of loyalty to the state;
• Having a legal source of income;
• Renouncing any previous citizenship.

Persons who had served in foreign security services, had demobilized from the Soviet army in Latvia, or had been convicted of serious crimes were barred from citizenship.

The passage of the law was greeted with relief by some deputies and disdain by others. Similarly, whereas European organizations welcomed the revised law, the Russian president Boris Yeltsin was highly critical of it.[90] President Guntis Ulmanis formally signed the bill into law in August with little fanfare and without comment, though the Baltic English-language newspaper suggested that the "signing of the law August 10 was . . . something of a victory for Ulmanis, who, along with centrist parliamentary factions, was determined to increase Latvia's ties with Western Europe even at the cost of antagonizing Latvia's nationalist forces who opposed compromises for the sake of European approval." Ulmanis's adviser on foreign policy noted that the law seemed "to be exactly what everybody wanted—that is, a law that reflects the situation that the CE and CSCE wanted in Latvia, and at the same time serves Latvia's interests."[91] The adviser's comment that the adoption of the law in this particular form served "Latvia's interests" highlights again that the content of interests was differently defined across Latvia's political spectrum: the temporal narrative about normality in this field of play was based on the reconstruction of a particularly "Latvian Latvia," whether or not it corresponded to "European traditions"; the spatial narrative revolved around Latvia as a modern European nation-state tied into the common European home; and the evolutionary narrative focused on the construction of a wholly new state based on successorship to the old Soviet Latvian state.

Conclusion

> Not for myself do I live out my fate,
> But for my nation,
> which will a choice make.
> —The Bearslayer in *Fire and Night*[92]

The political field was an important site of contention in the contest to determine the boundaries of post-Communist normality and the path of transformation in Latvia. The degree of competition was considerable because the stakes in this field were, in a context where the state was widely perceived to be the dominant vehicle of change, high. The (re)construction of normality in and through this field embraced imperatives of both elections and electorates, which were bound together because the successful realization of democratic elections depended on the provisional resolution of the problem of defining the post-Communist electorate. As well, in the elections, the resolution of this issue was a point of sharp debate, and, after the elections, the issue of the electorate continued to have a profound influence on Latvia's path of change because citizenship became a topic of international as well as domestic contention. In this chapter, I have tried to weave together the examination of these two issues because of this intimate, and to some extent determinate, tie between them.

I have sought in this chapter to embed the election contest and the contest about electorates in an analytical context that brings together, first, a conceptual scheme, highlighted by posters and platforms of the elections, which can help to illuminate the contesting notions of change in Latvia, and, second, the shadow cases that inform particular notions about normality. The former uses the images of the first post-Communist elections to define and demonstrate competing notions of normality. The legislative contest in the postelection Parliament reiterates the importance of these different visions of change in the legislative practice of post-Communist transformation. The examination and iteration of different narratives in this chapter also point to the relative lack of applicability of Western political categories. Multiple factors, including the demographic position of Latvians after Communism, the "small nation complex," the different notions of what constituted "national interest," and the continuing influence of Soviet notions of ethnic and class equality in some segments of society, contributed to the development of political categories and narratives that were obscured rather than illuminated by Western terms like "right" and "left."

The historical shadow cases suggest the centrality of historical precedents, those both negatively and positively perceived, in influencing notions of normality, particularly as they relate to the body of the citizenry. The discussion, for example, of the embrace of the 1919 Law on Citizenship by politicians in both the temporal and evolutionary categories, highlights the multiple uses of history. Again, the construction of narratives brings together events and renders them episodes in a particular story about the past, present, and future; the same historical precedent can, as that discussion shows, be read and rendered differently in different narratives.

In sum, the study of the post-Communist political field is not just the study of institutional politics. It is the study of a process of (re)constructing boundaries after Communism and (re)creating meanings in both political and social life. I have sought to examine these processes through the prism of the first post-Communist election contest and the contests over the electorate, which were, clearly, critically important sites of transformation for state and society. I have also tried to show that the narrative of opposition prefigured but did not inscribe the shape of post-Communist state and society. Rather, in the period after independence, the contest to define and (re)build normality pitted the visions unified in opposition against one another to mark the boundaries, models, and norms that underpinned Latvia's state and society in the years to come.

Transforming Boundaries: Space, Place, and Normality

In the late Communist period, spaces and places were not just neutral stages for demonstrations, but were important aspects of the symbolic language of opposition. The settings in which most anti-Communist demonstrations took place were messages in their own right: on the one hand, they created distance from the many Communist-era ritual demonstrations (like May Day) that did not use these sites. On the other hand, demonstration organizers and participants opted for symbolic places, like the foot of the Freedom Monument in Riga, which highlighted a link to a pre-Communist national past. In the case of the monument, the demonstrations were also an act of defiance, because gatherings or even placing flowers there were forbidden.[1] Writing on the "most sacred monuments of national heritage in Poland," Jan Kubik noted that "any spectacle near or making reference to them assumes, even if inadvertently, countless cultural and historical denotations and connotations of Polish national identity."[2] An analogous assertion can be made with respect to the Freedom Monument. Although, in contrast to the Polish sites, the Latvian monument is only six decades old, it is arguably one of the most sacred places in Latvian culture and history. In a collection of ballads assembled for the dedication of the monument, Leonīds Breikšs wrote: "Raise your eyes. Stop and look: Holy is this place. Holy is this moment."[3] Funded with private donations and completed in 1934, the monument fuses a multiplicity of significant symbolic elements. At its base, carvings show figures well known from national stories, histories, and myths. The monument's genesis in the first period of independence also made it a powerful symbol, and the words at the base, "For Fatherland and Freedom," were reminders through the Soviet period that Latvians, who for decades had neither, had the living memory of both. The monument, then, was not a neutral location, but rather an active purveyor of meaning that infused demonstrations with national content, even when the overt issues of the demonstration were, for example, environmental.

That the places at which demonstrations were convened were part and parcel of demonstrants' messages rather than just stages on which action unfolded is further highlighted by the fact that many of the demonstrations of the Interfront, which opposed both the Popular Front and Gorbachev's reforms, took place on the outskirts of Riga at the Victory Monument, a dedication to Soviet soldiers of World War II. Here demonstrators, many of whom were retired officers of the Soviet army or family members of officers, flew the flags of Soviet Latvia and the USSR, sang patriotic Soviet songs, and expressed their anger and frustration with the changes taking place in the republic and empire.

The importance of reasserting symbolic dominion over particular places in the period of opposition was highlighted again in the project of returning the streets of Riga to their prewar names, which was undertaken in the mid-1980s. David Kertzer wrote that "the notion that naming is a creative power, one that brings reality to being rather than simply provides a name for an already existing 'thing,' is found throughout the world and throughout history . . . the word creates the world."[4] In the case at hand, the creative power of naming was used less to create than to *re-create* a "normal" symbolic landscape, to call forth a historical memory, and to reassert the Latvian identity of the city.

The attempt to de-Sovietize and normalize through the transformation of space was also visible in the state policy of privatization that highlighted restitution of rural property to prewar owners.[5] The rapid decollectivization of state and collective farms opened the possibility of establishing a new regime of private property, which the state opted to do by grafting the prewar grid of private parcels onto the post-Communist map.

19   The Latvian farmer represented on the Freedom Monument

Land restitution, however, was not just a return of land as it existed, but rather an attempt to reconstruct the grid of proprietorship, to reestablish particular categories of economic power, and to simultaneously (re)construct and realize a social ideology of state and society more generally.

Tuomas Forsberg claimed that there is a tendency to view territorial disputes in an atheoretical fashion because "it is assumed that territorial issues [territories] are tangible, concrete objects," and "because of their tangibility, territorial disputes should be easier to bargain over than abstract issues." Forsberg, however, rejected this proposition, suggesting that the disputes are not just contests over objective boundaries, but rather that "territorial disputes have a lot of symbolic value."[6] Anthony Smith, among others, also recognized that, within nationalism, struggles around the bounding of physical space are also struggles about the interpretation of social space and time.[7] In Latvia, the link between the bounding of space and the interpretation of history was manifested in the dispute with the Russian Federation over a small territory to Latvia's east and Russia's west, called Abrene (in Latvia) or Pitalovo (in Russia). In Latvia, the legitimacy of Abrene/Pitalovo's 1944 transfer from the Latvian SSR to the Russian republic was disputed in the early post-Communist period, and the circumstances of the transfer rendered it a potent symbol of Latvia's occupation. Hence, the dispute embraced a contest over both the physical space and the narrative of history that this physical space represented.

In this chapter, I explore the notion that history, which cannot be recaptured in time, has been, in post-Communist states seeking to reassert the centrality of the national past, recaptured in space by re-creating the geography of the past in names, buildings, and maps. This is relevant to the project of (re)creating normality in the Latvian context, because space and place offer links between the present and the past through the representation of that past. The normalization of place and space apparently falls in the domain of a temporal conception of normality: space can be used to establish and capture a temporal continuity between present and past. The elevation and veneration of this continuity, in this case between prewar and post-Communist Latvia, are core imperatives contained in the vision of temporal normality. However, there is potential complementarity in this vision with that of the westward-looking vision of spatial normality, because, for example, in the arena of privatization, the nationalist-oriented desire to restore private property to "legal" prewar owners is not contrary to the modernization imperative of establishing a regime of private property as the foundation of a capitalist market.

This examination of the process of transformation in Latvia in the context of space and place proceeds as follows. First, I look at a little-studied but important process in the transformation, the battle to return the streets in Riga to their pre-Communist names. This process was undertaken in the late Soviet period and represents one of the early attempts to (re)map normality onto the space of Latvia through the symbolically significant eradication of Communist-era street, square, and park designations. Second, I address the issue of a border between Russia and Latvia that was contested in the early post-Communist period. The dispute over this territory was substantive, but highly symbolic as well. The state of Latvia stood on the legitimacy of its claim to the area, and its claim to the area was based primarily on a notion of continuity between the interwar and post-Communist states. Russia, on the other hand, refused to recognize the legitimacy of continuity and the illegitimacy of the Soviet occupation. The dispute over a physical space, then, also represented a fundamental dispute about history; Latvia's claim to the space was as much about normalizing the Soviet-Russian distortion of history as about taking back a territory. Third, I examine the contested and polarizing issue of rural land privatization, particularly the process of restitution of land to prewar owners. I highlight restoration as a mechanism by which the grid of prewar ownership has been re-created on the map of post-Communist Latvia and look at the ways in which this transformation of space is the product of a potent combination of notions of nostalgia, justice, and modernity.

I emphasize the importance of space and place to the project of (re)creating normality at sites widely perceived to have been deformed and distorted by the Soviet experience. I show that, rather than simply being a backdrop against which change was played out, space and place were (and are) fundamental parts of the transformation, embodying aspirations and symbolizing and structuring processes of change. The processes of naming, mapping, and restitution were part and parcel of the transformation process, some of which took place at a symbolic level, and some of which had material consequences for a significant part of the population. In sum, in this chapter, I focus on space and place as symbolically and materially consequential dimensions of post-Communist change.

Revolution in the Streets

> There is no social agent who does not aspire, as far as his circumstances permit, to have the power to name and to create the world through naming. . . .
> —Pierre Bourdieu

In this section, I examine the struggle that took place in Latvia's capital city of Riga over the names of streets during the period of opposition. I consider the significance of naming to the processes of opposition and transformation in Latvia. The sociologist Pierre Bourdieu wrote: "So far as the social world is concerned, the neo-Kantian theory, which gives language and, more generally, representations a specifically symbolic efficacy in the construction of reality, is perfectly justified. By structuring the perception which social agents have of the social world, the act of naming helps to establish the structure of the world, and does so all the more significantly the more widely it is recognized." Bourdieu was concerned primarily with the way that the designation of names of social groups is a product of struggle and a component of power relations, but his work is also useful for examining the way that social spaces are understood and identified. His notion—that the "categories of perception, . . . the names which construct social reality as much as they express it, are the crucial stakes of struggle, which is a struggle to impose the legitimate principle of vision and division"[8]—highlights what was at stake in the so-called battle of the streets in Latvia from the late 1980s through 1991. That is, by struggling for and winning the power to name, the anti-Soviet opposition seized the power not just to label but to (re)construct the symbolic environment of the city of Riga, to attach Latvian history and identity to space that had been permeated and defined by Soviet culture.

The importance of symbols in the constitution of political and social communities is widely recognized. The way that symbols are used to create and preserve a sense of "vision and division" has also received scholarly attention. Zdzyslaw Mach stated: "Every political group must have symbols which serve to identify it and its members and represent values which it pursues. These symbols are exclusive in the sense that they express the integrity and solidarity of the group, but also divide people into supporters and opponents, friends and enemies, emphasize differences between them, and define boundaries of the political and ideological domain of the group."[9] Symbols, then, serve the functions of representing a group, such as a nation, to outsiders and of telling group members "who they are, by demarcating what is authentically theirs from what is alien."[10]

When in 1940 and again in 1944 the Soviet army occupied Latvia, the USSR amply demonstrated the important relationship of symbols to power. Although the occupation regime, particularly in the Stalin era, relied heavily on coercion, brute force alone could not sustain the Soviet order. One way that social life was shaped was through the symbolic transformation of public spaces and the penetration of Soviet symbols into daily life. By the end of 1940, most of the visible symbols of the Latvian nation had been eliminated, replaced by the common symbols of Soviet states. The maroon-white-maroon Latvian flag and the prewar national anthem were prohibited. The International was accepted as the national anthem, though it was later replaced by a song written especially for the Latvian Soviet Socialist Republic. The hammer and sickle and the red star became the new symbols of state, as they were in the rest of the Union. The symbolic landscape was altered too by the change of street and district names, as well as the names of schools and factories. The map of downtown Riga was profoundly changed when the main thoroughfares were renamed in honor of Soviet figures like Lenin and Stalin.

The contest over street names in civil society and in the Riga City Council was a struggle for the power to construct the symbolic landscape of the city and a battle over whose vision was legitimate in the context of history. Michel Foucault claimed that what we recall of the past is a matter of how it is represented, and representations are the product of those in power.[11] The case of the opposition in Latvia, however, suggests not that representations flowed from power, but rather that by claiming dominion over representations, the opposition was paving a path and laying a claim to power. When the Soviet state ceded the power to represent (symbolically) to the opposition, it ceded its hold on the foundations of political power and legitimacy, which are built on the terrain of history. As Bourdieu has written, "Power comes through becoming authorized to provide a name for a thing, and thus to make it experienced in a new way."[12]

After the Soviet occupation of 1940, a number of streets experienced name changes, among them those whose names had links to religion. So, for example, *Bīskapa* (Bishop) became *Bezdievju* (Atheist), and *Mūku* (Monk) became *Darvina* (Darwin). These names were dropped during the wartime German occupation of 1941–44, and some were not renewed when the Soviet army reoccupied Latvia in late 1944. Hence, to follow through on the aforementioned example, *Bīskapa* was changed to *Muzeju* (Museum), and *Mūku* was renamed *Senatnes* (Ancient Past). After the reoccupation of 1944–45, many more names were altered: in 1950, for example, *Aspāzijas bulvāris*, named for a popular poet of the interwar period, was changed to *Padomju bulvāris* (Soviet Boulevard). In June 1950, the Riga City Council also issued an order to rename Riga's central thoroughfare, hitherto called *Brīvības* (Freedom). It declared (apparently without irony) that "*Brīvības*, as a street with an old and inappropriate name, is [to be] renamed *Ļeņina* (Lenin)." The new street combined a mass of Riga streets, including *Svērtuves*, *Kaļķu*, and *Brīvības* (which included *Brīvības bulvāris*, *Brīvības iela*, and *Brīvības gatve*).

Many of the interwar names had historical roots in Riga, some recent, others very old. For example, *Kaļķu* (literally, calcium) is mentioned as early as 1404. *Brīvības,* previously *Aleksandra* for the Russian Tsar Alexander, was so named in 1923, in honor of the July 1919 march into Riga of the Latvian Northern Army. In that year, the Northern Army, together with the Estonian army, had driven the German general von der Golc and his army out of Latvia and Estonia.[13]

In the period of Soviet rule in Latvia, over 150 streets, squares, and parks in Riga were renamed.[14] In this way, Riga became like so many other cities of the USSR, which shared the same street names, building adornments, and political monuments. These symbols followed a formula of uniformity imposed in all major spheres. Tomasz Goban-Klas and Pal Kolsto noted: "One of the most striking features of the system that the Soviet Union imposed on Central and Eastern Europe in the aftermath of the Second World War was the sameness of the political organization of their respective societies."[15] The authors did not specifically address the point, but the same could be said of the symbolic politics of the USSR and its satellites. Many streets were named for Soviet or Russian historical figures who did not have a connection to the territory or history of Latvia; some, like *F. Engelsa* (for Friedrich Engels) or *Gagārina* (for the Soviet cosmonaut Yuri Gagarin), simply reflected the Soviet tendency to name city streets in all Soviet republics with identical names. In Riga, for example, *Marijas,* named for the wife of Tsar Alexander II, became *Suvorova,* for the Russian general of the Russo-Turkish War of 1787–91. The historian Ļubova Zīle commented on this point in an interview: "There was no [good] reason to change everything. But in the Soviet period everything was changed, all the old names. They changed them to names that had nothing to do with Latvia: Suvorov had nothing to do with Latvia. . . . He had links to Russia, but not to Latvia."[16] Zīle's suggestion that "there was no good reason to change everything" misses the point that there was indeed ample reason to "change everything": the retention of historical Latvian names and symbols in the landscape of daily life would have legitimated a past that could not be compatible with the processes undertaken to define and legitimate a Soviet order that was externally imposed.

The participants in the contest over the symbolic landscape of Riga were, initially, *Latvijas Kultūras fonds* (Latvia's Cultural Fund, or LKF) and the conservative leadership of the *Rīgas pilsētas Tautas deputātu padomes izpildkomiteja* (Riga City Council), which was led by Alfrēds Rubiks. The LKF was established in summer 1987, in the wake of the previous year's establishment of the Soviet Cultural Fund, in whose statutes the task of furthering "the preservation of the historical names of geographic places and objects" was accepted. Stradiņš suggested: "This formulation also implied a recognition that the names of cities and villages, streets and squares are a component of the nation's historical memory, and they must be, from generation to generation, stable." The LKF followed a similar principle in its work and, shortly after its inception, formed a historical place-name committee *(seno vietvārdu komisija)*, whose chair was Jānis Stradiņš. Stradiņš stated: "The guiding idea of [the committee's] work was that a name is a vital component of a place, the most important designator of its character, history, and culture: with the loss of its name, the place loses its soul."[17]

In the mid-1980s, Rubiks had undertaken a massive physical restoration of buildings in Old Riga. The committee under Stradiņš undertook a symbolic restoration of the area, seeking to return prewar names to some of the streets of Old Riga. The committee, according to Stradiņš, worked on the premise that "in the context of the [physical] restoration of Old Riga, . . . it was necessary not just to renew buildings, but the entire cultural environment, a meaningful component of which are the historical names of streets and squares." The efforts of the committee met with a combination of success and rejection: at the November 1987 meeting of the City Council, some of the Cultural Fund's suggestions were accepted, including the renewal of the names of three squares. All names with religious connotations were rejected, including the proposed return of *Bibliotēkas* (Library) to *Anglikāņu* (Anglican) and *Muzeja* (Museum) to *Bīskapa* (Bishop). Also among the names "too religious" to renew was *Grēcinieku* (literally, Sinners), which had, in the Soviet period, taken the name *Imanta Sudmaļa*.[18] Despite the council's objection to the religious connotations of the name, it had come not from a reference to those committing religious malfeasance, but from the German Baron von Sundern. The street was originally named Sunderstrasse, which translates to Sinner Street. Later, when Riga's German-named streets were given Latvian names, the street's designation became the Latvian *Grēcinieku*.[19]

Although the LKF committee achieved modest success in its efforts to return prewar street names to Old Riga already in 1987, they met with greater obstacles in altering the symbolic landscape of central Riga. Stradiņš wrote: "An incomparably sharper conflict emerged around Riga's central streets, because the names of these main streets generally were names of persons and ideas that were holy to the ideology in power. It was felt that, changing these names would signal doubts about 'socialism's basic values.'" Echoing a common theme in the restorationist narrative, he suggested, however, that the City Council failed to accept that the task undertaken by the committee was not alteration but restoration: "not a word was said about the fact that the issue was not about changing names, but rather about the renewal of old names, whose eradication had in its time caused painful bruises on public consciousness." Addressing the issue of opposition to the street name project, Stradiņš suggested that many of those who were against the changing of street names were immigrants to Riga: "Many have not understood the point of 'renewal,' incorrectly seeing in that a threat to their interests and values." In any case, the Riga City Council kept its distance from the issue of altering the downtown landscape, avoiding examination of the issue.

Through part of 1988 and early 1989, the work of the committee was halted because of the Soviet census of 1989. The opposition, in early 1989, was also focusing more energy on the March elections to the Council of People's Deputies, the first competitive elections of the Soviet era, in which candidates associated with the Latvian Popular Front would also stand. The committee had expected the council to take up the issue again beginning in spring 1989, but the council refused to look at proposed changes at its May 1989 session, citing among the reasons "fear of high monetary costs, lack of time, the objections of some part of the population, [and] possible misunderstandings."[20]

Despite the inactivity of state structures in the realm of transforming the symbolic landscape, in civil society activity around the issue continued. Letters from inhabitants, particularly those of the older generations, to the committee and council spoke out about changes; the issue was broadly discussed in the media; and popular activities like concerts were also organized. On March 16, 1989, for example, a concert of popular music entitled "We Are for *Aspāzijas bulvāris*" took place. The concert commemorated the 125th birthday of Aspāzija, a Latvian woman poet renowned in the interwar period but marginalized by the Soviet regime, and asked for the renewal of *Aspāzijas bulvāris*, which had been renamed *Padomju bulvāris* (Soviet Boulevard). In spring 1989, at its first congress, Latvia's Cultural Fund also declared a change in its status, freeing itself from official structures and putting forth a declaration of sovereignty, which, in the words of Stradiņš, "[they] hoped would be followed by the evolutionary return of state sovereignty."[21]

On October 31, 1989, the City Council debated a number of important changes to the streets of the central city and Old Riga. At a "stormy session," the council accepted, among others, the following proposed renewals: *Gorkija* (Gorky) became *Krišjāna Valdemāra* (after Krišjānis Valdemārs, an important cultural figure in the Latvian "awakening" that preceded the establishment of the first independent Latvian state in 1918); *Padomju* (Soviet) reverted to *Aspāzijas; Komjaunatnes* (Young Communists) returned to *Jēkaba* (Jacob's); and *Anglikāņu* (Anglican) and *Mūku* (Monk) regained their prewar names. Also renewed was *Brīvības bulvāris* (Freedom Boulevard), part of Lenin Street, though the remainder of the thoroughfare retained Lenin's name. Other changes rejected by the council included proposals to renew the names of *Stabu* (Stake), a historical name[22] changed to *F. Engelsa* (F. Engels) in 1950, and *Tērbatas* (Tartu), part of the old road to Tartu, which was changed in 1955 to *Pētera Stučkas*.[23]

Although the City Council had changed a number of names by the end of 1989, the *administrative* declaration of renewal did not immediately translate into the *physical* alteration of the landscape. As Rubiks, his supporters on the council, and some Soviet newspapers suggested, the body did not want to budget scarce money to manufacture new signs when the changes were accepted. Hence, Latvia's Popular Front, the formal organization of the opposition, underwrote the printing of stickers with the renewed street names, and supporters of Front glued the stickers onto existing street signs.[24] Typically, the stickers showed the new name only in the Latin alphabet used by the Latvian language.

On the issue of naming some streets after Communist revolutionaries and political figures like Pēteris Stučka, the committee took a stance of compromise. As late as 1990, the committee, while it spoke out in favor of renewing most of the historical names of the streets in Old Riga and the downtown center, suggested that it would "find a place on the map of Riga" for the Communists Pēteris Stučka, Imants Sudmalis, and even Lenin, "because Lenin was closely associated with Latvia's revolutionary movement and was the leader of the first country that recognized Latvia's independence on August 11, 1920." The possibility of finding a place for Karl Marx was also not rejected.[25] Soon after, however, as the march toward independence gained momentum, these plans were quietly dropped.

Again, the street issue was temporarily put aside as the opposition prepared for the spring 1990 elections to the Supreme Soviet of Latvia. By April 1990, the Riga City Council had also elected a new Presidium and a new head, Andris Teikmanis, and the process of changing street names became more rapid. Another reason for the intensified effort was, according to Stradiņš, that the "20th [Latvian national] Song Festival was nearing, and in honor of this occasion, it was intended to settle [issues about] Riga's cultural environment." At an April session of the council, forty-nine street names and eleven square and park names were on the agenda. The process was by no means uncontentious, however, and deputies who were against the changes twice blocked the acceptance of changes. In a compromise reached a week later, the agenda was pared down to include twenty-five streets and eleven squares and parks. The remainder of the names, the committee and

City Council Presidium decided, would remain unchanged, at least for the time being. In a 1990 newspaper piece quoted in full in his book, Stradiņš wrote: "Because of V. Lenin's 120th birthday on April 22, the issue of renewing *Brīvības iela* [Freedom Street] was postponed until the May session."[26]

The issue of Lenin Street, named for the preeminent icon of Soviet power, is worth examining further. Stradiņš's claim that the issue of changing the name of Lenin Street, one of the city's central thoroughfares, was put aside because of Lenin's birthday is, in the context of the politics and climate of 1990, somewhat dubious. Alternative explanations for the postponement of changing the name more plausibly centered around the fear of the committee or council or both that ejecting Lenin from the heart of Riga could incite outrage and possibly retribution from conservative forces. Lenin, immortalized in the street name and the statue that stood at the head of the street, was among the last Soviet symbols that remained in Riga; the flag and anthem of Soviet Latvia and place-names for Soviet heroes and revolutionaries were disappearing representatives of Soviet political and ideological hegemony. The flag of prewar Latvia had been relegalized in 1988 and, as of February 27, 1990, flew over the building that housed the Supreme Soviet of the republic. By early April 1990, the Communist Party itself, the guiding light of the revolution, had split in Latvia, separating into progressive and conservative wings. Finally, the Supreme Soviet of the republic had, in July 1989, accepted a declaration of state sovereignty, maintaining that the laws of the Supreme Soviet were the highest laws in the land, a move that preceded by just ten months the newly elected Supreme Soviet's declaration in favor of full state independence. What remained of Soviet power in Latvia in spring 1990, then, was military force, which there was limited will to use, and the last powerful Soviet symbols in Riga—the statue of Lenin, extending his arm toward the street that still bore his name.

Stradiņš suggested that the "street battles" were about restoration rather than change as such, but exceptions were made to the rule of renewal. For instance, the *Maskavas* administrative district of Riga was renamed rather than renewed; presumably this was motivated by a desire to minimize the visibility of Soviet-associated symbols. Other changes were based on the desire to underscore Riga's membership in the community of European cities: Stradiņš wrote that "in [the committee's] opinion, it isn't necessary to renew all former names because earlier [in interwar Latvia] there were also hurried and poorly thought out street names given. . . . One need not forget that Riga is not just the city of Riga's inhabitants, it is Latvia's capital city; further, it is also a large European city; therefore, it needs to have appropriate names with European relevance."[27] The interest in reestablishing a

Latvian landscape in a European context was, in politics as well as symbols, a central concern of the opposition, which melded discourses of nationalism and modernity in anti-Soviet protest.

The changes of names in the landscape of Riga were components of the symbolic reclamation of historical memory and claims made about the identity of the city. The names of streets that existed during the period of independence almost invariably returned to their prewar names, a transformation accorded some importance, especially with respect to the main thoroughfares in downtown Riga whose prewar names were well known. Most new streets with politically insignificant names retained their names, but any names with "Soviet" connotations or links were changed. Kertzer noted: "Endowing certain spaces with sacrality is universal in the struggle for power, as it is in governance. Space is marked off in a way that not only brings to mind a certain view of history but also links those in the present to the sacred past."[28] The renewal of names on the basis of the notion that "ancient names are a component of the nation's historical memory"[29] highlights Kertzer's suggestion that space (and the process through which it is marked—by names) is a vehicle through which to marry the present to a "sacred past" and to stake a claim in the creation of the identity of the landscape and agents operating on that landscape.

Bourdieu argued that social science must "examine the part played by words in the construction of social reality and contribution which the struggle over classifications, a dimension of all class struggles, makes to the constitution of classes—classes defined in terms of age, sex, or social position, but also clans, tribes, ethnic groups, or nations." Indeed, this constitution of classes or other social groupings is achieved in part through their representation in the public realm. Groups, suggested Bourdieu, can be both validated and elevated by representation or, by the same token, cast in shadow. He wrote that through the political action of agents, groups can be made and unmade, and that "collective action [agents] can undertake to transform the social world in accordance with their interests—by producing, reproducing, or destroying the representations that make groups visible for themselves and others."[30] Among the representations that might be included with symbolic representations like names (words) are alphabets, the building blocks of the words that represent and structure social reality.

Below I discuss the symbolic reclamation of space by the anti-Soviet opposition in Latvia, not only by means of renewing names that linked the uncertain present to a Latvian national past, but also by means of erasing the stamp of Soviet power, destroying one of the representations that made a Russian (or Soviet) presence visible, by expunging Cyrillic letters from

the signs that carried those names. The early process of erasing Cyrillic
script from the landscape was carried out in a number of ways. First, as
noted earlier, the stickers printed by Latvia's Popular Front with the new or
renewed names of streets featured Latin script. Second, it was common by
1989 to see that the Cyrillic portion of street signs had been painted over
and obscured.

Many street names in Riga, particularly in newer areas of the city, were
not altered, and, hence, stickers were not made for them. On these signs, old
names, in both Latin and Cyrillic script, remained until the latter was erased.
The painting was undertaken by individuals; the state neither explicitly permitted nor prohibited the action. Most of the painting was done on the
corner street signs of the city rather than on the signs posted on private
homes, many of which had signs with the house number and the name of
the street in both languages. To paint over the Cyrillic script on one's own
home, according to one Latvian, would at first have been to invite possible
retribution, "a rock through the window," from passersby offended by the
effacement of the Russian name. Later, however, most Latvian homes with
signs did paint over the Cyrillic script. The widespread practice of painting
over the Russian names on street signs evoked an indignant response from
the editorial staff of the newspaper *Edinstvo* (Unity), the official mouthpiece
of the Interfront. In a photo essay featuring four shots of painted signs, the
paper published the following angry response:

> [Latvia's Popular Front] leaders sing sweet songs about every lan-
> guage being protected under the new language law! This shows the
> truth. This illustrates this "protection.". . . How can we expect the
> new citizenship law will protect the honor . . . of the tens of thou-
> sands who will not become first-class citizens. The *Edinstvo* editorial
> board requests the LSSR Prosecutor's Office to consider the publi-
> cation of these pictures an official request to start an investigation
> according to the law and to punish those who are responsible for
> this hooliganism and violation of the language law of the LSSR. In
> down to earth terms—save up some courage, noncitizens of "sover-
> eign Latvia"—more is to come.[31]

Edinstvo, like its parent organization the Interfront, saw the issue in the context of a narrative that did not question the legitimacy of the Soviet presence
or its symbols. The newspaper typically took a hard conservative stance
against the initiatives of the Popular Front, as well as the moderate wing of
the Communist Party.

The language law to which the photo essay refers is the law accepted by the Supreme Soviet of Latvia on May 5, 1989. The law, among other things, conferred on the Latvian language the status of a state language, though it was a law on *languages* in that it also recognized the status of minority languages. The law noted:

> In recent decades, the use of the Latvian language in state and public life has narrowed markedly. This requires that special measures be taken by legal means for the protection of the Latvian language. Only the status of state language can guarantee such protection. The state ensures this by the multilateral and fully valid usage of the Latvian language in state and public life, as well as its study. . . . At the same time, the state is concerned with respect toward all languages and dialects used in the Latvian SSR. . . . The law takes into consideration the fact that after the Latvian language, Russian is the most widely used language in the Latvian SSR and is one of the languages of international relations.

With regard to place-names, the law stated that "Latvian SSR place names are formed and given in the Latvian language." Finally, Section 6, on the "Protection of Languages," stated: "Those guilty of violating the citizens' right in choice of language, public humiliation, or premeditated distortion of any language in official documents and texts will be brought to accountability as established by law."[32]

Whether or not the language law under which *Edinstvo*'s editorial staff demanded protection proscribed the alteration of street signs is not fully clear because the language law, perhaps intentionally, was vague. Clearly, however, *Edinstvo* and the segment of the population whose views it both reflected and formed took the position that the new status of the Latvian language, certainly to the point that it lowered the status of the Russian language, jeopardized their interests. Furthermore, they used the issue of the disappearing Cyrillic script to build a narrative that rejected opposition initiatives toward Latvian sovereignty and elevated the notion that Soviet (and Russian) power in the region was historically legitimate and that steps toward the "Latvianization" of the state and social institutions constituted a threat to their well-being.

Indeed, a low-level conflict over street names and alphabets simmered beneath the battle of wills and words being waged in civil society and governmental structures. In downtown Riga, where streets had acquired more new names than in the outskirts of the city, some stickers pasted over old names were torn down, or paint was sprayed over the new designations. In the outskirts, where there were many signs with obscured Cyrillic letters, painters with a different point of view on the issue erased the Latin script from street signs, leaving only the Russian name beneath. This symbolic struggle over script highlights Bourdieu's suggestion that groups are made visible through representations (or invisible through their destruction), and representations can be used to create the social world and assert power. By erasing Russian names, painters, agents of an opposition narrative, erased the stamp of the group they perceived to be their oppressors and asserted their own dominance of the landscape. Similarly, those who obscured the Latvian names reasserted their own symbolic power and the preeminence of the Russian language and its status as the "means of communication between all Soviet nationalities."

The battle over symbols in the physical and political landscape, although little noted by those who study the region, constituted an important part of the contestation around the future of the republic and the historical terrain on which this future would be built. The process of transforming the symbolic landscape and "Latvianizing" landmarks by harnessing them to Latvian history, culture, and language and nullifying Soviet associations was a central dimension of returning the symbolic landscape of Latvia to a state of "normality."

Mapping Memory: The Histories of Abrene and Pitalovo

"In terms of most communication theories and common sense, a map is a scientific abstraction of reality. A map merely represents something which already exists objectively 'there.' In the history I have described, this relationship was reversed. A map anticipated spatial reality, not vice versa. In other words, a map was a model for, rather than a model of what it purported to represent."[33]

This quotation describes the mapping of Siam late in the nineteenth century, but its recognition of the map as a dynamic symbolic and political instrument rather than just a mirror of objective conditions is useful for understanding the mapping of nationhood in the Soviet and post-Communist periods as well. Mapping, as Thongchai Winichakul suggested, can be as much a process of describing aspirations and claims as a method of describing landmarks. Indeed, the symbolic process of incorporating the independent Baltic countries of Latvia, Lithuania, and Estonia into the Union of Soviet Socialist Republics began even before these countries were occupied in summer 1940: military maps from autumn 1939 and school maps from spring 1940 had already extended the borders of the USSR to include the three countries.[34]

The Soviet penchant for mapping aspirations also led, more recently, to somewhat less serious outcomes. In the early 1990s, several foreign mapmaking firms, eager to cash in on the possibilities of growing tourism in Latvia, prepared new maps of the country and surrounding areas by using the broadly distributed maps produced in the Soviet era. Many maps of the late Soviet period showed a completed highway between Riga and Moscow. The project, however, was terminated near the time that Latvia exited the Soviet Union, and the "highway" comes to an unceremonious end on a dusty road in eastern Latvia. Ignorant of this detail, however, foreign mapmakers included the road from Riga to Moscow, a route apparently taken by some foreign motorists similarly ignorant of the "missing" miles to Moscow.[35]

Narratives of nationhood typically place a strong emphasis on territorial issues, treating particular places and spaces as constituent parts of national identity. In Latvia in the 1980s and 1990s, place and space were important sites for the symbolic definition and redefinition of nationhood. The reclamation of history was part of this process as well. In the previous section, I discussed the successful process of "returning history" to Riga with the return of old street names. Here I look at attempts in early post-Communist Latvia to re-create the map of interwar Latvia in the geopolitical space of the late twentieth century. I take legal issues into account, but concentrate on the role that historical and modern borders played in the process of definition and redefinition of the Latvian nation-state in the post-Communist period.

In discussing the issue of Abrene/Pitalovo, I take this area to be more than a physical space. I take it to be a geobody, a term used by Thongchai to describe a geographic area that "is not merely space or territory. It is a component of the life of a nation. It is a source of pride, loyalty, love, passion, bias, hatred, reason, unreason."[36] As the concept of geobody suggests, Abrene/Pitalovo was a site at which political realities mixed with national histories, myths, desires, and hopes. The dimensions of the area were, hence, temporal as well as spatial: the frontier posts of history delineated borders that were quite different from modern frontiers.

A nation-state comes into existence through a variety of means; a state is a structural entity, but, as Benedict Anderson argued, a nation is an "imagined community."[37] It is not "imagined" in the sense that it is not real, only in the sense that it *becomes* real through a conscious rather than "natural" process of creation, which entails drawing boundaries that are cultural, linguistic, political, economic, and spatial. In this section, I use the case of Abrene/ Pitalovo to illustrate the power of the geobody and to examine how the dispute over this area was not only about mapping physical space, but about mapping nationhood and constructing (or reconstructing) the Latvian nation-state after Communism.

Because the name of the territory itself has been enmeshed in the historical stories of the area and the dispute over it, I use the Latvian designation Abrene where it was the "official" name, that is, during the interwar period. I use Pitalovo, the Russian designation, where it is the generally recognized name. In discussions not focused on any particular historical period, I refer to Abrene/Pitalovo.

Abrene/Pitalovo: History and Population in the Twentieth Century

The disputed territory on Latvia's eastern border is known in Latvia as Abrene and in Russia as Pitalovo (sometimes transliterated as Pytalovo). The Latvian historian Edgars Andersons wrote that the latter name is a Russianized version of the ancient Latvian name Pietālava, literally "near Tālava," a historical Latvian feudal state.[38] In this rural area, populated in the 1990s by roughly 18,000 people, the shifting boundaries offer a microcosmic view of the twentieth-century history of Eastern Europe. In this period, the territory has gone from being part of the Russian empire that blanketed a large portion of the Eurasian continent until the First World War, to being part of the Republic of Latvia in an interwar period characterized by small sovereign states, to being part of the Russian Soviet Federated Socialist Republic (RSFSR) and the Soviet Union from 1944 to 1991, to constituting an eastern edge of the Russian Federation, one of fifteen states to emerge from the former Soviet Union. This small territory has been occupied by the identities, ideologies, and historical narratives of four states and has, as I discuss further along, seen a population shift that radically splits the historical memory of its inhabitants into collective recollections founded in the pre– and post–World War II periods.

Before the First World War, the territory in question was part of the Vitebsk province of the Russian empire. The population of the area was ethnically mixed, with Russians, Latvians, and other ethnic groups making their homes there. In accordance with the 1920 Peace Treaty between the USSR and the newly proclaimed Republic of Latvia, a political border between the two states was fixed by a Frontier Commission made up of representatives of the two states.[39] The committee worked for two years before reaching full accord on the border in April 1923. At this time, its members accepted a final version of the 352-kilometer-long border. Abrene fell on the Latvian side of the frontier.

During the interwar period of independence, the Abrene area experienced an expansion, though it remained rural. The demographic composition of the area was, according to the Latvian state census of 1935, predominantly Russian. In the Abrene district there were 44,566 inhabitants. Of these, around 85 percent were ethnically Russian, and 12 percent were Latvian; the rest were Poles, Germans, and Jews. In the town of Abrene, Russians made up about 52 percent of the 1,242 inhabitants and Latvians about 38 percent.[40]

In 1940, when the Soviet army occupied Latvia and incorporated it into the USSR, Abrene was a part of the newly created Latvian Soviet Socialist Republic. The Soviet army was driven out of Latvia by the Nazis in 1941, and the German army occupation lasted until summer 1944. During the reoccupation of the late World War II period, the Soviet government made a number of changes in the existing borders of the occupied Baltics and neighboring states: Lithuania regained Vilnius, as well as the port city of Klaipeda; Estonia lost a portion of Narva and Petserimaa; and Latvia lost Abrene. Although a substantial portion of Latvia's territory, including Riga, was still occupied by the Nazis, in August 1944, Soviet authorities based in Daugavpils, a city in southeast Latvia, acted to move the border.[41] In response to a "suggestion" by the Soviet government, the renewed Presidium of the Supreme Soviet of the Latvian SSR turned to federal authorities with a request that they add to the territory of the RSFSR particular areas of Latvia with large Russian populations.[42] The following day, the Presidium of the Supreme Soviet of the USSR handed down a decree, "On the Formation of the Pskov Oblast' in the Territory of the USSR," which transferred the territory to the RSFSR. The decision of the USSR Presidium was accepted by the deputies of the Supreme Soviet of the Latvian Socialist Soviet Republic in October 1944.[43] The border between the two Soviet republics was normatively sealed two years later.[44]

The Soviet government based its claim about the legitimate transfer of territory on two basic premises: first, that the area given to the RSFSR was predominantly Russian and thus appropriately part of the Russian republic; second, that the move was based on "repeated requests" of the area's inhabitants to join the RSFSR.[45] Andersons rejected the notion that the transfer was a response to the wishes of the local population, because a plebiscite was never held, which would presumably have gauged the population's opinions on the issue. Furthermore, sources suggested that most inhabitants of the area, including local administrators, did not even know about the change until after the war had ended.[46] In a recent interview, Aleksandr Nikonov, who was first secretary of the Communist Party of the district of Abrene at that time, indicated that "it all began very unexpectedly. Simply, one day ... the leadership of the newly established Pskov Oblast' arrived ... introduced themselves, showed [us] the declaration from the Presidium of the Supreme Soviet of the USSR with [Nikolai] Kalinin's signature, and began to tell us how we would henceforth live and work." Nikonov added that "our first reaction was: what is this and why did we not know anything about this?"[47]

The territory, like other territories transferred to the RSFSR, underwent a fundamental internal redefinition. Among other things, the symbolic land-scape was profoundly altered. Place-names were changed; the town of Ab-rene and surrounding villages, as well as the streets, squares, and parks, were given new names. The Latin alphabet disappeared over time as well, re-placed by the Cyrillic script of Russian. Retrospective redefinition was achieved by creating a particular interpretation of history for local memo-ry—the area had not been annexed, but rather "given" by the Latvian re-public, and this transfer corresponded to the stated wishes of the local popu-lation. Consistent with this recasting of history, publications on the area and exhibits on local history and folklore typically excluded materials from or references to Abrene.[48]

The internal definition of the territory also changed as the living memory of the area's inhabitants changed. During the war and postwar periods, the composition of the population underwent a radical change. After the transfer of the territory to the RSFSR, many Latvians as well as Russians moved to the Latvian side of the new border. War and deportations further thinned the prewar population. Movement into Pitalovo from other parts of the So-viet Union undergirded a substantial change in population identity. Accord-ing to some estimates, only around 5 percent of the present-day population of the Abrene area is made up of prewar Latvian citizens or their descen-dants.[49]

One of the features that makes the Abrene/Pitalovo dispute novel is the fact that, from the Latvian side, the question centered around territory, ex-clusive of population. In contrast, many border disputes marry issues of na-tional frontiers with those of national minorities in the spirit of Ernest Gellner's theorized political principle of nationalism, "which holds that the political and national unit should be congruent."[50] The Abrene/Pitalovo questions revolved, at least from Latvia's official view, around a historical claim to the space, with no overt claims about the population, and a demand for the acknowledgment of the validity of that claim. The issue of congruence between a national (Latvian) population and national borders was tangential to the Latvian case.

Narratives of History

In a study of border disputes in and around the former Soviet Union, Forsberg brought up the issue of the "value" of territory. He discussed "value" in terms of security and economy, though he did not limit himself to those two; he recognized value in the fact that "control over territory can also be seen as a means to promote religion, national culture, and [a] political system in a given area." Forsberg argued that value is not an objective condition in a territory and that it may change depending on the "international environment."[51] Beyond this, one might also hypothesize a symbolic value that is constructed by agents in a dispute. Indeed, in this case one might ask what the symbolic value of Abrene/Pitalovo was to Latvia. What was its symbolic value to Russia, the legatee of the USSR? I address these questions below.

The dispute over Abrene/Pitalovo was more than a dispute about legal rights to a territory (though those were important). It was a collision of narratives about history and nationhood. In the Latvian narrative on Abrene, two particular features stand out. First, the dispute appeared to be less about wanting physical control over the territory Latvians called Abrene than about asserting control over history. There was a desire to legitimate the Latvian "story" of Abrene and to receive from Russia recognition of a historical injustice that could *symbolize* other historical injustices done to the nation.

On January 22, 1992, the Supreme Council of the Republic of Latvia passed a resolution "On the Nonrecognition of the Annexation of the Town of Abrene and the Six Rural Districts of the Abrene District." The resolution directed a delegation from Latvia "to resolve the Abrene issue during interstate negotiations with the Russian Federation, including procedures for the determination of the amount of and compensation for material losses caused to the still-existing property of the Republic of Latvia and the citizens of the Republic of Latvia in the town of Abrene and the six rural districts in the Abrene District." It asserted that the annexation was carried out during Latvia's illegal occupation and was a violation of the Latvian and Russian Peace Treaty of 1920 and the Latvian-Soviet Non-Aggression Treaty of 1932 and that the August 23, 1944, decree of the USSR Supreme Soviet Presidium, "On the Formation of the Pskov Oblast'," was invalid from the time of its adoption. It also declared illegitimate two additional juridical acts of 1944 and 1946, which transferred territory and altered the border. According to the document, the Peace Treaty of 1920 and the borders established on its basis were still legally in force. However, although the resolution was strongly worded, it did not move to demand the return of the territory. Rather, it asserted the fundamental illegitimacy of the annexation and asked in various ways for Russian acknowledgment of this point.

The second feature of the Latvian narrative around Abrene, one also mentioned earlier, was that the identity and history of the territory were divorced from the identity and history of the inhabitants of that territory, few of whom had historical links to a physical space called Abrene. Some ethnic Latvians were reported at the time to reside in Pitalovo and interest was expressed about their fate, but the *historical* space and population of Abrene rather than the *physical* (present) space and population of Pitalovo were the focal point of Latvia's claims.

In terms of the "value" of Abrene the historical space to Latvia, several points can be made. First, as the Supreme Council document suggests, an economic value was recognized and considered in the discourse around Abrene. Claims against Russia, the legatee of the old USSR, were made by both individuals and the state. The Russian government, however, has not to this point shown any inclination to compensate material losses sustained by Latvia or its citizens. Second, Abrene was valuable as a historical symbol. By winning recognition from Russia that the annexation was illegal, Latvia would have won a historical victory that potentially transcended the Abrene issue because a recognition of illegality in the Abrene annexation had larger ramifications. That is, it could have been extended to a recognition that the 1940 occupation of Latvia itself, of which Abrene was a consequence, was illegal. Russia, despite its recognition of the secret protocols of the Molotov-Ribbentrop Pact of 1939, has never conceded this point.

From Russia's side, the dispute over Abrene seemed to be about asserting its own historical narrative and about maintaining the legitimacy of those acts of which it was the primary legatee. Russia asserted that the area was and had historically been predominantly Russian. In this narrative, then, the inclusion of Abrene in the Republic of Latvia and, in fact, the independent existence of the Baltic countries themselves, was a historical anomaly that was largely explained by "the weakness of the newly formed state [USSR] and the pressure from the imperialist world."[52]

Maps, Laws, and Perspectives on the Future

The Latvian government did not put forth an active territorial claim on Pitalovo, but even symbolic historical claims were construed by Russia as provocative. In spring 1992, the firm *Latvijas karte* (Latvia's map) released a map of Latvia with its pre-1944 borders, that is, with Abrene included as part of the territory. The inclusion of Abrene evoked an indignant response from Russia. On April 18, 1992, the Russian Foreign Ministry sent the Latvian government a stern rebuke, saying that Russia would not recognize any historical or legal claims to Pitalovo by Latvia "because for hundreds of years already, nearly all inhabitants [of the area] have been Russian."[53]

It is worth reviewing at this point the discrepant bases on which Latvia and Russia based their claims to Abrene/Pitalovo. Russia, at least in the context of the map issue, framed its claim about the territory's legitimate place in Russia with an argument that the ethnic makeup of the area had "for hundreds of years already" been predominantly Russian. It is true that even in the mid-1930s, Russians did make up the largest part of the population. Russia also evoked the Helsinki Act of 1975, suggesting that Latvia had violated the principle of inviolable borders in this dispute.[54]

Latvia's claim to Abrene/Pitalovo was not based in the 1990s on an "ethnographic principle," as it was not based on that foundation in 1920. In a review of the history of the 1920 Peace Treaty between Latvia and the RSFSR, which addressed some border issues, Aivars Stranga wrote: "When Latvia's delegation asked for Pitalovo's official inclusion in Latvia, it well understood that the ethnographic principle could not be used as the foundation for its request, because the majority of the population in the Pitalovo and the surrounding areas was not Latvian." Latvia's decision to pursue the inclusion of Pitalovo, rather, was based on economic considerations: rail lines going through Pitalovo provided important connections between Latvian cities. According to this account, the RSFSR did not focus on so-called ethnographic principles in its concern over the territory either. Rather, A. Jofe of the RSFSR delegation was concerned about the military threat that could arise from the West and the role that Pitalovo could play in a Western attack on the USSR. At the time, the RSFSR received assurances from the Latvian delegation that Latvia had no aggressive intentions toward that state.[55]

Latvia's claim to Abrene in the 1990s—or, rather, its claim to the legitimacy of its claim—was framed primarily in terms of history and legality: the continued binding legality of the 1920 Peace Treaty between Latvia and the RSFSR and the illegality of the 1940 Soviet occupation and all juridical acts that followed. The 1920 Peace Treaty contained a provision in which the RSFSR "unreservedly recognize[d] the independence, self-subsistence, and sovereignty of the Latvian State and voluntarily and forever renounce[d] all sovereign rights over the Latvian people and territory."[56]

Because Latvia strongly asserted the continuity of its legal existence under the auspices of international law (a point implicitly accepted by most Western countries as they never recognized de jure the occupation of Latvia), it claimed that this treaty was still in force and, hence, regulated interstate relations between Latvia and the Soviet Union's legatee, Russia.

Russia did not accept this argument and disputed the notion that interstate relations were regulated in the 1990s by the 1920 treaty. Rather, Russia suggested that the 1940 entry of Latvia into the USSR nullified the 1920 treaty. Russia's stance on this aspect of the dispute was important because its claim that the Peace Treaty of 1920 was nullified by Latvia's entry into the Soviet Union was also *a claim for the basic legality of the 1940 incorporation of Latvia*. In other words, for Russia to accept Latvia's claim that the 1920 treaty was binding, it would have to acknowledge that the occupation itself was illegal.

In early 1997, Latvia and Russia agreed on the basic content of a limited border agreement. The agreement was limited in that it fixed de facto borders between the two states, but did not address tangential issues like compensation for those who lost property in the transfer of territory. Although the agreement was not perceived as favorable to Latvia, two issues appeared to push Latvia toward recognition of the 1944 border: first, the fact that Estonia had already resolved its border dispute with Russia about Narva and Petserii by recognizing the postwar border, creating a precedent for Latvia; second, that the 1995 Pact on European Stability asked countries to resolve their border disputes as a condition for joining international structures like the European Union. Most political groups in Parliament accepted the inevitability of the agreement, though the nationalist For Fatherland and Freedom group rejected any but the Peace Treaty of 1920 as a foundation for post-Communist Latvia's international affairs.[57]

De facto borders seemed to be a foregone conclusion by 1997, but tangential issues like compensation, restitution, and Russia's recognition of the illegality of the transfer of Abrene to the RSFSR remained unresolved through the end of the 1990s. The most probable scenario is that Russia will retain Pitalovo within its borders. Hence, the question that remains to be answered in the decade after the restoration of independence is whether Latvia will succeed in pressing Russia to acknowledge the illegal transfer of Abrene. Because such an acknowledgment would carry an implicit recognition of the illegality of the occupation of Latvia, even this symbolic victory appears unlikely. As recently as 2000, the Russian Foreign Ministry posited the "official" position that the "USSR sent its troops into the Baltic region only after the leaders there requested it."[58]

Mapping Normality

Earlier in the section, I put forth the notion that Abrene/Pitalovo was more than a physical space in the context of the border contest. Rather, it could be understood as a "geobody," a term defined by Thongchai. His notion that the geobody is "a component of the life of the nation" is important for highlighting the point that the dispute over Abrene/Pitalovo (as well as post-Communist border disputes elsewhere in the region) was more than a contest over physical space that might provide economic or military advantages. The contest over territory was underpinned in part by a desire to assert control over the history of a nation and the legitimacy of that nation's historical story. In this case, the claim was motivated less by a desire on the part of Latvia to acquire the territory of Pitalovo than to "correct" history. That is, Abrene was a component of national history and its annexation a facet of the occupation that cast a long shadow in post-Communist politics.

The process of mapping nationhood is a component of constructing national self-definition. However, notions of how the nation was to be defined in post-Communism and whether it was to be reconstructed on a template of the West or a template of the past were in conflict in the post-Communist period. Hence, whereas the Parliament accepted Resolution 69, "On the Nonrecognition of the Annexation of the Town of Abrene and the Six Rural Districts of the Abrene District," in 1992, negotiators in 1998, headed by a representative from the progressive party Latvia's Way, appeared to accept that de facto recognition of the border was a necessary step toward acceptance by European institutions that demanded the resolution of border issues. The radical restorationist party, For Fatherland and Freedom, on the other hand, did not want to back off the issue, asserting the primacy of the 1920 treaty in the regulation of interstate relations and borders. The dispute over whether the map of post-Communist Latvia was to be drawn from outlines of the interwar period or around paths that led to the common European home was not easily resolved in a climate where the past, as Anatol Lieven suggested in his book on the Baltics, "has a way of walking around in the present as if it were alive."

Fields of Change: Rural Property and Restitution

[Space] that has been seized upon by the imagination cannot remain indifferent space subject to the measures and estimates of the surveyor.[59]
—Gaston Bachelard

The prism of rural property and its transformation is a useful one for exploring some of the important dimensions of changing social institutions in post-Communism. Like other sites of change, the (re)creation of a regime of private property in rural areas has been a field of play defined by both visions of restoration and imperatives of modernization across Eastern Europe.[60] There are two processes in Latvia by which land made its way into private hands in the late Soviet and the early post-Communist periods. These processes, termed "privatization" on the one hand and "reprivatization" on the other, have not been smooth and have frequently come into conflict with each other. Privatization began in the late 1980s, when small amounts of land not being used by collective farms or other official institutions were distributed to rural inhabitants wishing to begin farming privately. These farmers were granted usufruct (use) rights, and the property was recognized as heritable, but users did not assume title. Reprivatization, or restitution, based on a principle of returning land to legal prewar owners, obtained the force of law in the early 1990s. By way of restitution, individuals could assume full title to parcels of land.

Among the problems that have arisen are conflicts between urban dwellers who want to repossess a piece of rural land owned in the prewar period by them or their forebears and rural residents who now make a home and perhaps a living on that land. One variation of this conflict played on the post-Communist stage is the conflict between rural inhabitants, both Latvian and Russian,[61] who work or live on a parcel of land and Latvian émigrés from the West who, in the post-Communist period, lay claim to that land on the basis of prewar ownership. Because working the land is not a prerequisite for receiving it, the potential (and, in some cases, actual) consequence is that those who have lived on the land and farmed it have limited legal claim to it. Furthermore, there is a problem that pits users of privatized land against legal owners of reprivatized land when the parties potentially or actually occupy the same parcel: in some cases, the law recognizes the rights of the user, in others the rights of the owner. Whereas some rural interests have taken the side of present-day users against prewar owners, others stand on the principle of restoration, suggesting that both the 1940 nationalization of land and the 1980s distribution of that wrongly acquired land were incorrect, if not illegal. For example, in a commentary written for the newspaper *Diena,* a retired farmer in Latvia suggested that the 1980s land handout was intended to placate rural interests in a time of upheaval, "when it could be felt that the nation was awakening and [it was apparent that] a fight for right would follow."[62] He compared it to the agricultural policy put in force after the 1940 occupation, under which land was nationalized, and ten hectares of land were given to farmers who were landless before the occupation. This was undertaken, he wrote, primarily to garner support for the Communist regime in rural areas.

Some post-Soviet states outside the Baltics have opted to decollectivize and privatize agriculture through other means, including redistribution and maintenance of some state-run agriculture, but in the Baltics, restitution has been a central pillar in the privatization of rural land. Although the rights of prewar owners are not paramount in every case, they are elevated in political rhetoric and have been an important component of a larger effort to assert continuity with the institutions, ideals, and social order of the past. Unlike some other initiatives, such as citizenship policies or protection of the internal market, which have created friction between political factions espousing different visions of change, this policy has created greater conflict at the microsocial individual level and less at the macropolitical level of party politics. In a sense, *localized* visions of normality are pitted against the visions of normality held by the political elite in Riga.

How can one explain the focus on restoration rather than redistribution in Latvian policy? First, the broad and comprehensive disgust with the Communist experience, the perceived barriers that it erected to progress and Europeanness, and the pain and injustice it brought to Latvia are notable, because in the early post-Communist period anything seen as "undoing" what the Communists did was likely to find a sympathetic constituency in Latvia. For example, the abnormal state of agriculture was represented by collectivization; consequently, decollectivization of agriculture was the "natural" instrument for reconstructing normality in the countryside and the Latvian economic order.

Second, one of the goals of land reformers, particularly those who espoused strong nationalist views, was to improve the economic lot of Latvians: Latvians seemed to be the principal beneficiaries of restitution because they made up most of the prewar landowners. Furthermore, the right to ownership was foreseen as extending exclusively to citizens, many of whom were also ethnic Latvians. Through the mechanism of restitution, in theory, property would make its way into the hands of Latvians, giving them greater economic power. Why it was not foreseen that these reforms would lead to sharp conflicts between Latvian individuals and families and that some Latvians would bear serious losses as a result is not clear.

The third salient point is the widely shared nostalgia about Latvia's agrarian past. Restorationist political parties and coalitions, embracing the vision of a return to interwar norms and conditions, highlighted both a return to the social and agricultural order of small family farms *(viensētas)* of the inter-

war period and an unqualified restitution. That tradition as well as economics was implicated in the vision of restoring *viensētas* in the countryside is
highlighted by this quotation from a 1990 conference, *Latviešu nācijas izredzes*
(Future of the Latvian Nation). After describing an elderly farmer he had
known, the speaker, Visvaldis Lācis, asserted: "Farmers such as A. have held
and will continue to hold Latvia on their shoulders. They, such men and
women, will come again in the future, if we understand that not in *kolkhozes*,
not in *sovkhozes*,[63] not in shareholding farms, but only in *viensētas* will we find
the keys to the barn door, with which we will make our way to riches that
go beyond grains or wool or honey." He also implicated traditional rural life
in the foundation and formulation of Latvian nationalism: "What is nationalism? In my view, nationalism is the pursuit by a nation of immortality—of
eternal survival. . . . This [nationalism] that grew from peasant farming
brought us to a point of national consciousness and its highest ideal—the
idea of an independent state." The linkage between rural life and Latvian
nationalism also formed a foundation for the notion that rural land was to
be held exclusively by members of the citizenry, which Lācis iterated:

> On the question about citizenship and land ownership rights I can-
> not agree to any compromise. Today, as in the [19]30s, when we
> occasionally brought into Latvia 30,000 [or] 40,000 foreigners, ag-
> ricultural workers, the citizens of other countries, we have to main-
> tain the motto of Kārlis Ulmanis, "Be the farmer of your own land!"
> *(Pašu zemei pašu arājs!)* The majority in Latvia's six largest cities and
> still other cities and towns has been given to foreigners. Let us not
> give to strangers our fields![64]

Strongly nationalist actors, however, were not alone in their insistence on
restitution as a core value, which did not meet with significant resistance in
more progressive political quarters either, a point that I discuss below.

The nostalgia about interwar agriculture and rural life was born in part
from the agricultural success that Latvia achieved in the interwar period,
when it became a notable exporter of agricultural goods like butter and
bacon to other parts of Europe. As well, it was influenced by the broad
elevation of Latvians' peasant heritage. A passage in a small history book
sold to help would-be citizens prepare for the history and Constitution quiz
required as part of the naturalization process highlighted this notion, declaring that the "growth of national wealth [in the interwar period] was significantly ensured by the persistent, even fanatical, work of farmers."[65] A
journalist covering the region in the early period of transformation suggested

that "the national-cultural image of the free hard-working peasant farmer was indeed the key motivation of the agricultural reforms in the Baltic in 1990–92."[66] In this context of veneration of smallholdings and rural tradition, the issues of productivity and efficiency became footnotes to the big story, which was the restoration of agricultural traditions and the hope that Latvian private farms rather than Soviet collective farms would come to define the countryside again.

Beyond this, the reanimation of peasant farming envisioned in the reforms can be linked to hopes for the reanimation of traditional family life and the rejuvenation of the Latvian nation, which was popularly diagnosed as suffering from a demographic crisis. In a conference on Latvian women held in 1992, one of the speakers addressed this issue:

> Already in the second half of the [19]20s there were 5.25 people on average in a farmer's family, [but] at the end of the [19]80s—only 3.2. Consequently, the family in the countryside has decreased to a minimum which does not ensure normal reproduction processes anymore. . . .
>
> The revival of the peasantry in Latvia is connected with both our hopes to provide the society with the necessary foodstuffs and to renew the traditional way of life in the countryside. This revival could also influence the stabilization of the family in our society. . . .
>
> Traditionally the farmer's family has been a social group characterized by not only living together, but also by working together, in the same household. Thus if compared to city life, there are larger, more stable families in the countryside, the generation ties are closer, the traditions are handed down from generation to generation, thus creating a more favorable cultural environment for the reproduction of society.[67]

The nostalgia that attached to rural smallholdings, then, stretched beyond a concern with the re-creation of the grid of private property. It was also animated by a concern about national demography.

In a chapter on the restoration of the pre-1959 property order in Romania, Katherine Verdery stated: "Law 18 re-creates the property situation as of 1959 for a society existing some thirty years later. Thus it reconstitutes the farms of households that were viable units thirty years ago but whose members have now died, emigrated, married, and otherwise substantially changed their relationship to the land."[68] In Latvia, this is true as well, and restitution has been even more complex because of the longer period that has elapsed since land was nationalized and because so many émigrés are involved in the reclamation of land. In such a context, it is worthwhile to ask why families and individuals, many of whom live in Latvia's cities or even in Western countries, want to repossess agricultural land. The reasons are manifold, but among the most important are the following. First, in the economic context of post-Communism, the compensation offered by the state as an alternative to restitution was, when the policy was put into place, paltry. The uncertainty surrounding the value of currency in the period and the drag put on its value by inflation translated into an environment in which land, perceived to have greater stability and value than Latvia's currency, was preferred even by those who had no possibility or intention of working it. Some hoped to sell or rent the land or to pass it to other family members capable of working it.

Second and no less important were reasons of nostalgia: the desire to reclaim a physical representation of a better time. The desire to possess something of one's own past and Latvia's past was a powerful motivator, especially for elderly claimants. That many, particularly émigrés to the West, were willing to spend substantial amounts of money for local attorneys, surveyors, and even bribes (cognac and chocolates were favored ways to grease the wheels of bureaucracy) to get back land from which they would never earn a profit and on which they would never live is reasonable evidence that the drive, for some, to repossess their prewar space was driven by an emotional rather than practical imperative. Intricately enmeshed with this nostalgia was a sense of righting an injustice: those who had to leave their homes quickly, fleeing the Communists or being deported to the Soviet interior, took few possessions and almost invariably lost everything they left behind. The need to take back something unjustly taken from them was relevant to understanding why, for example, a Latvian émigré pensioner, with no means to use the space, wanted to reclaim land turned, in the Soviet period, into a garbage dump.[69]

Land restitution has created less friction between politicians than between political decision makers in Riga and local administrators, as well as farmers in the countryside and prewar owners of land plots. I discuss each of these in turn. Whereas policies on land reform have, from the start, been handed down from the Parliament in Riga, the administration of restitution is locally handled by *zemes komisijas* (land commissions). These commissions, while bound by decisions made at the federal level, are not necessarily sympathetic to the policies that have governed decollectivization, privatization, restitution, land use, and taxation. The policies of land reform enacted in Riga have created a host of problems for local rural administrators. A member of the land commission in a southeastern town bluntly termed the reforms enacted "foolish and wrong." Local officials are concerned about land going out of production as it is transferred from active farms to landholders unwilling or unable to work the land. Furthermore, officials are more likely to be sympathetic to the needs and claims of local farmers they know than strangers who arrive from cities or abroad. As a result, the restitution of legal rights to land has often dragged out for years.

As well, in the rush to reclaim property after the policy was instituted, land has been returned to people who cannot work it, cannot sell it, and cannot afford the taxes levied on the territory. Some of the land is agriculturally worthless because it is overgrown with brush or flooded. In other cases, recipients have established lives in urban settings or are too old or ill to work the land. To prevent speculation in the land market, laws were introduced to proscribe the sale or rental of land for a time after land was repossessed. Even if this were not the case, however, the rural land market remains weak. In the words of a land commission official, "Who would [an owner] sell it to? There are no buyers." Taxes on the land are also a salient issue: those who have repossessed their property are now responsible for paying taxes on it, whether or not they work or live on the land. For some, the taxes are unmanageable. Their option in this case is to sell or disclaim the land; they may lose the land as well as any chance for compensation. A farmer told me:

> If earlier everyone wanted to get their land back, now we have the question of what to do with this land. Unhappy is the one who gets his land back and cannot use it: he already has a tax debt that he needs to pay. This process is still developing, but in the future there will be many people who will have to give up their land because they cannot pay the tax bills on that land. For example, in this district, for one hectare the tax is just under two *lati*: so if your property is fifty hectares, you owe one hundred *lati* per year in taxes. It may not matter what kind of land that is; it may be farm land, or woods, or a swamp.

In some instances, then, property owners may end up, as a result of their reclaimed property, in an even worse financial state than before.

Finally, although it fit with imperatives of de-Sovietizing Latvia and returning rural life to its peasant heritage, decollectivization has had consequences in agricultural production and the organization of rural life. A farmer in southeastern Latvia offered the following assessment:

The land reform here in Latvia was foolish. There was a single
principle [in carrying this out]: it was all based on the principle that
kolkhozes had to be eliminated. It's true, there was much in the
kolkhozes that was not as it should have been. . . . But to take and
in a single day destroy all that productive potential—those complexes, the animal husbandry complexes with thousands of animals—to take and eliminate that without replacing it with
something. . . . I understand what they wanted. They felt that private
property was important, that it was holy, that it had to be returned.
At that time, then, they had, at all costs, to eliminate the kolkhozes.
. . . This has driven us in to the ditch. Today, we have not even
reached the level [of production] achieved in the kolkhoz time, the
bad kolkhoz time. There was a lot wrong there, but it could have
been changed in a rational way. The politicians—concerned about
their [popularity] ratings—they did it this way.

In fact, agriculture has suffered severe declines in the post-Communist
period. Whereas agriculture constituted about one-fifth of the gross domestic product (GDP) in the late Soviet and early post-Communist periods, by
1993 it had fallen to 11 percent of GDP and by 1996 to just 9 percent of GDP.
Some studies have suggested that just 5 to 8 percent of rural enterprises in
the field of agricultural production are commercially viable. Furthermore,
Latvia has become a net importer of agricultural products, as many of the
goods that are produced on the new or revived smallholdings, which average
just 19.7 hectares,[70] are used by the immediate or extended family of the
farmer rather than marketed.

In considering issues of restitution, it is worthwhile to look at the creation
of prewar ownership and the organization of a private property regime in
the First Republic of Latvia. The motivations and mechanisms that underpinned land reform in that period were, as I show in the following section,
different from those of the late twentieth century. Hence, despite the desire
of some to re-create the norms and institutions of the interwar period, models have been selectively chosen. In this case, legislators opted to re-create
the map of the agrarian past by returning property to prewar owners, but
they disregarded the political and economic politics of redistribution that
created the grid of rural ownership. Next I discuss the politics and policies
and results of interwar reform and offer a comparison of the models of interwar and post-Communist agrarian reform.

Creating Ownership: Interwar Agrarian Reform

The issues of rural inhabitants and rural land loomed large in the post–World War I period, as Latvia became an independent state for the first time in history. Although before the war approximately 59.7 percent of the total population had been rural, a wartime population shift resulted in proportional growth: in 1920, about 76.5 percent of the population resided in rural areas. The need for reform was highlighted by a number of political and economic considerations. First, according to Andrejs Plakans, "The Latvian government remembered how the landless had been attracted by Bolshevik promises of land in Latvia as well as Russia." The high percentage of landless persons in rural areas—estimates place the proportion at 40 to 50 percent[71]—made this a highly salient issue, as did a historic sympathy for left-wing ideas among country dwellers and some urban intellectuals.[72] Second, much of the rural land that was in private hands was owned by non-Latvians, mostly Germans and, in the Latgale region, Poles. An estimated 48 percent of this land was concentrated in large estates: in the western region of Kurland *(Kurzeme)*, of the 570 large estates, 24 percent were between 10,000 and 70,000 hectares. Only 39.4 percent of land for cultivation was in the hands of peasant farmers.[73] Latvians, who constituted 72.8 percent of country dwellers in 1920, were hence overrepresented among the landless, and, according to Plakans, "notwithstanding the laws it had adopted for the protection of minority nationalities, [for the national assembly] to allow these relatively wealthy non-Latvians to control some half of all agricultural properties would have been to commit political suicide." Furthermore, many of the German barons and Polish landlords had been among those working against the creation of an independent Latvian state and had benefited, to that point, from the centuries-old agrarian order in which Latvians had been serfs, tied to the land but landless.[74] Third, in the wake of the devastation wrought in Latvia by the war, the state had a strong interest in creating active farms that would cultivate the soil and support a national economy with a weak industrial base. These reasons clearly precluded reestablishing the agricultural economy on the base of the estates of the early century.

Agrarian reform in Latvia was adopted in three parts, beginning in September 1920. The first article created the State Land Fund "to establish new and to enlarge existing small farms, to meet the needs of economic enterprises and of social and cultural institutions of various kinds, and to expand the area of cities and townships."[75] The second article declared the nationalization of "crown lands, manors, and forests." With this act, 51.5 percent of

Latvian territory was gathered into the Land Fund. The remaining 48.5 percent stayed in private hands: about 81 percent of this space belonged to small
farms, and 16 percent was constituted by the diminished manors, fifty hectares of which could be retained by their owners.[76] The issue of compensation
for nationalized land was hotly debated in the national assembly; parties on
the right suggested a package of compensation for land taken into the Land
Fund at 1920 market prices, while parties of the left and center rejected
compensation of any kind. By a margin of three votes, the latter prevailed,
and, except for a state agreement to take care of debts owed on the confis-
cated property, no compensation was granted. The aggrieved owners of manorial estates in Latvia took their case to the League of Nations, but their
1925 petition was unsuccessful.[77] In any case, much of their prewar land was
already in the hands of new owners, because redistribution was undertaken
even before the complaint was settled: by 1925, 70.9 percent of the rural
population were landowners, compared with just 38.8 percent while Latvia
was part of the Russian empire.[78]

The land reform was based on a principle of redistribution to the landless
population, most of whom were Latvians. The mechanism for allotting parcels prioritized persons who had been in the armed forces and country
dwellers who could show that they were landless. In line behind these
groups were those who had farmland but asserted that their holdings were
too small to support their families. Land not so allocated was put to use by
local administrations or the national government.[79] With the redistribution
of land, the number of private smallholdings rapidly multiplied. Whereas in
prereform Latvia there were about 150,000 peasant farms, by 1935 their number had grown to over 275,000, at which point the proportion of landless in
the countryside was only about one-fifth. Despite the fact that most holdings
created by the redistribution were small (85 percent were under thirty hectares, or seventy-four acres),[80] farms of the new landowners (*jaunsaimnieki*)
employed one-quarter of the agricultural workforce.[81]

There was trepidation at the time of the reform about radically altering
the long-standing organization of rural life. Indeed, both locally and abroad
the "opinion was voiced that the abolishment of the large landed estates
would cause disturbances in agricultural production and that the new small
farms would not provide an adequate living for their owners."[82] To a good
extent, however, the reform was successful in meeting its goals. First, it made
substantial progress in addressing the problem of landlessness, particularly
among the titular population, and put in place the foundations for the em-
bourgeoisiement of at least a segment of the indigenous rural population.
Second, the area of arable land and the number of farm animals reached

unprecedented levels (which declined again in the early Soviet period),[83] an achievement that was important for establishing Latvia as a successful agricultural economy both in terms of the internal market and exports. Among others, hectares of wheat, oats, and potatoes grew, and new crops such as sugar beets were brought into extensive cultivation. Dairy farming expanded rapidly, and by 1935, Latvia was exporting over 16,000 tons of butter annually, a quantity surpassed in Europe only by Denmark, Holland, Sweden, and Ireland.[84] Third, in the words of a Latvian history text, "When the rural proletariat became landowners, the action not only meant redress for age-long social injustice, but also made the people immune to Communist propaganda."[85]

The notion that a historical injustice was righted by the land reform appears in a more recent history text, printed in Latvia in 1996, as well: the author suggested that the agrarian reform "renewed historical justice, returning the manorial land stolen from the people."[86] This point is worth highlighting because it bears a striking similarity to the rhetoric of justice that underpinned the land reform of the post-Communist period where, again, reform turned on the notion that the land taken from Latvians was to be returned and, through this mechanism, justice restored.

The land reform of the interwar period was not without negative consequences. Indeed, it created issues that, to anyone following post-Communist land reform, are familiar. First, although most smallholdings were productive, they also experienced problems related to their size: farming machinery was often out of financial reach for little farms, the work was labor intensive, there was a shortage of credit resources, and the smallholdings tended to take on a lot of debt. Plakans noted: "By 1939, there was a high inverse correlation between size of holding and indebtedness: on holdings of less than fifteen hectares, 137 lati were owed per hectare, and on holdings of more than one hundred hectares, 37 lati." Thus, he added: "Although the agrarian reform had defused the *political* problem of landlessness, it had enlarged the *economic* problems of smallholdership."[87]

In a revisitation of the past, the present period also finds the broad displacement of large, centrally organized farmsteads by family smallholdings and trepidation about the ability of these smallholdings to survive, to acquire modern farming equipment, and to produce comparably to or better than farms operating on economies of scale. Indeed, as I discuss below, much of this trepidation is not misplaced. Many rural households struggle with poverty; access to modern or even working equipment is far more limited than it was on large Soviet farms; and agricultural production has precipitously declined.

Although there are similarities in the rhetoric, circumstances, and problems of the agrarian reform of both the early pre- and post-Communist periods, there are also important differences. Most notably, the notion of righting an injustice was present in both periods, but in the earlier period it was realized through redistribution, and more recently it was to be realized through restoration. In the interwar period, a postmanorial property regime was fashioned by distributing land to mostly rural persons who worked on that land but did not own it. Justice, hence, derived from transferring economic power from the hands of manorial landlords to the landless rural proletariat, generations of whom had tilled the soil for someone else's benefit. In the 1990s, a post-Communist property regime was being fashioned by restoring rights to prewar owners of private parcels, regardless of the relationship of the "legal owners" to the land in the past half-century. In this case, justice came from renewing the economic power of those who were directly deprived of it by the Soviet regime. Through this action, normality was ostensibly (re)created in three ways: first, the very basis of the hated Communist regime—the abolition of private property—was crushed. Second, the map of the past was, at least in theory, renewed. Third, a step toward Europe was simultaneously taken, because private property is also the basis for and the demand of modernity and its institutional enforcers such as the International Monetary Fund and World Bank.

In the following section, I turn to the institution of the Communist regime and its consequent abolition of private property and transformation of the organization of rural life in Latvia. This, together with the above section on interwar reform, provides a historical background to and basis for further discussion of the problems and potentials of post-Communist privatization and reform in the countryside.

Rural Land in Soviet Latvia

The Soviet period in Latvia changed rural life in a number of important ways. The changes came in phases, one in the early occupation and World War II period, a second near the end of the war, and the last in the late 1940s.[88] The first phase of reorganization of the Latvian countryside took place shortly after the dissolution of the independent Latvian government in summer 1940 and was, according to a Soviet-era history text, "one of the most important links in the chain of large and important revolutionary and socialist transformations performed . . . by the Latvian Communist Party and the Latvian SSR government."[89] A Declaration Concerning Land was passed on July 22, 1940, and was followed a week later by a "special decree" that took farmland in excess of thirty acres as well as land owned by churches, monasteries, and congregations into a state land fund.[90] Private holders could retain the thirty hectares of land at this point, but the rest of the property was redistributed to country dwellers who were still landless. The declaration followed these practical decrees with a self-lauding exclamation: "From this day on there is not and will not be a place on this land for those who have lived on the sweat of the working peasantry, there will be no place for exploiters—big landowners and their supporters."[91]

The newly created private farms were relatively small—no more than ten hectares each. A Latvian historian writing in the West stated that this, "in view of local conditions, was not sufficient to sustain a family." Spekke further stated: "Moreover, although promised, no aid was given to the new farmers in the form of loans, or building material for the construction of farm houses, with the exception of the establishment of the so-called Machine and Tractor Stations and Horse-Lending Centers, which for payment undertook to work the fields of the new farms."[92] That the first phase of agricultural transformation in the Soviet period did not give birth to new successful smallholdings is, arguably, a marginal issue; the creation of a new class of prosperous private owners could hardly have been the goal of the reform. Rather, as a Soviet text suggested, one of the aims of the change was to win the support and loyalty of those still without land or with little land and to pit them against the rural bourgeoisie:

> The strongest support of the Ulmanis' fascist regime was the country bourgeoisie *(budži)* who held key positions in Latvian agriculture. Weakening the influence of the country bourgeoisie in the economy and politics and restricting the *budži* was an extremely important task of the proletarian dictatorship. This task could be solved only with the help of undivided support of the landless peasants and the middle peasantry. Providing farm labourers and smallholders with land actually determined the consolidation of [a] union between the working class and the peasantry.[93]

The nationalized land was redistributed in the fall of that year, but the new rural order was short-lived and was annulled by German authorities, who occupied Latvia the following summer.

The Soviets drove out the Germans and reoccupied much of Latvia in summer 1944. At this point, a new phase of redistribution was undertaken by the Soviet government. Under the decree of September 7, 1944, which altered the earlier decree, an old farm could not occupy more than twenty to thirty hectares; land in excess of this amount was nationalized by the state. Furthermore, all land belonging to "enemies of the people" and people who had fled Latvia and abandoned their land was to be seized, and no more than five to eight hectares were to remain in the possession of anyone who had "collaborated with or supported the Germans." The particulars of this decree, like the determination of how much land would be left to an old farm or whether a landowner was guilty of collaboration, were left to local authorities. The transfer of land under this decree was substantial: 738,849 hectares were severed from private farms, 273,294 hectares were seized from "enemies of the people," and 368,538 hectares of abandoned land changed hands. Somewhat less land was, at this point, "voluntarily ceded to the state": 92,625 hectares fell into this category.[94]

In this period, a number of new farms were created, and some existing parcels of private land were even expanded, because under the 1944 decree, the area of new farms could reach up to fifteen hectares, whereas previously the limit had been ten hectares. The total number of individual agricultural entities privately held, however, declined from over 75,000 in 1940 to 69,770 in the period from 1944 to 1945.[95] Despite the decline, the individualistic character of peasant farming, rooted in the existence and persistence of small personal plots in the tsarist period and strengthened in an interwar agricultural organization founded on smallholdings, remained a salient issue. Since 1940, the Soviet position in Latvia had been that "collectivization shall not be enforced upon peasants against their will."[96] However, because of the traditional nature of smallholdings, the fact that properties acquired in the interwar period were in many cases the first that previously landless generations of peasant families had owned, and rumors about the difficulties and problems of life on collective farms (of which there were already a few in Latvia and, of course, many in the rest of the USSR), most peasants resisted the idea and did not volunteer to cede their land to the Soviet state.[97]

The system of private farm ownership continued to exist for several years into the Soviet occupation, but the state undertook measures to pressure peasants to add their land and labor to collective farms. Among the instruments the state employed were the imposition of a heavy tax burden on individual farms and the requisition of farm products by the state, with little left for the peasant farmer.[98] The first state kolkhozes or collective farms were established in 1946 and 1947 and were set up in different regions to serve as models. In contrast to individual farms, collective farms were provided with a variety of facilities for workers' use and an array of farm equipment. For example, the Machine and Tractor Stations (MTS) provided tilling services, farms were provided plentiful supplies of fertilizer and seed, and workers received good salaries.[99] Despite the combination of disincentives and incentives designed to lead the peasants toward collective farming, most continued to resist collectivization: in spring 1947, Latvia had only four kolkhozes. In early 1948, the number climbed to 49 and later that year to 599, but even this represented the consolidation of only a small fraction of Latvia's farms.[100]

The failure of the campaign to pressure or entice farmers to give up private holdings of their own volition was clearly apparent to the Soviet authorities by the end of 1948, when fewer than 5 percent of farmsteads had been consolidated into kolkhozes. At this point, the government took several actions. First, the rhetorical campaign targeting the country bourgeoisie intensified. They were denounced as "enemies of the community," and citizens were entreated to "unmask" and denounce them. The working masses were implored to participate in this campaign, and "the press and radio featured stories about 'enemies' who had managed to become members of a kolkhoze because of lack of vigilance on the part of the toiling people and who tried to undermine the kolkhoze from within."[101] Second, in March 1949, the Soviet government instituted a wave of deportations that tore entire families from their land. Historians estimated that between March 24 and March 30 of that year about 50,000 persons were deported from Latvia and sent to camps and villages in the Soviet north. This action not only "liquidated the *kulaks* [the Russian word for the rural bourgeoisie] as a class," but also put additional pressure on the resistant smallholders who remained to cede their land and labor to collectivized agriculture. Third, Communist Party functionaries from urban areas were dispatched to rural areas to foster the process "because the number of local activists there was considered too small."

The new tactics employed by the state to intensify the consolidation of farms and farmers into kolkhozes proved effective. The number of kolkhozes climbed into the thousands: by the end of 1949, they numbered 4,103, and by March 1950, a year after the kulak deportations, there were 4,118 collective farms in Latvia.[102]

An understanding of the early Soviet land reform and collectivization in Latvia is important for grasping some of the reasons that reprivatization in Latvia is fraught with problems. In Latvia, collectivization proceeded in the wake of the mass displacement of populations and alongside the Stalin-era practice of mass deportations. Furthermore, many rural dwellers, particularly younger farmers who had worked private parcels in the interwar period and the very early Soviet period, remained resistant to collectivization practices and propaganda and opted to emigrate to the cities, leaving their rural land and lives behind. Hence, collectivization of the land often involved not the collectivization of land and the integration of former private farmers of that land into the new state farms, but rather the integration of the land without the farmers. This, as might be expected, has complicated the return of agricultural lands to former owners, both those in residence in Latvia and those who emigrated abroad and their descendants. Much of the land to be returned has not been connected in any tangible way for half a century to the people who claim it now. Land reform in the post-Communist, in contrast to the post-tsarist period, is not a matter of recognizing and institutionalizing the right to property of those who toiled on the land for the good of another (in that case, the manorial landlord), but rather of reinstituting the property rights of people who, in many cases, have been disconnected from the land. The rights of those who have, on the other hand, toiled on the land for the good of another (in this case, the Soviet state) are recognized but not prioritized in a reform guided by the notion that justice lies in renewing the map rather than the principles of the interwar agricultural order.

Rural Land and Perestroika

During most of the Soviet period, private property as an institution was abolished, but small private plots of land for personal use existed and were widespread throughout the USSR. These plots were normally used for small gardens or orchards and sometimes for the numbers of livestock (according to early regulations, two cows, two calves, one breeding sow with piglets, and ten sheep or goats) that could be privately held. The limits set at the time of collectivization for private gardens were between 0.25 and 0.60 hectares per household. The Soviet government was aware of the value of these plots to rural people and closely regulated their use and allocation, issuing decrees that the state could reduce or repossess personal holdings if, for example, farmers were spending too much time on their own plots to the detriment of the kolkhoz. As well, perhaps in a nod to Soviet "family values," single people were not allocated private plots.[103]

Millions of Soviet citizens, urban as well as rural people, held private plots, though the urban plots were more restricted in their use. For example, by law the plots of urban dwellers were smaller than those of *kolkhozniki*, and no permanent habitable structure could be built on the private plot (a rule that was regularly violated). These personal and valuable spaces constituted only about 3 percent of the fully cultivated land in the USSR, but they were, particularly in contrast to many kolkhozes, extremely productive, generating a substantial proportion of the Soviet Union's vegetable crops. In the late Gorbachev period, privately held plots and farms accounted for one-quarter of the agricultural production of the USSR.[104] Notably, by this time, the small personal plots were no longer the only privately held spaces of agricultural production.

Important changes in usufruct (use) rights began in the early 1980s. James Bater described these changes:

> Over the years, there were experiments in which a small area of the *kolkhoz* as well as *sovkhoz* was turned over to a few men, or contract groups, to cultivate according to their estimation of which crops would do best. Gorbachev sanctioned more of this type of activity in 1983, before taking over as Party leader. Where such decentralized control was linked to a share of the harvest, the results were invariably the same—substantially higher yields than from similar quality land farmed by salaried *sovkhoz* employees, or regular collective farm labour brigades. In 1987, legislation was introduced which extended the concept of agricultural contracts embedded in the 1983 decree to families. This legislation permitted families to lease land for periods up to 15 years. The incentive of higher personal income, combined with autonomy in decision-making, was a potentially powerful force for change in Soviet agriculture. But these initiatives were clearly too little, too late.[105]

Although these alterations in policy and practice had some effect on yield and on notions of personal autonomy, these changes were incremental rather than fundamental in a period when the latter held more attraction. In this context, some republics, including Latvia, undertook their own versions of reform in rural areas. Latvia won limited economic autonomy from the Soviet center in January 1990, but even before that, changes were introduced to the countryside. In 1989, the Supreme Soviet of Latvia accepted new legislation, the Law on Peasant Farms, which allowed the creation of private farms in the republic. At that time, land was given for private use without regard to prewar ownership. Notably, however, the rights to the land were usufruct, and the limitations on private ownership in Soviet law remained in place. Individuals and families could own buildings on particular parcels, but land, while heritable, was not tradable because the state retained formal ownership at that point.[106]

By 1990, land-use rights had been granted at no charge to over 7,500 persons wishing to establish private farms. For the most part, the parcels were allocated from areas not considered to be important for the operation of the collective or state farms that administered them. Would-be private farmers were typically those "with known claims on the land and the strongest desire to establish their own farms."[107] In the wake of this action, the number of private farms in Latvia increased rapidly, numbering close to 6,500 in May 1990, one month before the next round of reform legislation was passed.[108]

The farms of the so-called *brešu* farmers *(brešu zemnieki)*,[109] which were created by the 1989 legislative action, produced additional problems with restitution in Latvia, as those who were granted use rights in the wake of the 1989 reform were loathe to give them up to prewar owners claiming rights to the property. Problems arose because though the 1989 reform instituted by the Supreme Soviet of Latvia granted private usufruct rights to agricultural workers, the 1990 reform introduced a process of granting private property rights to prewar owners. In a notable number of cases, the parcels of land for which these rights were granted were the same, grafting a historical map of interwar ownership on a new map of late-Soviet private farming.

Restoring Rights and Justice: Private Property in Post-Communist Latvia

The population of Latvia is closely tied to the land, a fact only marginally affected by the changes in post-Communism. In 1989, 30.8 percent of the population lived in the countryside; in 1999, the proportion was 31 percent.[110] Many rural dwellers are also ethnically Latvian. Finally, even after the heavy industrialization of the Soviet period, agriculture still accounts for a notable proportion of national income. All of these factors are salient for understanding why rural land reform in the late Communist and early post-Communist periods was and continues to be of great consequence to politicians and populace alike.

A year after the reforms granting usufruct rights to private farmers were enacted in Latvia, two new laws (re)establishing ownership rights to land were accepted in Latvia's Supreme Soviet. The first law, *Par agrāro reformu Latvijas Republikā* (On Agrarian Reform in the Republic of Latvia), was passed in June 1990. This law, "recognizing that the methods of forced collectivization of agriculture in the republic were illegal, decree[d] that [it was necessary to] (1) reorganize the relationship between land and ownership in agriculture [and to] make an agricultural reform. (2) Within the context of agricultural reform, the state [was] to do a land reform, an economic relationship reform, [and] an agricultural administration reform."

The second law, *Par zemes reformu Latvijas Republikas lauku apvidos* (On Land Reform in Country Districts of the Republic of Latvia), was passed in November of the same year. The goals of this law were "to reorganize the legal, social, and economic relationship between land use and ownership in the country within the context of gradual privatization, to support the renewal of the traditional Latvian rural way of life, to ensure the use and protection of natural resources, to preserve and expand the productivity of the land, [and] to expand the production of high quality agricultural products."[111]

These laws together provided for the establishment of a regime of full private land ownership, which had not existed since its abolition in 1940. The reform was to proceed in two phases: first, land was to be allocated to "physical and legal" persons for use without full ownership rights. This phase was foreseen as lasting from 1990 to 1996. Second, persons to whom the land was allocated were to receive legal ownership, and this law specified that such legal ownership might be assumed through "the renewal of land ownership rights or the allocation of private title for compensation with or without compensation." This phase of reform was to go on for ten to fifteen years, beginning on the first day of 1993.

These laws foresaw the allocation of private land to legal and physical persons "for pay" and the renewal of the legal rights of Latvian citizens and of those who were Latvian citizens at the time Latvia was occupied (specified in the law as June 21, 1940) and of their descendants to land that was lost after that date. The latter had priority in receiving a parcel of land "whether or not, at the time this law came in to force, [claimants] had or had not been allocated the land for current or long-term use" and could receive it, theoretically free of charge. Exceptions to the right of claimants to land within historical borders included land on which there was already a developed farm, if there were no buildings belonging to the (restitution) claimant on that parcel; land on which the person in residence had legally purchased or built a homestead; land needed for state defense or nature conservation; land on which historical, cultural, or archeological monuments were situated; land on which there were "industrially important" raw materials; land requested by localities; land needed for experimentation, research, or education. Behind restitution claimants, land was to be allocated to new owners for the following purposes and with the following order of priority: (1) to expand existing private farmsteads; (2) to raise individual houses for persons using the land who did not have such a house; (3) to expand towns; (4) to expand the land of cooperative farms (the descendants of state and collective farms after those fell out of favor). Those who did not want or could not get back land within historical boundaries also were offered the options of "equivalent" parcels of land (as determined by local land committees) or compensation in cash.[112]

Agents of restitution in Latvia have been primarily district or town land commissions, who, by the 1990 laws, were granted the power and responsibility for local distribution and restitution of land. These commissions examine the evidentiary documents, evaluate claims, and work with surveyors who measure and bound the new private parcels. The body is also responsible for finding "equivalent" parcels where the original territory claimed by a prewar owner is unavailable. Surveyors are also an important part of this process; they measure out parcels based on the topography of claimants' memories, land-claim documents, and ground rules laid down by local committees. Another important cadre of agents in the restitution process is that of attorneys, many of whom have been locally retained by émigrés in the West to "put things in order" for them in Latvia. The attorneys then act as go-betweens for the parties involved, which include local land committees, claimants, and sometimes the occupants of the land. The complexity and lack of clarity of some laws and the relative recency of the entire process have created a situation in which claimants often rely on local attorneys to file and prepare documents and carry out other tasks that the attorneys themselves are ill-equipped to understand. In the hope of making money in difficult times, not a few lawyers with no experience or training in property law have made a dash into the field.

The laws passed since 1989 have had a potent effect on the multiplication if not the modernization of family farms. From a total of 3,931 in 1989, the number of private farmsteads grew to 17,538 in two years. At that point (1992), the direction of this growth favored smallholdings: 39.9 percent of farms were between 10 and 19.9 hectares. In the next largest category, 24.5 percent were farms between 20.0 and 29.9 hectares, and 19.5 percent were very small farms, under 10 hectares. Decollectivization had already had a marked effect by this time; only 6.7 percent of all farms were 40 hectares or larger.[113] The continued development of these small- to medium-sized private farms is a product, to a large extent, of the directed policy of the Latvian state. A 1996 publication by the Organization for Economic Cooperation and Development noted:

> In Latvia, restitution and privatization have encouraged the emergence of family-type farms. In order to promote this type of farm-

ing, similar to the prewar structure, any approved application for land, whether for restitution to previous owners or for a new individual farm, had a higher priority than continuing use of the land by a collective or state farm. As a result, individual farms and household plots are now the cornerstone of Latvian agriculture, operating on over 80% of agricultural land with an average size of 20 hectares per family farm.[114]

Although restitution as a core practice of the privatization effort has been little contested in the political field, there has been a lack of agreement between parties favoring a more open market and those favoring varying degrees of protection of the internal market and farm supports in Parliament. The lack of consensus on this issue was one of the factors leading to the collapse of the leading coalition in Parliament, established after the 1993 elections, between Latvia's Way, which favored fewer supports, and the Farmers' Union, which favored more. This political issue of agricultural support has two notable components. First, parties and coalitions favoring a path of restoration in post-Communism also tended to favor greater support and protection of agriculture. In the interwar period, agriculture was the mainstay of the Latvian economy, and a return to agriculture in this vision is a return to the economic and social roots of Latvian life. Over the half-century of occupation, however, the potentials and power of agriculture have markedly changed. Whereas family farming was the norm in the interwar period, the collectivization of agriculture has had an effect on farming skills in the sense that the "all-around" knowledge needed by independent farmers was replaced by a farming environment that often required only a narrow set of skills to perform an assigned task. Quite a few farmers in the post-Communist context may be lacking not only equipment to run a modern, independent farm, but adequate skills as well. Furthermore, agricultural space has contracted over the last sixty years: the World Bank estimated that from 1935 to 1990, over one million hectares of agricultural land went out of production, a 32 percent drop in the number of hectares. Over this same period, on the other hand, the hectares of forest have expanded by 60 percent.[115]

Second, the clear predominance of ethnic Latvians in rural areas and in the occupational category of agriculture may have some effect on the centrality of the support issue, particularly for more nationalist political organizations. Dreifelds noted: "Russian-language publications have sometimes seen the support of agriculture and the apparent failure of support for industry as a clear case of governmental ethnic bias."[116] This statement must be qualified by noting that the support of agriculture by decision makers has often been weak and ineffectual (certainly farmers in Latvia see it this way), but industry, numerically and proportionally dominated by Russian speakers, has also fared badly. The fact that most factories were built as "middlemen" in the production chain (that is, they processed or prepared goods from raw materials supplied by other republics) is one key reason for shutdowns and slowdowns, though there is lack of will in government, increased by pressure from international lenders, to rescue sinking industries. Certainly, these Soviet-built industries have few supporters, and the lack of political and economic capital among the Russian-speaking proletariat helps to ensure the marginality of this issue.

The issue of restitution itself has been less contentious than the support of independent agriculture in Latvia, but restitution has raised issues of consequence and conflict between the administration at the center and that at the rural periphery. Conflict has arisen between the needs and interests of national parliamentary politics, conducted in the comfort and distance of an urban center, and that of small rural communities that must reconcile the visions and decrees of the Saeima with local conditions and the need to use land efficiently and to see that those who use it have adequate access to it. In the following section, I illustrate, through the experience of one Latvian farmer, the core issues and problems that country dwellers face in the post-Communist political and economic context of Latvia.

Stories from the Field: Practicing Property Rights

The elevation of property rights of prewar owners has created a mass of practical issues and problems in rural areas, particularly in cases where a prewar owner insists on historical boundaries that cross land being worked by others or otherwise in use by groups or individuals. The following example illustrates such a case, which, though humorous from one viewpoint, is an issue of real consequence for local people.[117]

In a rural area of southeastern Latvia, the local garbage dump was until several years ago located off a dirt road near the main highway that passes through the town. In the wake of the reprivatization undertaken by the state, the prewar owner of the parcel of land that had become the local dump handed in a request for the restitution of the land. The local authorities offered the property owner an "equivalent" parcel elsewhere in the district, but the owner stood on her rights to the parcel within its "historical boundaries." Having no other options, the local authorities granted her request and returned the parcel.

As a result of the return of the land, which was being used as the local dump, the new owner assumed legal responsibility for the parcel. Two problems, however, quickly became apparent. First, as there was no other local dump, residents continued to dump their garbage in and around the area. Second, as the legal owner of the land was not in residence in the town, or even in Latvia, the use of the land was not supervised. The dump began to migrate beyond the boundaries of the now-closed and gated space of property and onto the dirt road used by farmers living nearby to travel between their farms and the highway and town.

Local deputies, apprised of the situation, resolved to call the property owner and demand that she take responsibility for the rapidly growing garbage heap on the small road. It was quickly determined, however, that the party responsible for the road itself was not the property owner, but rather the *ceļu eksplūtācijas iecirknis* (local road commission), which had kept the rights to the road and the immediate area around it for itself. As late as summer 1998, the situation remained unresolved; local people did not have a legal garbage dump nearby; and garbage continued to pile up and make its way onto the road.

As indicated earlier, the laws passed by Parliament make provisions for a host of exceptions to restitution within historical boundaries, but this case did not fall in that category. The fact that the individual with a historical claim to the land would apparently not take care of it and the additional fact that the space returned was used to meet a community need (which garbage-disposal clearly is) were not accounted for in the law. The massive growth of absentee landownership in rural areas, attributable to the large number of émigré and urban claimants to prewar property, has had other important consequences as well. Some of the agricultural land returned to prewar owners remains fallow. Absentee owners do not return to the land themselves and often cannot rent or sell it either, because of legal obstacles to private sales and a lack of buyers. As well, absentee plots in rural areas invite illegal exploitation of the land; for example, those parcels on forest land (which are numerous because, as noted earlier, a million hectares of interwar agricultural land have reverted to forests) are inviting to those who make money by cutting down trees and selling them for export or local use. The Latvian farmer interviewed for this section noted: "In some of these locations, there is no one who oversees the land. In our district, many forests are cut down and taken away [from these absentee estates]. It isn't that we are all corrupt. But there isn't anyone to watch over the land; the forest guards can't control it. . . . Most of the land just stands fallow. Maybe someone gets some money stealing trees off some parcels, but much of the land just grows over with brush and doesn't get used."

The following case study of rural land transfer in the post-Communist period helps to illustrate some of the complex dimensions of land reform. This case, like many others, shows the conflicting demands and interests created by the parallel institution of processes of privatization and reprivatization in Latvia. It also shows how the field of private ownership in rural areas is populated by agents with vastly different interests: historical owners, new farmers, and old inhabitants, among others. The structure in which this play takes place is of importance as well because it is the product of political interests at the federal level. Land reform was a fundamental part of the transformation of Latvia that began in the late Soviet period. The desire to institutionalize normality in this field is premised on manifold bases: first, the desire to do away with the collectivized farms of the Soviet period and to replace them with independent family farms like those that characterized the interwar period; second, the desire to set down a social and economic regime based in private property; and, third, the desire to restore the property rights and physical property of prewar owners who lost the land to Soviet occupation. That these bases for agricultural reform are at least as often conflictual as complementary is illustrated by the story of Juči, a smallholding in southeastern Latvia.

The farm called Juči came into the possession of the Gailītis family in the late nineteenth century, while the territory of Latvia was part of the Russian empire. Nellija Kalniņš's (born Gailītis) grandfather, a peasant farmer, purchased Juči from a German baron who had held the land. At that point, it was sometimes possible for peasants to gain private possession of land.[118] Her grandfather purchased the land and later divided it between his two sons, Jēkabs and Jānis. The larger portion was given to Jēkabs—this farm was called Juči. The smaller portion, Lower Juči, was given to Jānis. Nellija, Jēkabs's daughter, was born and grew up at Juči. Jēkabs tried to farm the land, albeit with difficulty after the early death of his wife. Later, Jēkabs gave the land to Nellija and her husband Kārlis Kalniņš; they took possession of the house, and Jēkabs lived in a small house by a pond. Kārlis did not farm the land; he was an engineer at the sugar factory at Krustpils. The gardens at Juči were cared for by paid help and did not produce in quantity. At this point, the Kalniņš family lived in an apartment near the factory, which was a short distance from Juči.

During the late phase of the Second World War, the family moved to Juči, where they hoped they would be safe from the Soviet and German armies fighting for control of the territory of Latvia. Juči, however, was not safe. At one point, German tanks rolled from the wooded hills onto the farm. The family left Juči and went to Vietalva with Kārlis's family, but Vietalva was also not safe because the Soviet army was firing heavy artillery in the area. The family then returned to Juči, but both the German and Soviet armies were nearby and were shooting at civilians as well as soldiers. Opting to seek safety elsewhere, Nellija and Kārlis took a horse, a cow, a few possessions, and their three small children and left their home at Juči for the last time.

In 1944, Nellija and Kārlis and their children sought to leave Latvia altogether, moving through Riga, which had already been reoccupied by the Soviets, then to the port city of Liepāja, and from there to Germany and the Allies' refugee camps. Jēkabs remained in Latvia and continued to live in the small house by the pond at Juči until his death in the 1950s. Nellija and Kārlis lost touch with relatives in Latvia, and after Jēkabs's death, the connection between the family and Juči was severed for forty years.

Nellija and her grown children visited Juči for the first time in 1992, in the post-Communist period. At this time, the farmhouse was inhabited by three families: two Russian and one Latvian. The small house previously inhabited by Jēkabs was home to an elderly Lithuanian couple. By this point, the Kalniņš family had already gathered and handed to the district land committee the documents required by law to reclaim the property nationalized by the Soviet authorities and inhabited by families who had had no prewar connection to the place. The reception the Kalniņš family received from the families then living at the farm was courteous but chilly. Juči was not then an active farm; there were small garden plots around the house and baby chicks in the house, but the house was officially a forest guard's house, not considered part of a farm. The buildings and surrounding land had not been incorporated into a collective farm.

Although the legal owner of the restituted property, Nellija Kalniņš, already in her eighties and living since the 1950s in the United States, would and could not come to live and work at Juči, Nellija's family sought to transfer use rights and property rights to most (though not all) of the land to Nellija's nephew, Pēteris Kalniņš. Pēteris himself had recently been involved in a land dispute about the property on which he was living before coming to Juči, and partly because of that, he agreed to come to the restituted property at Juči. Before turning to the issues raised by the case of Juči, I bring in the case of Pēteris's previous home and land, in which restitution did not take precedence. Pēteris told this story himself:

> In Limbaži, [the town in which I lived], I purchased an abandoned house—this was in 1990. At that time, city dwellers wanted to buy

country homes. At that time, you could not yet get back your [pre-war] land, but you could buy a house somewhere. . . .
I had the chance to buy this house from the district—it belonged to the sovkhoz [state-owned farm]. I bought it legally, no one lived there, no one used it. It was going to ruin at that time. I bought it, and we planted a garden around it, and we went there from our city apartment. . . .
Then the awakening began, and the existing laws changed, and you could get five hectares of land—we bought that too. I started to work that land too. Then one fine day a letter arrived inviting me to go to court. This was in connection with the land I had purchased. It was completely unexpected. . . .
In this case, the property owner had not contacted me. It was being handled by a lawyer who was trying to get back for people, some of whom lived abroad, some land here in Latvia. The lawyer turned immediately to the court asking to get the land back. I had to arrive in court without ever having been contacted by the claimants to the land.
[But] the court recognized me as the legal owner of the land: I had bought it legally and in accordance with the law as it existed at that time. The historical owner did not get his or her land back; it was given to me. I could have kept it. They did get it back though. I gave it back, and some of the descendants live there now.

In this case, the dispute between the inhabitant of the land and the claimants for restitution was resolved in favor of the former, because a habitable structure—the house—was located on the land owned by Pēteris, and such domiciles, legally purchased or otherwise obtained, were protected under the new laws. As seen later, one of the reasons that Juči had restitutable land was because the farmer legally working that land did not have a house on it. In Limbaži, by contrast, there was a house that Pēteris had legally bought and that could not, by law, be taken from him: he was entitled to keep the house and some of the land surrounding it *(piemājas zeme)*.
After it was decided that Pēteris and his wife, Ieva, would come to Juči to live and work, Pēteris began to come to the farm from his home in Limbaži to work on the house. He spoke about his early time at the house and problems that have arisen for others in analogous circumstances:

I came here [to Juči] and spoke to the inhabitants. I said that I have a sincere interest in sharing this house with you all and asked them,

What space can you make for me here? They gave me a room in the attic, which I slowly fixed up. One of the inhabitants of the house came to me and said, Landlord *(saimniek)*, how much rent do I need to pay for living in this house? I said this depends on how much space you use. . . . If you use more space, this costs more. This family saw that paying rent—they were pensioners—would be difficult for them. At this time, it became possible for them to go and live with their daughter, and so they did that. We were lucky that the other families too were understanding of our situation. They could see that we were serious about coming here, that we have not just come to scare them, . . . that we really wanted to live here and work here. In a short time they too found themselves an opportunity to live elsewhere.[119] This is not, certainly, typical in Latvia. I know of many cases where this thing is settled with pitchforks and matches and fires. We were lucky though. . . .

There are still many legal owners who do not live in their homes. Let's take our case. What if these pensioners had not had a place to go? What would we have done? In our district, for instance, there are not free apartments, free homes that could be assigned to these people or traded. . . . The opportunities are limited.

In the case of Juči, Pēteris, the new legal occupant of the house and land (he was not, at that point, the legal owner because ownership rights were held by Nellija), was able, through diplomacy and auspicious circumstances, to take full possession of the house in a relatively short time. The law as well was on his side, though the tenants could legally have remained in residence for seven years. By law, however, he had the right to take control of the house and eventually inhabit it exclusively.

The agricultural land around Juči, however, presented a separate problem and introduced another agent with his own interests and rights into the picture. At the time that Nellija submitted documents for the restitution of her interwar property and several years before Pēteris arrived at Juči to live and work, several hectares of the agricultural land was already in use by a *brešu* farmer, who had legally obtained usufruct rights to the land under the 1989 reforms that reestablished private farming in Latvia. Pēteris described the situation:

We did not and could not get our land back within its historical boundaries because on our land a *brešu* farmer was already farming—they are those who got land for use in the first period [of land reform]. We could farm on our own territory, then, only in the case that we somehow moved him off of our land. The law at one point in time was on the side of the *brešu* farmers, and to move these farmers off of the land [they were working] was nearly impossible. And then, in the body of law, there appeared a point that specified that if a *brešu* farmer did not have a house on the historical land, then the priority in getting the land reverted to the historical, legal owners. Then, at this moment, we could seek to get our own land. This is a classical example, with our neighbor, B.: his house is on another piece of land, not on ours. Therefore, we could legally fully move him off of our land, out of our historical boundaries. We did not do that, our lawyer did not do that, and now it is too late to do it. . . .

[The cases when this occurs—when land has been legally distributed to new farmers, the *brešu* farmers, and then, legally offered to prewar owners] is characteristic [of this process]. In our case, this is a classic example. If his house was on this land, we would be fully dependent on him, if he would allow us [to use the land]—as we now allow him to do. We have dealt with him in a humane way, but if we stood on the letter of the law, we could push him out of our boundaries fully. There are a lot of examples of this happening too. On the whole, it is dependent on whether there is a house on the land.

Legally granting different parties the usufruct rights and ownership rights to the same land highlights the clash of priorities that arose in the period of the "awakening." On the one hand, the 1989 reforms represented an attempt to restore a space for private farming in Latvia after nearly half a century of centrally planned, collectivized farming. The map, in this instance, was drawn to accommodate those who wished to and had the means to begin farming independently. On the other hand, the reforms begun in 1990 represented an attempt to restore the extensive grid of independent ownership that had existed in the interwar period. The map of the agricultural past, thus, was grafted on top of the map of the reformed agriculture of the late Gorbachev period.

The case of Juči presents a story premised on the importance of repossessing land within its historical boundaries. This is, as I earlier noted, an issue that revolves around powerful notions of both justice (a return of what was taken illegally and by force) and nostalgia (a return to what symbolizes a happy and, to an extent, idealized past). These notions have affected decision makers in Parliament and individual decisions about reclaiming land.

Pēteris commented further on the policy and notions around restitution of historical boundaries:

> In our situation [the restitution principle] is relevant. In our case, we were interested in getting our historical property back—not a centimeter here or there, but ours. If today, this were put in front of us, if I were asked, would you take your land, would you take another parcel? Well, the global politics was this: we have to return things exactly as they were. As I said about the kolkhozes—this all should have been done in steps. I would have moved more slowly away from the kolkhozes. Maybe doing it more slowly, things would have looked differently.[120]
>
> If we had waited and done it [land reform] today, or last year, and then given prewar owners the opportunity [to get back land], then . . . if someone was offered thirty hectares of bushes, they wouldn't take them. But at that time, five or six years ago, people were rushing, without considering what was on that land—like the person who got back the land with the garbage dump. On her land, there is a dump, and we know that she has no tractor or cars— maybe she only has a wheelbarrow. But she stood on the principle that she had to get that land, that she had to have the historical boundary. That was the spirit of the time, though—if she were today given this dump, maybe she wouldn't take it. She would take equivalent land or would not take it at all because she knows she could not utilize it. . . .
>
> Furthermore, after the Soviet experience, people wanted some- thing—we went from owning everything and nothing to another extreme. For older people, who themselves lost the land, they wanted their pieces back. We got our independence quickly and rather simply. It wasn't so hard. And one day we were just free, and we could get back what we had—and we wanted it. . . . The land- owner is not rich, though, he is worse off than he was. That is the result of this politics.

Pēteris's comments reflect some of the contradictions that run through this process. He was clearly critical of the process of reform and many of the consequences wrought by restitution, but he expressed a sense that he would have liked to repossess the Juči land within its historical boundaries. This is not as contradictory, however, as it seems if one considers his position: why, after all, does the *brešu* farmer have any more right to the land than he does?

Both have a legal claim to the land, but Pēteris's claim is buttressed by a historical tie to the land that B. does not have. Furthermore, his point that after half a century of "owning everything [referring to the public ownership of land and industry under Communism] and nothing" people were eager to have something for themselves is salient: in this instance, Latvians particularly had the opportunity not only to possess private property legally at no (immediately obvious) cost, but also to regain a piece of the past that had been brutally torn from their hands.

There is a third dimension to the problems and issues of the division of space at Juči: the division of legal title to the property. Although most of the agricultural land at Juči goes to Pēteris, who lives and works at Juči, the family of Nellija, the historical owner of the place, would like to keep legal title to the few hectares of land that hold the small house, pond, and birch grove. The family wishes to do this to ensure its rights to visit and stay at Juči, even in the event that Pēteris or his descendants choose to leave or sell the farm. In other words, the land, to which Nellija is the legal heir, must be granted through administrative channels to Pēteris so that he may gain legal title to the land; Nellija's children, however, wish to retain a portion of land on which Pēteris would have use rights but not title. This final division of space at Juči has caused additional problems with the official registration of the property in the *zemes grāmata* (Land Book) in which titles are registered. This is in part because new laws that continue to be handed down by Parliament change the demands that must be met by claimants and committees. Claims may thus drag on for a long time in cases that claimants, on meeting old demands for documents and the like, are asked to meet new ones as well. By summer 1998, the registration of the Juči land in the Land Book, the final step in the process, had not yet been completed.

In an article on the transformation in Latvia, Andrejs Plakans wrote that the collection of tasks that the "Latvianized political elite" of the early transformation period wanted to address included the desire to eliminate the "remnants" *(atliekas)* of the Soviet period; to restore institutional continuity with the interwar period of independence; to absorb Western assistance and Western ways; to supervise the transition to a market economy; and to create conditions for the continued survival of Latvian-language culture.[121] A study of the laws, actions, and outcomes of the transformation of rural land, its use, its ownership, and its organization, highlights the fact that in this field of transformation all of these desires have come into play. Notably as well, some of these desires, such as the wish to "restore institutional continuity" and to achieve a "transition to a market economy," can be contradictory as well as complementary. In this instance, the desire to restore a grid of ownership taken over from the interwar period sometimes runs up against a desire and need to make rational use of land and to structure agriculture as a foundation of the new economy. The wish to restore the interwar map of private ownership and the wish to restore the productive capacity and success of agriculture of the interwar period are not necessarily compatible. Furthermore, the goal of rapidly eliminating Soviet-era remnants such as the collective farm can also be implicated in undermining the successful transition of agriculture in a market context that favors economies of scale over small-scale productive capacity. Whereas the reanimation of smallholdings is judged by some to favor Latvianness in both a demographic and cultural sense, the poverty wrought by the rapid transformation of the rural order economically undermines the Latvian population that makes its home in the countryside. In trying to reconcile all of these aspects of normality, rural land reform has brought new problems that highlight the difficulty of reconciling the visions of normality elevating spatial and temporal models of change.

Conclusion

The power of space and place in the transformation in Latvia runs visibly through the last decade of change. To some degree, the sites of change on which I have focused are similar in that they show the strength of the temporal vision of normality. On the other hand, they highlight different types and degrees of contest over the definition of normality. The return of old street names to the city of Riga, consistent with the unity of the opposition period, did not evoke any contestation of note in the social movements challenging the Soviet order. Rather, contesting this effort were conservative Communist forces. The stakes in this case involved the control of the symbolic landscape of the capital city, and the touchstone of legitimacy for the opposition was located in the symbolic order of the past and the perceived appropriateness of names for the city. The contest, then, was, from the opposition perspective, about asserting the particular (and normal) culture and history of Riga against the Soviet transformation of the city into one of many bearing the same street names and monuments as many other Soviet cities.

In the story of Abrene/Pitalovo, there is another set of issues. As in the issue of street names, there was a powerful symbolic component, and the dominant notions about change appeared to be consistent with the temporal vision of normality. The issue was symbolic, because assertions from the Latvian side about the illegitimacy and illegality of the transfer of Abrene to Russia in 1944 represented assertions about the illegitimacy and illegality of the occupation of Latvia itself in the 1940s. Russia's acceptance that the transfer was wrong would constitute an implicit admission that the occupation was not legitimate. Up to this point, Russia has not conceded this point in any political forum and has continued to hold the position that the Baltics requested membership in the USSR. There was a strong component of the temporal vision of normality in Latvia's push for repossession of Abrene, because the return of Abrene/Pitalovo would have represented a "normalization" of both geography and history.

Consistent with the shared notion that the Soviet order was illegal, the principle of asserting the illegitimacy of the transfer (and, implicitly, the occupation) was shared between organizations in the spatial and temporal categories. But there was a parting of ways beyond this point. Though some nationalist organizations like For Fatherland and Freedom maintained the position that all territory belonging to the interwar state must be returned to Latvia, political organizations like Latvia's Way showed a strong willingness to concede the de facto loss of the land to Russia. The inclination to recognize present-day borders stemmed at least in part in this narrative from the desire to resolve territorial disputes, a requirement of membership in the European organizations in which Latvia coveted membership.

The problem of privatization and reprivatization of rural property is clearly among the most complex of any confronted by state and society. Like the issues of street names and territorial boundaries, it is powerfully symbolic. Unlike those issues, it entails acute material consequences for large segments of the population. As there is some degree of complementarity between the dominant notions of normality in the issues of street names and border issues, there is also a degree of complementarity in this area, so that the imperative of building a foundation of private property prioritized in the spatial vision can be reconciled with the imperative of creating continuity with the interwar prioritized in the temporal vision. In contrast to the street and border issues, this issue entails a substantial degree of domestic conflict, though it appears to be less between the visions that dominate the political field than between the policies emerging from the political center that are born of those narratives and *local* visions of normality. Hence, I suggest that in this area there might be the formation of a local vision of normality, which holds up economic rationality and local notions of justice (such as land for those who have worked it and can work it) against the rationales that underpin extant policies.

One of the figure clusters visible from the front of the Freedom Monument is a group entitled Work. At its center is a powerful figure clutching a *gudrības zizlis* (wand of wisdom) with a cascade of oak leaves spilling down from it: he represents the Latvian farmer. That land and work on the land are broadly associated with Latvian culture and history is reiterated in the Freedom Monument, where the farmer holds a position equivalent to the Latvian warrior who stands, sword in hand, on the other side of the inscription, For Fatherland and Freedom. The desire to "normalize" this venerated cradle of history and tradition was and is powerful in Latvia, though the visions of how this is to be done are not all the same. Whether this can be best done by looking back, as in the case of the street names, or by balancing the imperatives of the past with a practical approach to the future, as in the approach to resolving the boundary dispute, remains, at this point, unclear.

5

(Re)Constructing Gender in Post-Communism

Atop the spire of the Freedom Monument in downtown Riga stands the figure of a woman, her hands over her head and three stars between her palms. In the Soviet period, it is said, some city guides told tourists that the figure was Valentina Tereshkova, the first Soviet woman in space. Among Latvians, however, she is popularly known as "Milda," and her significance is different. Not only does she face the West, but her back, for nearly half a century, had been turned to Lenin, who faced East. Milda is not the only female figure on the monument: just below her is Mother Latvia, shield and sword in hand, and to her right is the Latvian mother who bears the sons who will grow up to be heroes. However, there is no figure that represents all women on the monument. Throughout the twentieth century, women in Latvia also appeared in a multiplicity of roles, and notions about gender roles shifted during this period. At the end of the century, these notions again underwent transformation, as ideas born of the Soviet order were shed and replaced by other notions, both old and new.

In this chapter, I again revisit the dominant narratives of transformation that have underpinned the attempted (re)creation of "normality" in post-Communist Latvia. In this case, I focus on gender roles and norms, specifically as they pertain to women. In this setting, the identity of "difference" highlighted in the political field—that of historical citizenship and ethnicity—is complicated by the introduction of another identity of "difference": gender.

The search for Latvia's future in its past, a theme discussed throughout this work, has been significant in the field of gender norms. Though the direction of change in the political field has been fiercely contested in a public arena, the field of gender has been the site of what Peggy Watson termed a "silent revolution" where "the exclusion of women and the degrading of feminine identity . . . are not contingent to, but rather a fundamentally constitutive feature of the democratization of Eastern Europe."[1] A prominent component of the (re)creation of normality in social life has been the (re)creation of a gender regime that highlights *domestication* on the one hand and *commodification* on the other. The former has entailed a reinstitution of pre-Soviet gender norms and roles; in this vision, women play their most visible role as mothers, as bearers of the nation and keepers of the family. The latter has entailed the institutionalization of the modern market, where profits underpin action and power rests in capital; in this context, women's bodies have become commodities of value to be exploited and sold. Clearly, the dual processes of domestication and commodification, which I elaborate in this chapter, have affected the opportunities and roles available to women in post-Communism.

I argue that the field of gender roles is one with a low level of contest. This differentiates it from the political field, where conflict between different narratives of change—temporal, spatial, and evolutionary—was well defined in the early post-Communist period. In the field of gender roles, there exists a complementarity between the dominant narratives; for example, the movement out of the workplace and into the home (and motherhood) foreseen by the temporal vision is consistent with the need to shed "excess" employment in the drive for greater efficiency and competitiveness in the marketplace. A competitive free market is, as I have noted, a key component of the spatial vision. The demographic "crisis" of the Latvian nation is a concern of both dominant narratives and further strengthens the complementarity of visions on women's (re)domestication. There is also some sense

20　The Latvian mother and her sons on the Freedom Monument

among some women that going home is, after the mandatory employment of the Soviet period, liberating. Though problematic for the Western feminist vision, it has sway in the post-Communist context.

The issue of commodification of women in the new market economy, as evidenced by the rise of pornography and prostitution, also presents a contrast to other fields of change. Conflict is low, largely because the stakes are perceived to be low, and commodification has not emerged in public discourse as a "social problem." In part, this can be explained by the predominance of non-Latvian women in the sex market: these are clearly not the mothers of the nation. The tremendous profitability of the sex market as well helps to make it attractive rather than repulsive to those who seek to acquire a lifestyle of modern affluence; even a close relative of a prominent Latvian politician was several years ago said to own a sex club.

I begin this chapter with a brief review of the social position of women in interwar Latvia. Particularly because the interwar period has become a touchstone for the definition of normality, an understanding of this period is important. I follow this with a look at the theoretical notions that undergirded the social organization of gender in the Soviet period and a discussion of the way that the Soviet order reconfigured gender relations and reorganized the gender regime, albeit without eliminating fundamental inequalities. The Communist period of occupation in Latvia is, as in every field of post-Communist change, a shadow case. That is, the wholesale rejection of the Soviet order entails the rejection not only of authoritarian political structures and the command economy, but also of the organization of social life. In terms of women's roles, this rejection is salient because the "asexualization" and "overemancipation" of women wrought by this period are widely decried. The restructuring of the social organization of gender occurring in this period and the way that this has affected and continues to affect changes in the post-Communist period are considered. Finally, I examine the way that "normality" in the gender regime is being (re)constructed from both the idealization and rejection of particular historical experiences and the institution of modernity in the new state. To highlight my points, I consider the issues of social welfare and prostitution in post-Communist Latvia and show how the narratives about normality and change in post-Communist Latvia concretely affect women's lives, opportunities, and citizenship rights.

Women and Gender in the First Republic of Latvia

The Latvian sociologist Anita Kalns-Timans wrote in a conference paper that "the effect of years of Soviet rule, with its 'pseudo-feminism,' the rebellion against Soviet rule, plus the idealizing of the pre-war period, may lead to increased control and lessened chances for women relative to men."[2] This idealization of the prewar period is highlighted in this section because, as I have shown in earlier chapters, history and nostalgia are driving forces in post-Communist social change in Latvia. A close examination of the social history of this period is beyond the scope of this work, but a brief review of women's status in the interwar period can help to provide a context for a discussion of the appeal of this experience to the architects of post-Communism.

In literature on women and gender equality that emerged in the socialist period, the improved status of women under socialism was lauded. Some of the pronouncements were little more than the substitution of words for deeds, but women made some gains in this period as well. In other spheres, though, women experienced losses. To evaluate the "gains" and "losses" of the Soviet period, I look at the basic rights and prerogatives that women had in the interwar period in Latvia. First, women in independent interwar Latvia achieved a number of important citizenship rights. In 1918, with the establishment of the independent state, the franchise was extended to women and men twenty-one years of age. Furthermore, the 1922 Constitution enshrined equal political rights for men and women. Hence, whereas in states like Bulgaria and Hungary, women got the vote only with the advent of socialism, in Latvia (and some neighboring states such as Poland), women enjoyed full political citizenship after World War I. On the other hand, women participated in political life as voters, but few were in positions of power in the political hierarchy. The 1920 elections brought six seats (3.9 percent of the total) to women in the state administrative body and six seats in the Riga City Council. A woman was elected to the Saeima (Parliament) for the first time in the 1931 elections. The civil rights of women were also more limited than their political rights because, even after the passage of a new Civil Law in 1935, husbands retained, by law, the decisive decision-making role in the family.[3]

Second, though socialism brought, in theory and practice, the right (and obligation) of women to work, in interwar Latvia many women had already worked for pay. According to the 1935 census of the Republic of Latvia, 84 percent of women aged twenty to fifty-nine years were working.[4] In 1934, about 56.2 percent of women were working for wages, the second-highest rate in Europe at that time. Women's wages were only about 68 percent of those of male wage workers,[5] and most were concentrated in "women's" fields like teaching and secretarial work. Women however increasingly had access to higher education and began to move into "nontraditional" fields that had higher pay and prestige as well: for example, in 1931, the first female attorney was sworn in.[6]

The history of women's attachment to the formal labor force, thus, is strong but mixed. The data available suggest a rather high percentage of women working, but the dominance of agriculture in the interwar economy means that many of these women were working on independent farms. Whereas the family farm was, in many respects, an equal opportunity employer, women had fewer opportunities in nonagricultural occupations. Opportunities for urban women were further diminished by a 1937 government decree on the employment of state office workers. In the decree it "was determined that married women, if they had no children, had to leave their jobs, and so the family had to live on the husband's wages. The wife with children had to stay at home anyway in city conditions. In part, these regulations had arisen from the growing rate of unemployment that [led to] . . . steps to fight unemployment."[7] The decree was not legally binding, but signaled the higher priority assigned by the state to male employment.

Third, compulsory education for all children aged six through sixteen years was accepted in 1919. Even before this decree, however, girls as well as boys had enjoyed relatively broad educational opportunities in the Russian empire. In the 1890s, for example, grammar schools for girls were available, and, by 1897, 77.9 percent of women in Vidzeme (the northeast quarter of Latvia, which includes Riga) were estimated to be literate. This percentage was equal to that of men in the area and much higher than that of women in Russia proper, which was only 13.7 percent.[8] As noted earlier, women's opportunities for higher education were growing as well.

This brief overview of women's status in the interwar period raises several notable points. Although women had political and civil rights, the former were weakened by underrepresentation in decision-making bodies, and the latter were weakened by the prioritization of decision taking by the husband. Furthermore, women were economically disadvantaged by horizontal and vertical segregation in occupations and by unequal pay. That said, the status of women in Latvia was not worse than in most European states at that time. And in some respects such as suffrage, literacy, and education, it was even better.

The lament that women were "overemancipated" by the Soviet social order can be heard in Latvia in the post-Communist period, and it seems to imply that it might be appropriate to return to the "normal" place of women during the interwar period. How, then, to read this model in the aftermath of Communism? On the one hand, women in the interwar period enjoyed rights analogous to or better than those of neighboring European states, and

Latvia represents a progressive state in this era. On the other hand, the changes that took place in Western Europe during this period, in which women entered the professional labor force in great numbers and assumed positions of power in political and economic structures, are in clear contrast to the prewar experience of Latvia. If the interwar period is taken as a model in terms of its *progressive quality*, it can potentially satisfy a nostalgic need and meet the needs of women as well as the state and market. If, however, the model is understood *literally*, women appear to be political beings without real power, economic beings without economic independence, and social beings defined in terms of their activities in the private sphere.

Marxism, Leninism, and the Woman Question in the USSR

Before turning to issues of social and economic policy that affected women in general and Latvian women in particular in the Soviet period, I look at some of the theoretical notions that underpinned the Soviet state's response to the "Woman Question." The approach of Marxism-Leninism, the ideology of state, linked all forms of inequality, including gender inequality, to what was believed to be the preeminent form of inequality: class. Class inequality was linked to the existence of private property and exploitation that derived from the concentration of private property in the hands of the few to the detriment of the many. The abolition of private property—which is described by Marx and Engels in *The Communist Manifesto* as "the final and most complete expression of the system of producing and appropriating products, that is based on class antagonisms, on the exploitation of the many by the few"[9]—would, in turn, lead to the elimination of class inequality and the inequalities that they believed derived from it. Marx's work, consequently, engaged the issue of gender inequality only minimally; it was, after all, presumed to derive from class inequality and hence would disappear together with that.

Friedrich Engels examined the status of women in the family relationship, likening it to the position of the proletariat in relation to the bourgeoisie. In this context, he spoke of the issue of bourgeois marriage, which he harshly criticized. On the one hand, it was excoriated as a site of oppression, where the "marriage of convenience often enough turns into the crassest prostitution—sometimes on both sides, but much more generally on the part of the wife, who differs from the ordinary courtesan only in that she does not hire out her body, like a wage-worker, on piece-work, but sells it into slavery once and for all."[10] The woman in this relationship was, Engels believed, little more than a servant to the interests of the male oppressor. In *Origin of the Family, Private Property, and State,* Engels wrote:

> In an old unpublished manuscript, the work of Marx and myself in 1846 [*The German Ideology*], I find the following: "The first division of labor is that between man and woman for child breeding." And today I can add: The first class antagonism which appears in history coincides with the development of the antagonism between man and woman in monogamian [*sic*] marriage, and the first class oppression with that of the female sex by the male. Monogamy was a great historical advance, but at the same time it inaugurated, along with slavery and private wealth, that epoch, lasting until today, in which every advance is likewise a relative regression, in which the well-being and development of the one group are attained by the misery and repression of the other.[11]

This family form was also targeted as a site for the reproduction of property relations that favored the privileged classes. Engels posited that through the (enforced) monogamy of bourgeois marriage, heirs of indisputable paternity were produced who went on to inherit the wealth of their fathers: that is, wealth passed from generation to generation, from the hands of individual males to those of their male progeny. Hence, marriage and female monogamy were instruments of oppression and means to ensure that wealth remained in bourgeois families rather than benefited the community at large.

Engels also believed that mutual love in the bourgeois marriage was undermined by property relations. His work idealized the proletarian gender relationship, which he claimed was not distorted by the possession of private property. Instead, he wrote, "Here, all the foundations of classical monogamy are removed. Here, there is a complete absence of all property, for the safeguarding and inheritance of which monogamy and male domination were established. Therefore, there is no stimulus whatever here to assert male domination."[12] Buckley, however, argued:

> Engels and Marx both neglected the possibility that forms of domination could arise which were not the result of economic arrangements. They did not explore the dynamics of the superstructure under capitalism to see how it could construct, perpetuate, and reinforce gender roles. Marx and Engels believed that the ruling ideas of every epoch are those of the ruling class. From this we would expect that the superstructure of capitalism carried images of male

and female roles, which were, to some extent, adopted by the working class.[13]

The legal hurdles that forced women (and men) to remain attached to the family unit, like complicated divorce proceedings, were, in the new order, to be dismantled so that the marital relationship would be entered into and maintained freely rather than through institutional means. Engels addressed this point:

> What will most definitely disappear from monogamy . . . is all the characteristics stamped on it in consequence of its having arisen out of property relationships. These are, first, the dominance of the man, and secondly, the indissolubility of marriage. The predominance of the man in marriage is simply a consequence of his economic predominance and will vanish with it automatically. The indissolubility of marriage is partly the result of the economic conditions under which monogamy arose, and partly a tradition from the time when the connection between these economic conditions and monogamy was not yet correctly understood and was exaggerated by religion. . . . [After the coming social revolution, men and women] will be spared the experience of wading through a useless mire of divorce proceedings.[14]

The early socialist theorists believed that economic participation was the "key to full citizenship." Though women entered the labor force as wage workers under capitalism, they experienced this economic participation as oppression because they, like male workers, were exploited by capitalists. These women workers, it was posited, would join their male counterparts in a revolution to shed the yoke of capitalism. So women as workers had been oppressed under capitalism, but women as workers under socialism would be emancipated, albeit not from work, but from capitalism. Marx and Engels argued that "the solution was not to return to some golden age of the past, when women were safely confined to the home, but to draw them ever more fully into the industrial system."[15] Ultimately, after private property was abolished and a socialist order established, women would enjoy emancipation not only from the oppression of capital, but from their subjugation to men and male interests.

Marx and Engels condemned the bourgeois family and highlighted women's full participation in the formal workforce, but Marxism was squarely pronatalist and did not disconnect women from the role of childbearers.

Women were envisioned as generators of products and progeny for the good of socialism. The reconciliation of the roles of mother and worker was imagined as taking place in a context where domestic labors, rather than being a burden to women, were socialized.

V. I. Lenin followed Marx and Engels in their belief that capitalism underpinned the inequalities of gender relations and that socialist revolution would bring with it equality of the sexes. Lenin, however, paid greater heed to the policy matters that would be part, theoretically and practically, of this new equality. He supported the creation of a legal foundation for emancipation in the new Soviet state, which included easier divorce, access to abortion, and paid maternity leave for working women. In terms of civic rights, women and men were granted full equality before the law, superseding the tsarist civil code that subjugated the interests of the wife to those of her husband, and equal franchise, where it had previously been limited to those holding property.[16] The alterations in the civil code that gave married women a standing on par with that of men began to address domestic inequities, but did not change the realities of the domestic labor that was performed almost exclusively by women.

The pragmatic institution of the new order was slowed by the travails of the civil war. The socialist revolution met with resistance both inside and outside the territory of what was to become the USSR. In this context, policy matters were subordinated to the practical task of extending the tentacles of revolution and consolidating the gains made by Bolshevik revolutionaries. After Lenin's debilitating stroke in 1922 and his death in 1924, Josef Stalin ascended to power, and the continuation of the revolution and its promises and consequences for women came under his purview.

Though much early Bolshevik activity relating to women's emancipation embraced the eradication of restrictions on women's family attachment, movement, and inheritance, the Stalinist era saw a marked change. Buckley noted:

> Whereas the years immediately after 1917 were characterized by upheaval, spontaneity, and open debate . . . the 1930s and 1940s brought a stifling of discussion. By 1930 a clamp squeezed debates into rigid lines. Discussions about topics such as the appropriate path for socialist economic development or the meaning of artistic expression ceased; so did serious efforts to examine the relationship between women's liberation and socialism. . . . Stalinism resulted in a termination of serious discussion of the woman question; at best, isolated critical remarks were made in obscure sources. Stalinism provided

a series of hollow phrases about female roles that could be regurgi-
tated whenever appropriate.[17]

Rather than being further discussed, in the 1930s the Woman Question
(zhenskii vopros) was declared "solved." However, behind the bright veneer
of Stalinist pronouncements, policies that had brought women increased
control over their lives were being reversed. For example, the loose controls
on divorce of the 1920s were replaced in the 1930s by attempts to curb family
separation. Motherhood was elevated as a socialist duty, and abortion was
duly criminalized.[18] Equality of the sexes was no longer tied to specific policies that opened avenues of choice to women, but rather linked to the larger
structural changes taking place in society: what was good for society was
good for women, and equality was no longer an issue that demanded an
agenda apart from that set forth (by Stalin) for society at large.

The cult of motherhood highlighted women's role as mothers, but the
drive for industrialization and collectivization in Stalin's USSR underpinned
the elevation of women as a force in the socialist labor collective. Gail Lapidus stated:

It was not . . . a revolutionary program of emancipation that brought
about the profound changes in women's roles of subsequent decades.
Nor was it the slow but cumulative effect of broader economic and
social changes. The transformation of women's roles was, to a considerable degree, the indirect result of the inauguration of the First
Five Year Plan in 1928, the collectivization of agriculture that accompanied it, and the emergence of new patterns of authority under
Stalin.

The forced collectivization of agriculture, with its stunning impact on authority structures and social relationships in the rural
milieu, and the massive entry of women in to the industrial labor
force during the 1930s . . . were the central features of this social
transformation.[19]

It was in this historical period that the Baltic countries were incorporated
into the USSR and in this context that the roles of women (among others,
of course) were radically recast. The ideological foundations of the Bolshevik past were amalgamated with the political and economic imperatives of
the Stalinist present to structure the place of women in the USSR and its
newest territories.

Gender and Status in Soviet Latvia

Socialism reconfigured gender relations and, to a large extent, did this consciously. It can be argued that although the gender regime of socialism changed gender relations, it did so not by eliminating inequity but by mapping it onto different structures. First, women entered the workforce in unprecedented numbers, but they occupied positions in the workforce that were typically poorly remunerated and of low status: women made up the bulk of teachers, medical personnel, clerks, and secretaries. These were jobs that were defined as "women's work." In all sectors of the economy, even those dominated by women, positions higher on the pay and authority ladder were typically held by men. The result of this horizontal segregation and vertical stratification was that, despite the elevation of a doctrine of equal pay, women's wages were on average lower than those of men.

Lapidus pointed out another dimension of the vertical segregation of the workforce that affected Soviet agricultural workers across the USSR. She quoted a Soviet commentator who, in the 1970s, noted that "a peculiar division of labor has arisen between men and women: the sphere of mechanized work is a male privilege and that of manual labor is reserved to women."[20] That is, in the occupational division in agriculture, women performed largely unskilled tasks, while men worked in more highly skilled and better paid mechanized jobs.

Second, the equal citizenship enshrined in the Soviet order did not translate into a significant degree of political power for women. As noted above, when Latvia was incorporated into the USSR in 1940, women had already been enfranchised for twenty-two years.[21] The vote was not, therefore, a new development in the emancipation of women. Under Soviet rule, more women were elected to republic-level positions than had been elected to national bodies in interwar Latvia. For example, in the 1950s and 1960s, women made up about 30 percent of the Supreme Soviet of the Latvian Socialist Soviet Republic.[22] Despite this visible change, the highest echelons of power such as the Central Committees of the USSR and the republics continued to be disproportionately occupied by men. Even more important, the single-party candidate slates and the severely circumscribed scope of issues that could be debated rendered the political power achieved by women little more than a facade for the closely held power concentrated in the hands of the small Communist elites that controlled the country and administered the republics.

Furthermore, the enforced passivity of civil society precluded public activism in the name of women's interests. In the 1950s and 1960s, women's councils were organized to address social issues like alcohol abuse and family health, but the dependence on and supervision of these councils by the Communist Party limited their potential for independent initiative to effect changes that could have improved the lives of women and families.

Third, women continued to take responsibility for home tasks, assuming a double burden that few men bore. Earlier, I noted that although in the theorized visions of early Marxists domestic tasks were to be socialized, they were still the domain of women, and a lessening of women's burden did not seem to entail an increase in the male workload. So though women were envisioned, together with men, as workers, women also continued to appear in the roles of mothers and caretakers of the family. As Barbara Einhorn noted, there was no "equivalent definition of men as workers *and* fathers."[23] In practice, this meant that women continued to be responsible for domestic labor. The socialization of child care, for example, freed many women to enter the workforce, but the burden on women was hardly lessened because the need to do housework, cooking, shopping, and the like remained virtually unchanged. The perpetual shortage of consumer goods and the well-known phenomenon of endless lines for those goods further exacerbated the condition of many already overburdened women.

Women's dominance of the domestic arena, the private sphere, has been recognized, however, as a position of some power in the socialist period. In a time when there was little or no independent civic life, the private sphere carried particular significance. Einhorn suggested: "Under state socialism, many people invested the family with meaning as the source of dignity and creativity in a society characterized by alienated labour processes. There was a tendency to idealize it, construing it as a harmonious collectivity pitted against the difficulties and strife of coping with the shortcomings of daily life, in a unity of interests against the intrusive state and over-politicized public domain."[24]

The private sphere was also an important space for the transmission of information and in countries like Latvia where national culture and history were distorted by the requirements of Soviet ideology, for the transmission of national identities that were ignored or persecuted in the public sphere. A small 1991 survey highlighted this point. The survey sought to discern the "socio-psychological characteristics of the modern Latvian woman" and posed, among others, the question, "What are some characteristics of a wife and grandmother in a modern Latvian family?" Respondents were asked to name three characteristics. Together with expected answers such as "Women take care of the family" (which was first for Latvian wives and mothers), answers such as "Preserver of Latvian traditions" and "Preserver of family traditions" also scored high, particularly for Latvian grandmothers.[25] The survey, as constructed, was not representative, but it points to the notion that women were strongly associated in the Soviet period (as they continue to be) with the private sphere, which, at least in this period, was also a site for the nurturance of Latvian identity, because the public sphere was focused on the construction of the *homo sovieticus.*

It was not only through ideology (socialist or traditional) or the assumption of "natural" sex roles that women came to dominate the private sphere. The Estonian sociologist Anu Narusk wrote that in the Soviet period "war and political deportations caused an abnormal scarcity of men, thus transforming women into heads of households."[26] In the USSR as a whole, after World War II about 30 percent of households were headed by women.[27] In Latvia, as in the rest of the Union, the gender imbalance remained "abnormal" through several postwar decades. The 1959 census in Latvia, for example, found an overall female-to-male ratio of 1,278 to 1,000. The imbalance was particularly pronounced in the middle-aged groups: among those thirty to thirty-four years, the female-to-male ratio was 1,427 to 1,000; among those aged thirty-five to thirty-nine, it was 1,597 to 1,000; in the age category forty to forty-four, it was 1,468 to 1,000. The imbalance declined in subsequent age groups until the sixty and over age group, where it again rose dramatically.[28] Though the late Soviet period saw the reestablishment of a more balanced ratio, it nonetheless remained below Western European ratios. For example, in 1989 in Latvia, there were 951 males per 1,000 females in the age group fifteen to fifty-nine years. For comparison, in Denmark the number was 1,034 males per 1,000 females, and in Sweden, 1,035 males per 1,000 females.[29] In 1996, the female-to-male ratio stood at 1,160 to 1,000. In the last decades, the explanations for the residual imbalance lie not in war, but in greater male alcohol abuse, accidents, and suicides that have contributed to a twelve-year gap between the life expectancy of females (75.6 in 1996) and males (63.9 in 1996).[30]

Fourth, women's *choice* with respect to being a mother or worker or both was not salient to the socialist project: women were not actors, but objects, taking on the roles ascribed to them by the state patriarchy. Women were the beneficiaries of policies that facilitated their movement into the labor force and that eased some of the burdens of child care, but the provision of rights and opportunities varied according to the "needs" of the socialist state. Whereas socialist ideology contained a program of equity that foresaw the opening of avenues by which women would achieve economic independence from men, this was clearly not the only explanation for the increase of female participation in the labor force. Lapidus pointed out that the "vast economic expansion touched off by the First Five Year Plan in 1928 and the all-out commitment to rapid industrialization in the following decade required an enormous increase in the size of the labor force." From 1928 to 1950, the number of women in the labor force nearly doubled from 24 percent to 47 percent and remained above 50 percent after 1968. The need to bring women into the labor force was compounded by the population losses of the 1940s. With essentially full employment among males, women were sorely needed in the workforce. Even in periods that the labor shortage was less severe, a "woman who restricted her activities to the household was considered dependent, incomplete, and even unpatriotic." [31]

Decisions about motherhood were also guided by the state's perceived needs at least as much as by women's own choices. For example, abortion was legalized by the Soviet state in 1920, criminalized in 1936, and then legalized again in 1955. The early legalization had taken place in an ideological context of emancipation, but the criminalization in the Stalin era reflected a return to a concern for the state-defined collective good where motherhood was described as a social responsibility that should not be avoided. The "right" to an abortion upheld earlier was recast: "Abortion under socialism was not a right at all. The superior right enjoyed by Soviet women was the right to maternity under good conditions." The 1955 relegalization took place quietly because, although pronatalism was still on the state agenda, underground abortions were identified as a threat. Buckley suggested: "Abortion was being legalized not so much as a right for women as a corrective against resorting to illegal abortions." [32] In other words, the possibility for women to control their fertility, particularly in conditions where contraception was not easily obtained or was unreliable, was contingent rather than absolute, and the needs of the socialist state dictated rather than supported women's access to abortion.

In the USSR in the mid-1980s, Gorbachev spoke of the importance of securing "living and working conditions for women that would enable them to successfully combine their maternal duties with active involvement in labor and public activity." Gorbachev went on to define (infamously) among the "rights" of women, the opportunity to return to their "truly womanly mission." [33] He proposed, among others, a shorter workday or week for mothers in the labor force, a longer paid maternity leave, and more paid days for mothers staying home with ill children. [34] Together with these "rights," there were, in this vision, "duties," which included "housework, the upbringing of children, and the creation of a good family atmosphere." [35] The participation in the formal economy had, ostensibly, led to women's neglect of this role.

Ideology has long been wrapped around practical policies rather than being their foundation, and, as in earlier periods, women were objects, not actors, in the policy equation. This call to reproduction, with its concomitant economic incentives, was not a response to female initiatives. Rather, there was fear in the European-dominated structures of governance that the faster-growing Central Asian nationalities would become demographically dominant: one-child families had become the norm in many European areas, including European Russia, Latvia, and Estonia. That pronatalism was, at least to some extent, targeted to particular populations seems apparent from Susan Bridger's observation that around that time articles in women's magazines intended for a Central Asian female audience highlighted the advantages of women's participation in the labor force, while those for the European USSR stressed the joys of motherhood.[36]

Gorbachev defined gender equality in terms of difference, with duties and rights being categorized as "womanly" (and presumably "manly"). Many women (and men) embraced these identities of difference. The notion that women could be disadvantaged by a large-scale exit from the labor force was rejected by women like Tatiana Tolstaia, who wrote in 1990 that in Russia "there is no inequality of power between the public and private spheres, and women are more likely to choose to stay at home than to follow a career, since careers are pursued primarily for power rather than money and that women have enough power as it is." Furthermore, she suggested that "women's exclusion from the public sphere has been a privilege rather than a site of oppression since the 'public world' has been rendered devoid of any authentic worth."[37]

Tolstaia's argument cannot be dismissed because, as noted earlier, the sense that the private sphere is a locus of power where women stand atop the decision-making hierarchy is real. However, the "privilege" of remaining outside the public sphere, though it may have been present in the Soviet system that stripped both genders of genuine civic power, seems hardly to be true in the post-Communist period where both political and economic power are available in the public sphere. Gorbachev's reiteration of "womanly" roles, duties, and norms for women, thus, began the domestication of women that has continued and grown in the post-Communist period, though, as seen later, the motivations are very different.

Gender and Normality in Post-Communism

Although as I have shown in previous chapters the dominant narratives of transformation have often been at odds with one another in the field of political life, the temporal and spatial narratives share several points with respect to the "normalization" of the gender regime that have had a profound effect on women in post-Communist Latvia. First, the notion of "natural" or "normal" sex roles, whether associated with the past or with modern Europe, is widely shared in society and reflected in the narratives of post-Communist change in Latvia as well. Second, the two narratives of change have largely shared a nation-centered orientation that both reinforces and, arguably, expands women's subjugated status in society and submerges the "woman question" beneath the "national question," which continues to preoccupy political and social life. Third, the extent to which free markets are balanced by welfare provisions and local markets are protected from foreign competition has varied in the spatial and temporal visions, but both dominant narratives have essentially embraced the capitalist market and private property. Provision for consequent social dislocations, many of which have been borne by women, has, however, fallen largely outside the scope of ideology or possibility in the post-Communist state.

The "equality of difference" argument that some of Gorbachev's comments reflect has continued to be influential in the post-Communist period across Eastern Europe, though it is, predictably, posed in contrast to the Soviet order rather than seen as a continuation of any part of it. Although the assumptions and implications of the notion of "equality of difference" are variable, all are essentially premised on a sense that the Soviet-era asexualization of norms, roles, and behaviors was abnormal.

The notion that the Soviet period engendered an asexualization of gender roles is widespread and has been noted by women as well as men. The *National Report on the Situation of Women,* produced in Latvia in preparation for the United Nations Conference on Women in 1995, lamented the "destruction of individuality brought on by socialism generally [that] led to the asexualization of behavioral norms, disdain for women and traditionally 'feminine' work, ignorance of female characteristics."[38] In a 1992 paper given at a conference on women in Latvia, the criminologist Dzidris Seps suggested: "Society is made up of two genders. How well society functions depends on the harmonious integration of roles for men and women. Separately, the two genders are different in many significant ways. This was not taken into account by the socialist leaders and planners as they strove to bring about equality, in what now is seen as so many vulgarized slogans for establishing equality between men and women."[39]

The "equality through difference" argument highlights the notion that women's nature and roles are complimentary to, though different from, men's and also sees "female characteristics" as a source of power, particularly in the private sphere. Hilary Pilkington quoted Filipova, who argued that the "love for the close, natural wiseness, a sensitivity to beauty, self-sacrifice in the name of creation—these are all primordial female character-istics which are particularly valuable in our cruel, breaking time."[40] Seps claimed that "women's emotional perception of the world is more intuitive. Informative theory of emotions as developed by P. Simonov notes that women have an advantage when it comes to better orientation to everyday situations, however, they have more difficulties in dealing with unusual situ-ations. The advantage which women have in dealing with problems also helps to provide a favorable climate for their role as mothers." He continued: "The male, on the other hand, is expected to act more in terms of the rational mode, to experiment, and to find new ways of solving problems. . . . The girls orient their conduct more along the lines of women's role, they are less likely to experiment in ways which depart from the traditional life style. However, once girls lose their orientation it is more difficult to return them to normal behavior patterns."[41]

Women's organizations as well have largely accepted and even enshrined the notion of "difference." The Latvian Women['s] Organization Coopera-tion Council, for example, included in its Program of Action the assertion that "society comprises two equally important sexes, each of which in figures represent[s] its own half of society. Women and men strongly differ as to their mentality, desires, interests, life experience, and self-expression." Fur-thermore, among their "activity lines," the Council included the shaping of "public opinion as to the correct comprehension of the notion of equality (not to be mixed up with alikeness)."[42]

More recently, the *Latvia Human Development Report 1995*, prepared in con-junction with the United Nations Development Program, but authored pri-marily by local researchers and writers, featured a chapter on "Women in Transition." Though the chapter, like the conference essays, argued for the importance of equal rights and opportunities for women in the new order, it also suggested that "[a] good portion of a woman's life is occupied by bear-ing and raising children, caring for the home and family. For men, raising children and caring for children do not require leaving work. *This division of labor is natural and acceptable to all.*" The idea that this particular division of labor—with men as producers and women as reproducers—is "natural and acceptable to all" is tightly bound to the notion also iterated in the chapter that "the [Soviet] state deformed social relations between the sexes."[43] Thus the abnormality of the gender regime of the Soviet order is replaced in a post-Soviet vision by the "natural" gender regime, where women are defined by motherhood and family life.

The notion iterated above—that a set of "normal" and "traditional" behaviors exists for males and females—underpins the idea that the spheres
inhabited by men and women and the behaviors appropriate to those spheres
differ. Women's roles in the private sphere are elevated as important. As
Pilkington pointed out, "The 'equality through difference' argument illustrates an important point: the recognition of a division between public and
private does not in itself entail the subordination of the private to the public."[44] It appears that many women accept the private sphere as their domain,
while the public realm is perceived as the male domain. A 1989 survey of
women in Latvia suggested as much: the reply to the question "Does the
man have the dominant role in your family?" received more negative responses (52.6 percent), but the question "Do men have the dominant role in
Latvia's society?" received a positive response of 75 percent. Comments on
the latter question included the following: "That's the way it should be if a
man [is] manly," and "Looking at the government, it's comprised most of
men, but that is normal and sensible, because women, after all, are more
emotional."[45]

Though the association of normality with traditional gender norms and
roles is often linked with a nostalgia for the past in which this was (purport-
edly) so, the normality of this equality of difference can, as well, be associated
with the desire to "return to Europe," so often heard in the post-Communist
space. For example, the former Hungarian secretary of education Kata Beke
put forth the notion that "in the rich store of historical examples . . . the
European model of marriage has proven to be the most successful and
resilient. Because it corresponds to humanity's two-sexed nature, to the set
of complementary differences hidden in our genes. Because only here [in
Europe] can a new generation grow up in a normal—that is, two-sexed
world."[46]

Two things are of particular note in Beke's quotation: first, her elevation
of the naturalness of complementary relations and functions of men and
women ("in our genes"); and second, her linkage of these organic relations
with "Europe," the destination of Eastern Europeans seeking modernity.
The "normal world," hence, is traditionally gendered *and* modern, nicely
accommodating the spatial and temporal narratives in a single vision of gender relations in post-Communism.

Women's roles in the private sphere are elevated as important for society
and the nation, but it is notable that the "democratization" of the public
sphere is not widely foreseen as including women. This is problematic not
least because women are, on a large scale, excluded from the economic and

political power that can profoundly affect the conditions of their life and work.

Women and Nation

The narrative of temporal normality has elevated a historical model for change, seeking Latvia's future in its past. Its leanings have been decidedly nationalistic, prioritizing a collective national good and practicing politics that have privileged the Latvian nation above other collectivities (and the individual). As in the historical and contemporary nationalisms of its neighbors, in Latvian nationalism women have been held to be the bearers of the nation and, hence, have been valued primarily as mothers. Though temporal normality has not rejected the participation of women in the economy and public life, it has highlighted a "natural" maternal role for women in the life of the nation.

In a work on gender in Eastern Europe, Peggy Watson noted that "the 'regaining' of a traditionally prescribed gender identity is an important aspect of the nostalgia for 'normality,' which has been so often expressed as what people most hope for from change in Eastern Europe."[47] Furthermore, as Einhorn pointed out, "Women's reproductive and 'feminine' nurturing roles are seen as crucial to the survival, not of a particular social system—as they were under state socialism—but of the national or ethnic community."[48] Women are, thus, encouraged by popular sentiment and state policy to "have babies for the nation." As expected, the reception to neotraditionalism, especially where it affects women's prospects for gainful employment and personal choice about childbearing, has been mixed. In Latvia, however, neotraditionalism has an additional dimension that has fostered a broader constituency than might be expected for the elevation of women's role as mothers and motherhood as a national duty: whereas Latvians made up about 75 percent of the population in the interwar period and had a positive rate of growth, since the early 1990s, Latvians have had a negative growth rate and still make up under 60 percent of the population. The widespread sense that Latvians are becoming a "minority in their own country" and are "dying out" has underpinned the centrality of procreation and motherhood as public rather than private issues and has given traditionalist claims greater legitimacy.

Essays from *Fragments of Reality: Insights on Women in a Changing Society,* a book that emerged from a conference on Latvian women in 1992, reinforce the aforementioned point. Whereas most participants clearly advocated equal rights and opportunities for women, the portrait of the woman in "her role as guardian of future generations" of Latvians permeated the text. A physician wrote: "We [Latvian women] have to be proud of ourselves, who else but we can rejuvenate our nation by giving birth to healthy children and bring[ing] them up for [the] future [?]"⁴⁹ Similarly, following a discussion of the poor health status of many mothers and young children in Latvia, two psychologists stated:

> That all testifies that the health conditions of our nation and our genofund for our future generations is so degraded that there is a threat to our nation's survival. To avert this threat women have to assume a larger responsibility in taking care of their health, giving birth to children, and bringing up physically and mentally fit children. [The Latvian author] Augusts Deglavs wrote in 1910: ". . . [the woman] is of great importance as a bride, wife, and mother. . . . The key to the future is in the hands of the next generations! But mothers have to take care of the next generations so that they are able to use the keys."⁵⁰

On the other side of the "traditionalist" coin are those voices that embrace the "natural" role of women as mothers without attaching concern for the education and economic independence of women. In a 1990 conference organized by the nationalist political organization Latvia's National Independence Movement, the issue of procreation loomed large in discussions about national survival. Jānis Mauliņš, who read a paper entitled "The Most Important [Thing]—A Strong Family," suggested:

> It is an old truth that he wins, who has the ability to see what is important. What, then, is the most important for the survival of the Latvian nation? The number of children. The birth rate. . . .
>   The hot-blooded slogans about independence will do nothing if there are no children. . . .
>   We need to awaken people's shame about their weakness and selfish pursuits. But first we need to understand what's most important. Then we will triumph.⁵¹

The speaker evoked "selfishness" and a missing sense of "shame" in those who would not bring forth children for the sake of the nation, but others sought the roots of the low birthrate in physiological and psychological and social phenomena. For example, the speaker Jēkabs Raipulis, who read a paper entitled "Only We Can Protect the Latvian Nation," noted:

> There is a disturbingly high level of never-married men of repro-
> ductive (over 16) age: for quite a while, this has been 23%. . . . Of
> those men who never marry, only a small number remain bachelors
> by choice. Some of these do not find mates because of their shy
> personalities. . . . Many more remain bachelors because of the lack
> of [marriageable] women. That is especially problematic in the
> rural areas, from where young women go to the university or to
> [work in the cities]; those who return to the countryside with an
> education no longer wish to marry [common laborers]. From un-
> married teachers and other educated women, a class of "spinsters"
> is created.[52]

Raipulis highlighted the issue of never-married men in Latvia and suggested that although the failure of men of "reproductive age" to marry may be explained by the "shy personalities" of some males, the lion's share of the blame goes to women. The reason for women's reticence to marry appears, in this speaker's view, to lie in the fact that "educated women" do not desire to couple with less educated men. He never overtly stated that women's higher education should be limited, but he clearly saw the issue of education as a salient one in the context of national survival.[53] Later in the paper, he added:

> It is especially important to consider the complicated situation of
> the intelligentsia in the national context. Latvian university students
> marry infrequently and have even fewer children. After finishing
> the university, many educated women stay unmarried or else in late
> marriages have few children with worse health than those born to
> young mothers. Furthermore, professional wages and the supply of
> housing [both poor] also do not further the creation of large fami-
> lies. This situation invariably leads to the diminishment of the geno-
> fund.

Paradoxically, while women are being elevated as mothers and entreated to reproduce for the good of the nation, they are being chastised for their perceived failure as mothers, wives, and socializers. The Estonian sociologist Anu Narusk stated: "Overemancipation is blamed for social problems such as divorce, men's drinking, juvenile delinquency, the decline in morality, and so on."⁵⁴ The Hungarian sociologist Maria Adamik also noted the trend of attributing negative social phenomena to women's actions or failures, writing that women are blamed "for the increasing mortality of middle-aged men, the rising divorce rate, the falling birth-rate, and the generally decreasing stability of families."⁵⁵

In this context of assigning blame to "overemancipated" women, other issues related to structural problems of Communism and post-Communism are marginalized. For instance, some have recognized the role of widespread ill health on fertility and childbearing, but male impotence or sterility is attributed, on the one hand, to factors like alcohol abuse (which, as Narusk noted, may be blamed on women) and, on the other hand, to environmental or job-related exposure to radiation or chemical mutagens. The male who, as in Raipulis's account, is not normally at fault for his failure to marry is also not at fault for his failure to procreate. Women in these states, many of whom also suffer from poor health and poor health care, are more likely to be held accountable for their physical problems. For example, Raipulis suggested:

[Because of their] lack of knowledge about personal hygiene, many girls suffer from gynecological illnesses that result in sterility. As a result of poor knowledge about sexual relations, as well as the short-age of contraceptives and the lack of knowledge about how to use them, there are many unwanted pregnancies. For every child born in Latvia, two are liquidated through abortion. Many women be-come sterile after this procedure. Abortion is particularly dangerous when it is [a woman's] first pregnancy.⁵⁶

While the lack of contraceptives is noted by the speaker, it is women's fail-ure to "know" about hygiene, sexual relations, and contraceptive use that stands out in this account. Women, then, shoulder the blame not only for having few or no children by choice, but also, in some cases, for their physi-cal inability to procreate.

The narrative of spatial transformation embraces notions of Europeanness and a Western model of modernity. The marketization imperatives of the spatial narrative have created a space for the massive opening of the market, the decline of regulation, and a broad sense that private capital, its abun-dance or lack, is the determinant of quality of life. On the other hand, the temporal and evolutionary narratives have leaned toward greater regulation and protection *of* the market and greater protection of the populace *from* the market. Spatial narratives and initiatives have, however, dominated this sphere.

In the arena of the free post-Communist market, women surface as the primary household consumers of the cornucopia of goods and services available in the new economy. Women in Latvia make a substantial proportion of the decisions that determine household purchases, and, as in the West, advertisements for household appliances (many relatively new to Latvia, such as modern dishwashers and clothes washers) are aggressively marketed to women, suggesting that therein lies female freedom and contentment. Whereas the free market gives women access to goods about which they could only dream in the Soviet period, it also undermines women's ability to independently afford such goods, as I discuss further along.

Symptomatic if not symbolic of the free market narrative is the concomitant appearance of women as consumables, as salable products valued for the services they provide to boys and men on the market of sexual exchange. Prostitution, pornography, and a full spectrum of erotica have taken a prominent place in the new market of post-Communism in Latvia. Pornography has declined in popularity after a massive influx of materials early in the period, but the sex trade continues to be the site of staggering exploitation and profit. The trade benefits from both the freedom of and the dislocations caused by the capitalist market: the widespread tolerance afforded new forms of commodification (like the commodification of bodies and sex), the need for new forms of economic support in an environment of widespread unemployment and paltry wages, and the profit potential of sex seamlessly meld together in this environment.

Out of the amalgam of Latvia's dominant narratives of change, a unified picture emerges of the privileging of the historical nation and modern market, the treatment of the "feminine" private sphere as a site for realizing the needs and interests of the nation, and the vision of the "masculine" public sphere as a site for realizing individual (usually male) desires and aspirations. Here women appear as objects rather than agents of transformation. In the nationalist vision, women are producers in the home economy, and the fruits of their labor are coveted not because they ensure that women as such will survive and thrive, but because the interests of the nation and its subunit, the family, will be advanced. The value of women in the sphere of market is not so much as the producers of commodities (because with the growth of unemployment, male employment becomes the priority) as it is as consumers or consumables in the free market. The places structured for women by these visions are complementary rather than contradictory, then, because the "need" for women to go back home engendered by the traditionalist vision legitimates the "need" for (some) women to exit the workforce, a need created by the decline of employment opportunities in many sectors of the labor market.

The dual processes of domestication and commodification, which are linked to these visions of transformation, are illustrated in the following sections by a closer examination of two areas of post-Communist life: social welfare policies and the domestic sex trade in Latvia. In the remainder of this chapter, then, I examine two spheres in which change has taken place in post-Communist Latvia, describe some of the effects on Latvia's women, and consider their relationship to the transformations taking place in Latvia as well as elsewhere across Eastern Europe.

The state's action in the area of social welfare suggests an inclination to link economic aid with mechanisms of control, particularly with respect to mothers, and to regulate women's options with respect to maternity, child rearing, employment, and familial separation. Conversely, once women leave the home and enter the labor market, the state virtually disappears, and the market itself assumes the primary managerial and regulatory role. In the "man's world" of business, sexual harassment, capricious hiring and firing based on gender, age, appearance, and the granting of sexual favors, and the exploitation of women in the massive sex industry have received little or no legislative attention or regulation.[57]

I suggest that both the domestication and commodification of women are processes directly related to the transformation of political and economic structures and that the privileging of national interests over all others entails the development of a masculinized public sphere that shuts women behind the doors of kitchens, bedrooms, and bordellos. The case of women in Latvia can help to evaluate how the existence of large nontitular populations affects political ideologies and practices, including those relating to gender roles and women's opportunities and disadvantages. Furthermore, I consider how Latvia's dominant political narratives of temporal and spatial normalization are woven into policy and public discourse on social welfare and prostitution: the explicit comparison of these two areas highlights their relationship not just as two "women's issues" but as political, economic, and ethnic issues in Latvia.

Mothers and Others in the Marketplace

Social welfare policy in post-Communist Latvia in the 1990s has been driven by a mixture of the narratives of temporal and spatial normality and the pressures of budgetary shortages and the market economy. The revival of a traditionalist patriarchal family order in which mothers remain outside the labor market and stay home with children rather than bringing them to child care centers (as was common in the Soviet period when most working-age women were in the labor force) has received some legislative support. Accordingly, the child allowance given by the state to parents until the restoration of independence was quickly canceled for families in which both parents worked full time, despite a strong sentiment among families with young children that "all families have a right to child care benefits during a child's first three years of life, regardless of whether the mother has paid employment or not during this period." Under the new legislation, benefits were offered only to those mothers who stayed at home with the child or children. Leaves or benefits for fathers were not addressed in the legislation. The value of the benefits was (and continues to be) low. A survey of parents of young children taken by the Institute of Economics, however, suggests that although half of two-parent families felt the benefits were "insignificant," one-fifth found them to be "a significant help." In over half of single-parent families, the benefits were believed to be of importance to the family budget.[58]

At about the same time that these benefits were discontinued for working mothers, nearly half of public preschools were closed, which forced some women to leave their jobs. In 1985, 61 percent of preschool-aged children (one to six years of age) attended preschools, and in 1990, 48 percent were enrolled. By 1991 the number of children in public preschools dropped to 38 percent, and by 1993 just 28 percent of children attended.[59]

Unaffordability may explain some of the drop (the cost has remained relatively low, but wages are often low as well), but the number of public preschools available for young children has also fallen dramatically in recent years: in 1990 there were 1,123 such establishments; by 1993 the number had fallen to 647. The figures have not improved since: in 1995 the reported number of preschool establishments in Latvia was down to 608.[60] Some rural areas in Latvia have no preschools at all. Few private child centers and preschools have been established to take the place of those lost since 1990. The primary reason for this, according to Dr. Pārsla Eglīte of the Latvian Women's Study and Information Center, is that, with low wages and no tax breaks, most parents would not be able to afford the cost of private establishments.[61]

Social welfare policy in Latvia, as it relates to young women, could be construed as pronatalist in direction. The "family policy" passed by the National Legislature in 1995 and revised in 1996 foresaw the availability of a maternity benefit, a birth grant, a child care allowance up to the age of three years, a monthly family allowance for children up to the age of fifteen, and a reduction in parental income tax for each child. The revision included, among other things, an increase in the per child allowance for successive children up to the number of six.[62] Such policies seem consistent with both the claims of the traditionalists and the broad popular notion that the state should encourage and support childbearing. The allowances, however, even taken together, are very small, though a marginal increase in the child allowance was later passed for those born after 1998.

This pronatalist slant has had no notable effect on childbearing choices made by families, and all ethnic groups in Latvia, with the exception of the small Roma population, have experienced declines in the natural growth rate: the last year in which Latvia experienced a positive natural growth rate was 1990, when the rate was 1.2 per 1,000. Though the birthrate in Latvia remained relatively low after World War II, in the post-Communist period it has dipped below that of any prior period. In 1980, there were 53.2 births per thousand women fifteen to forty-nine years of age. In the mid-1980s, the birthrate reached a postwar high of about 61 per thousand women in this age category. In 1990, the rate dropped to 59 per thousand and declined precipitously thereafter, down to 50 per thousand in 1992 and just 30 per thousand in 1998.[63] The total fertility rate in Latvia has fallen below the rate needed for a population to replace itself, and at least one study has projected a population decline of between 7 and 11 percent by 2010.[64]

Though popular rhetoric embraces motherhood, the imperative of economic growth engendered by free market politics and policies makes the position of women, particularly mothers, precarious. In the post-Communist sociopolitical and economic context, women, especially those with children, are more likely than men to be represented among poor people. First, they are more likely to be solely responsible for children after a divorce or in the case that the parents never marry. Second, they are more likely to be employed in positions with low remuneration in spite of their higher educational attainment as a group. Women suffer from a wage gap in all sectors of the economy: overall, women earn 78 percent of the male wage, and, in the public sector, where women outnumber men, they earn just 73 percent of the male wage.[65] Third, because women have an earlier age of retirement and a life expectancy ten to twelve years longer than men, they make up 70 percent of pensioners, most of whom are poor.[66] The widespread lack of savings and meager state pensions mean that pensioners who receive no outside help (from, for example, adult children) may be among the very poor, some of whom beg on the streets and many of whom suffer from the lack of nutritious food and other basic needs. Even with the increase of pensions in 1996, the value of the support was still equivalent to only 52.8 percent of the full subsistence-level basket of goods and services and 74.3 percent of the crisis basket.[67]

Although women appear to be more vulnerable to poverty, the state's focus on economic growth and a free market has largely marginalized issues of social welfare that affect women of childbearing age in spite of the discursive elevation of motherhood. For example, the maternity allowance is available only to women who have been actively employed in the official job market during the previous year. Because 10 percent of births are to women between the ages of fifteen and nineteen, it is reasonable to assume that most of these young women, 75.9 percent of whom were economically inactive, will not receive the allowance. They are not, however, the only ones who can be denied the allowance. By official estimates, in late 1995, 40 percent of all women and 25.7 percent of working-age women (twenty to fifty-nine) were "economically inactive."[68] This drop in women's labor force participation is also notable for its stark contrast to earlier levels of participation. Among young women aged twenty to twenty-four, for example, the employment level fell from 80.6 percent in 1989 to 46.1 percent at the end of 1996. Among women aged twenty-five to forty-nine, the rate of labor force attachment fell from an average of 93.6 percent to 70.38 percent in the same period.[69] Among women who were and are working, some work in the "informal" economy (for example, selling flowers on the street) or on private, self-supporting farms, neither of which permit them to qualify, in many cases, for allowances. The purpose of limiting the benefits of those who are not attached to the formal economy, according to Dr. Pārsla Eglīte, is to "force people to pay the social tax,[70] to force people to work in the official labor market [as opposed to the unofficial or second economy]."

There is a maternity leave legally available for working women and the "guarantee" of a job on return, but employers may bypass the law by simply eliminating the position the day after a woman returns. Unemployment benefits are available for nine months, and, though benefits vary depending on a number of factors, they are typically low and decline as the months pass. Thus benefits for the fourth to sixth months of unemployment are 80 percent of the initial payment and for the seventh to ninth months, 50 percent of the initial payment.[71]

In considering the structural conditions in which women make choices about, for example, whether to abort or to carry a child to term or to conceive a baby at all, the medical facilities available to women must also be considered. The poor state of health care in the former USSR and East Bloc is well known, but the particular problems of maternity care have received comparably less attention. These problems are, I suggest, relevant to the examination of the issue of childbearing. As I show in this chapter, women are broadly encouraged to bear children for the health and good of the collectivity, whether that be the socialist collectivity or the nation, but structural conditions under which this is an attractive option continue to be absent. In this picture, the conditions under which women give birth are relevant. The words of a female respondent to a survey on childbirth in Latvia illustrate this point. The woman said: "I should like to have another child, yet I can't forget the indifference and humiliation of the first childbirth. I have the feeling that nobody needs the possibility for a woman to bring children to the world in a [humane] way."[72]

To what extent the system of socialist medicine in the USSR wrought conditions under which medical personnel (most of whom are women) treat patients, including mothers-to-be, with disdain is difficult to ascertain. Clearly, however, the system was not deficient only in terms of supplies, but also in terms of providing patients information about and comfort in childbirth. A nonrepresentative 1992 survey of women who gave birth between 1990 and 1992 ($N = 470$) found that the majority of women had not received information about birthing in advance. One respondent wrote: "At the consultations . . . nobody told me anything, but when I arrived at the maternity hall, I was showered with reproaches that I did not know how to act. The doctor said that women who do not know how to do anything must not give birth to a child." Another mother who experienced a difficult birth described her situation as follows: "My baby did not want to be born, everybody was tired of me. I had to listen to various remarks [such as]: Why do you need a child if you cannot bring him forth? It does not hurt her, she only plays a role. Take her off the table, let her go on lying in torture. She does not want to press out the baby, she is not unable to do so, etc."[73] Reportedly, conditions have improved in recent years, though the state of knowledge, technology, and comfort for birthing women continues to lag behind that of the West.[74]

In sum, then, small families continue to be the most attractive option despite government pronatalist incentives and policies. The combination of difficult material conditions, conflicting demands of home and family, inadequacy of family housing options, many women's desire to work outside the home, lack of child care options, and low quality of health facilities are all salient factors in understanding this choice.

Childbearing is not the only "private" issue that has been forced into the public arena in Latvia. Two policies in particular seem to reflect the push toward reestablishing the prevalence if not the dominance of the traditional patriarchal family unit in Latvia. First, as the divorce rate in Latvia is high, there has been a desire to reduce divorce. The process of divorce is now lengthier and more costly than in the Soviet period, and all divorces must be court approved.[75] In fact, the divorce rate has recently dropped; after peaking in 1992 at 5.5 per thousand inhabitants, it fell to 2.5 per thousand in 1998.[76] Some of this may be a product of the policy; certainly, some of the drop is related to a fall in marriages over the same period.

Second, the special child allowance for single mothers, established in the postwar USSR to encourage births, was eliminated in 1991. The discontinuation of this allowance, which was supplemented in 1981 with privileges like a shorter wait for apartments, reflected, among other things, a concern with the increase in births to unmarried mothers apparent since 1985. Although the real number of children born to single mothers actually declined around that time, the percentage of all births that were to single mothers increased and was reported to be 19.6 percent in 1992.[77] Statistical data on unmarried mothers also showed that many were Russian and had a low level of education. This was not a segment of the population among whom the state was eager to encourage births. However, the proportion of births outside marriage, unlike the divorce rate, has continued to climb: according to preliminary 2000 census data, the proportion is now close to 40 percent.[78]

In *Cinderella Goes to Market: Citizenship, Gender, and Women's Movements in East Central Europe*, Barbara Einhorn stated that a "traditional family unit is being envisioned by East Central European societies in transition, as the focal point of the search for identity and new values. This vision casts the family as the smallest unit in the wider ethnic community, invoking its central and salutary role in the process of establishing new mores. The family is thus seen as a crucial element in the claim to national identity and self determination."[79]

The popular vision of this traditional "unit," the site at which both citizens and citizenship values are (re)produced, is belied by reality. This ideal family is, as it was in the socialist period, a utopian construct, and legislative visions clouded by a mythologized past and imagined radiant future drive social policies that potentially undermine the viability of existing family units, whether they be made up of one or two parents. In a traditionalist vision, divorce is seen in the context of the idealized nuclear family, which engenders the "solution" of saving families by slowing or stopping divorce. An alternative vision, one that has not commanded attention on the stage of political transformation, sees divorce in the context of economic and social life and recognizes the nexus between personal choices and structural conditions in both the Soviet and the post-Soviet periods (the high rate of divorce is not a new phenomenon). Such a vision recognizes the reality of family life and the stresses entailed by the structural context. Among young families especially, the housing shortage means that new families, many with children, are forced to live with parents in crowded conditions. In the Soviet period, the shortage was driven by a lack of apartment units (some people waited on lists for up to twenty years); in the post-Communist period, the somewhat greater availability of units is undermined by their prohibitive cost. The low average age at first marriage in Latvia makes the cost issue a salient one as well, because young couples may still be in school or may be working for low wages; thus they may face budgetary stresses and even the threat of poverty. The rate of unemployment among younger adults has also typically been higher than the unemployment rate generally.

Writing on gender discourses and policies in the former Soviet Union, Anastasia Posadskaya characterized the direction of family policy as it relates to women as follows: "New legislation on the family by the central government and local administrations presupposes and encourages women's family attachment rather than career options."[80] Indeed, the "presupposition" noted by Posadskaya emanates from both nationally particular historical experiences and the structure of new states themselves. In a work on the birth of modern Turkey, Carol Delaney suggested that "the concept of nation-state is itself gendered, and therefore the gender inequality vis-à-vis the nation is not an accidental feature but is inherent in the notion of the nation as it has been historically conceived in the West."[81] Hence, the movement of women out of the workforce and back to the home in Latvia is not just a process emergent from the historically specific temporal narrative about normality. Indeed, it is a process that, because it mirrors what is widely conceived of as the "natural order of things," is inherent in the structure of the modern nation-state and in the dominant narratives of post-Communist transformation that privilege the nation.

The inequitable division of power between men and women that existed but was theoretically condemned under state socialism is enshrined in post-Communist society. If the Communist system itself was "abnormal" (as many suggest), so too was the "overemancipation" of women; hence, the very idea of post-Communist normality carries within itself the seeds of gender inequality planted and nurtured in the soil of restored nationhood.

Bodies for Sale: Sex and Transition

The rapidly expanding free market and free market politics and policies in Latvia, which have wrought unemployment, a decrease of state support for the needy, the rapid rise of prices, and the development of a competitive, capital-driven business environment, have also fostered conditions ripe for the massive expansion of the sex business in Latvia. Several factors are of particular note here: first, the economic hardships disproportionately borne by women; second, the commodification and marketability of sex; third, the lack of comprehensive and enforceable laws and regulations in this sphere and the state's laissez-faire approach to the prominent and profitable sex trade. In this section, I also highlight the argument that the aforementioned factors can be better understood by bringing the diverse ethnic composition of Latvia's society into the analysis.

The proportions of the post-Communist sex trade in the mid- to late 1990s are worth noting. In Latvia's capital, Riga, a city of over 800,000 people, about one-third of Latvia's population, there may be between 4,000 and 10,000 prostitutes;[82] criminologists have estimated that 4 to 5 percent of women aged fifteen to twenty-nine years work in the sex business in some way. Police data show that some women working as prostitutes are in their forties and fifties. In 1995 in Riga, there were over five hundred known bordellos, sex clubs, and other establishments offering sexual services.[83]

As advertisement of sex clubs is permitted (though sex clubs themselves are not permitted to operate under a law that requires businesses to be registered with the state), the mass media are full of offers of sexual services. A study by Baltic Media Facts of advertising in Latvia showed that in March 1995, *Ledi Lukss,* a well-known sex club in Riga, placed more ads than *Mikrofōns* (Latvia's leading record company), Kellogg's (the American cereal manufacturer), and Philips Latvia (the German maker of home appliances) combined.[84] Indeed, the competition for clients is fierce, and the ads often offer perks to appeal to the seekers of sexual services, such as a "third hour free" and free champagne.[85] The criminologist Andrejs Vilks noted that "there are enough [advertisements] and they are interesting enough, that this [seems] a product—one that appears to us normal. Here they say, 'this is the best' and so forth [as in other ads], though this is for prostitutes."[86] Notably, sex establishments are not the only ones who profit from the peddling of bodies in the media: a police report from 1995 found that in every issue of the weekly Russian-language newspaper *Reklama,* fifty to seventy sex clubs had placed advertisements. These weekly advertisements brought in an estimated Ls 2,500–3,000 for the newspaper.[87]

Riga is the center of the sex trade in Latvia, but other areas have also experienced the expansion of this industry. In a 1997 newspaper interview, a madam in the southeastern city of Daugavpils suggested that women from all walks of life are entering prostitution: "[Women] are prepared to go who are 35, even 40, tall and short, thin and fat, attractive and ugly." She added that most of her women are not professionally educated, but that "some are saleswomen, accountants, who cannot find work in their fields" and that she "even had one girl who was a student at a university in Riga." The woman, who, by her own admission, organized women in the city for "export" to clients abroad, commented that "it is better to work as a prostitute than to go hungry" and that "the desire to go abroad and offer sexual services is very great."[88]

The economic hardships engendered by the transition to a market economy are widely believed to be the primary explanation for the expansion of prostitution. In an article on women in post-Communist Eastern Europe, Gail Kligman noted that "especially in this period of transformation, secondary economic activities remain critical to economic survival or betterment."[89] This point is iterated and recognized in Latvia by both society and law enforcement officials who have contact with prostitutes. The head of the *tikumības policija* (morality police), the body formerly responsible for policing in this area, described the expansion of the sex business as a "phenomenon of this period of economic reorganization."[90] An officer in the police department suggested that "material circumstances are the determining factor [in women's entering prostitution]."[91]

A survey of workers in the sex industry conducted by the Criminological Research Center in Riga inquired about motives for entering prostitution: "In response to the question of which factors are most salient in explaining the growth of prostitution, 79.3% of respondents replied 'getting money to live.'... In difficult economic circumstances, the wish to earn [money] should not be understood as a wish to acquire luxury goods and so forth, [but rather], in this [economic] situation, the wish to earn should be understood as a need to earn the basics for oneself and one's family."[92] Two officers with the Morality Police in Riga listed the following as the most frequently cited reasons female prostitutes give for entering sex work. As in the Criminological Research Center survey, economic need was the dominant reason. Economic hardship explanations fell into several categories: some, especially single women, cited an inability to find a job that would permit them to support children, elderly parents, or both; some, mostly Russian women, who came to Riga during the occupation or were born of parents who immigrated at that time and never learned Latvian, cited the inability to find a job now that Latvian-language knowledge was required at most places of work; some cited the inability to earn enough money at a day job—these women went on the street after working an "official" job during the day; a few cited the need to earn money to complete or enter higher education. Some other reasons frequently cited were also materialistic, but do not necessarily reflect a response to economic hardship. These included a desire to make money to purchase expensive clothing and cosmetics; a desire to get rich quick; a desire to meet a man and marry him.[93]

The difficult economic conditions fostered by market transition policies and practices explain only part of the expansion of the sex industry. A fuller explanation requires consideration of the legal, political, and discursive context in which this business has flourished. As noted, a section of Riga's criminal police force (known until 1998 as the Morality Police) is assigned responsibility for policing the sex industry, but it operates with few resources and in a legal context where prostitution is neither clearly illegal, where it could be controlled by force of law, nor legal, where it could be regulated, taxed, and/or limited to particular zones. Some aspects of the sex trade, though, are legally forbidden. As noted earlier, sex establishments advertise freely, but they are largely unregistered businesses and, hence, can theoretically be prosecuted for the operation of an unregistered establishment. Prosecution, however, has been very uncommon up to this point: in 1996, of thirty-seven criminal cases prepared by Riga's Morality Police, only two were for the unregistered operation of a business. In addition, "forced" prostitution, the sexual use of children, and pimping are illegal. Even so, the lack of resources of the policing unit assigned to this area, the size of the unit (four workers in 1998), and the legal difficulties inherent in gathering evidence and prosecuting suspected criminals mean that even extant laws are inadequately enforced. Though the head of the policing section estimated that up to 40 percent of prostitutes may be coerced to work in the business, this has not translated to criminal prosecutions of those who are doing the coercion. In fact, most criminal cases prepared by the police were against the prostitutes themselves. In 1996, thirty-four of the criminal cases prepared by the policing unit were against prostitutes for refusing to seek medical aid for venereal diseases.[94] Until early 1998, only four or five pimps had been prosecuted.[95]

Child prostitution is illegal, but the law officers are authorized only to bring children to a state children's home after finding them, and the children are free to leave when they wish. Many girls return to the streets; many have nowhere else to go. The proportion of juveniles in the sex trade, as noted earlier, varies, though the government estimated it to be 12 percent in 1997. A study by the Latvian Family Center suggested that juvenile prostitutes are troubled by more than economic hardship; the survey found that 80 percent of young prostitutes had been sexually abused at an early age.[96]

Legislation dating from 1987, which made prostitution an administrative offense, was abolished in 1995, an act that gave prostitution the curious status of being neither legal nor illegal. In noting the abolition of this law, it is interesting to consider the conditions under which prostitution was made illegal in the late Soviet period:

> Whereas at the time of the revolution prostitution was regarded as a social evil rooted in capitalist inequalities and insecurities for which the prostitutes themselves bore no responsibility, it was now interpreted as a result of moral failings for which the women must take the main share of blame. Accordingly, lawyers, security chiefs, government officials, as well as journalists argued in the press for the criminalization of prostitution; consistent with the view that it was a theoretical impossibility, prostitution had until this time gone unmentioned in the legal code.[97]

Public opinion, again, seems to have shifted from condemnation of individual moral failure to recognition of structural failure to ensure a "normal" life for many women. As a policewoman told me: "If she [the prostitute] could live and earn normally, she would not go out there [on the street]."[98]

Despite overwhelming confirmation from surveys and anecdotal evidence that "at this time, prostitution is driven by individuals' poor material conditions," neither public sentiment nor projects put forth by researchers and legislators have focused on economic solutions to what is largely a problem with *economic* roots. Rather, the debate has centered around whether prostitution should be legal or illegal. The same researcher quoted at the beginning of this paragraph concluded:

> Priority must be given to a law that legalizes prostitution as a trade and guarantees women's sexual freedom. Individual work and individual businesses would be the most appropriate form of this work. . . . We should institute punishment for the prohibition of women's sexual freedom, for failure to pay taxes, and for other [similar] crimes. . . . Such a law could be modeled on the Republic of Latvia's [1918–40] punishment law (1933), which has, without reason, not been renewed.[99]

Notably, though the author suggested that the root of prostitution's expansion is to be found in the current economic situation, this issue was raised in none of his suggestions for minimizing the problem. Rather, he advocated a renewal of earlier laws on prostitution and suggested that prostitution be legalized and women's "sexual freedom" be enshrined, though the existence of such freedom in a context where women go into prostitution to alleviate desperate economic circumstances is questionable.

Various subthemes have emerged in the debate over legality. In the one illustrated below, issues of economic opportunity and equal citizenship for vulnerable women are submerged beneath a discourse of "rights" that echoes the position asserting "sexual freedom" noted above. The notion of prostitution as a "human right" has been put forth, as in this memo, "Question of the Legalization or Criminalization of Prostitution," from the methodological section of the Latvian National General Prosecutor's Office: "One could speak about human rights—can one punish a person for the fact that she sells herself for money, if, of course, no harm is done to anyone else?"[100] Ultimately, the prosecutor's office came down on the side of legalization. At the very least, suggested a deputy on the Riga City Council, prostitution is broadly construed as a question of freedom: "Most of our fellow citizens feel that this question is not worth discussing. Let each do as he wants [to do]. Indeed, why restrict this free choice[?]"[101]

Other positions taken by public officials and specialists highlight particular practical concerns. Many share a favorable stance toward the legalization of prostitution. The former Minister of the Interior, Ziedonis Čevers, favored such a move as a way to rein in the spread of acquired immune deficiency syndrome (AIDS) in the country. Other venereal diseases are of concern as well: from 1987 to 1993, the incidence of gonorrhea rose in Riga from an estimated 116.6 per 100,000 persons to 204.2 per 100,000.[102] Some officials support legalization as a means to halt the movement of street prostitutes into downtown areas and to curb the influence of pimps and organized crime in the sex business. Another "specialist" on prostitution issues has suggested that the city of Riga could "supplement its budget" by opening a public house and collecting rent.[103]

Prostitution and its rapid and massive spread in Latvia are construed, then, as presumably unfortunate but nonetheless inevitable by-products of marketization and "democratic development."[104] In this sense, prostitution is broadly accepted, at least tolerated, and public and professional discourse has, rather than questioning the trends in post-Communist development that have pushed women otherwise unable to make a living in Latvia into prostitution, narrowly defined the issue as a juridical one.

Though the current state of juridical limbo in which prostitution exists is widely seen as problematic, legalization itself presents issues that go beyond moral considerations. The head of the former Morality Police pointed out that "it cannot be legalized because the U.N. Convention forbids it."[105] Indeed, the United Nations Convention of 1949 takes a stand against trade in

human beings and human exploitation, a formulation that appears to proscribe state-sanctioned prostitution.

The problem of growing prostitution has elicited little interest or concrete action from the male-dominated state, but it has not found its way onto
the agenda of most women's organizations in Latvia either. For example, the
1993 Program of Action of the Latvian Women's Organization Cooperation
Council, a body uniting over a dozen women's organizations, highlighted
issues of equality, education, and economic independence for women, but
did not raise the issue of sexual exploitation of women.[106] Similarly, the
Future Strategic Goals iterated by the Latvian National Preparatory Committee for the 1995 United Nations Conference on Women included the
strengthening of social guarantees for families and increased opportunities
for women's participation in political and social life, but failed to address
the commodification of women in the sex trade.[107]

Though the issue has not been iterated in public discourse as an ethnic
one, it is notable that a substantial proportion of prostitutes as well as pimps
are non-Latvian. According to the estimate of an officer of the Morality Police, the proportion of prostitutes in Riga who are Russian (or Russian speakers) may be as high as 90 percent. The percentage of non-Latvians in Riga is
also high—about 60 percent[108]—so their domination of the market is more
easily explained than is their overrepresentation. Several factors are salient in
considering the issue of overrepresentation. First, as noted by the Morality
Police, some non-Latvian prostitutes indicate that their lack of Latvian language knowledge makes it difficult to find work. This problem may be compounded by the fact that those non-Latvian women (and men) without
citizenship are barred by law from holding civil service as well as selected
other jobs. Second, though ethnic Latvians dominate the political sphere, ethnic Russians dominate the sphere of business, both legal and illegal, in Latvia.
Thus the widespread shadow economy, which, according to Ministry of Fi-
nance estimates, constitutes 20 to 50 percent of the gross national product and
employs 14 to 20 percent of the labor force, is predominantly Russian. Ole
Norgaard noted that an important "legacy of the Soviet period is the widespread use of informal networks and mutual, unregistered, and often illegal
favors, which was an important aspect of the planned economy."[109] The continued operation of informal networks in ensuring economic survival or betterment may explain to some degree why, in a business dominated at the top
by Russians, the lower echelons are also populated by Russians.

Third, the proportional overrepresentation of non-Latvian women
among prostitutes in Latvia may contribute to official ambivalence toward
the issue. The massive expansion of the sex business presents concerns ranging from associated crimes like the sale and use of narcotics to the exploita-

tion of economically vulnerable segments of the population, but the issue has not generated much interest in the public sphere. As noted above, ethnicity has not surfaced in the discourse around the issue, but there may be salience in the silence as well. The dominance of the commercial sex business by ethnic "others" (non-Latvians) may allow Latvian-dominated political structures to cast the issue of prostitution as a juridical rather than a national (Latvian) one and to marginalize it as not fundamental to state and national interests. It is worth noting, however, that the lack of legal regulation of business (particularly where it affects women) is the norm rather than the exception. As suggested earlier, regulation of sexual discrimination or harassment in the workplace (where women of all ethnicities are found) has not generated interest in Latvia (or, for that matter, in neighboring post-Communist states), suggesting that the link to ethnicity and the "othering" of the sex trade, while it may well be present, is not entirely clear.

Sex and sexualized bodies have, from the early post-Communist period, been a tremendous source of profit. Though prostitution was not nearly as widespread in 1991 and 1992 as it was by the mid-1990s, these years saw a massive expansion of pornography. Indeed, the distribution of pornographic images was not limited to the everywhere-available glossy magazines bedecked with women in various stages of undress. Even mainstream publications followed the trend. Valentine Moghadam noted that "with the end of government subsidies and the proliferation of new and independent presses engaged in a fierce battle for survival, many newspapers [and magazines] began to adorn their articles with nudity."[110] From a less economistic perspective, Watson suggested that "the pornographic icon [was] . . . the new symbol of freedom."[111]

Pornography, though still widely available, is no longer novel, and a rapidly saturated market has led to a decline in both purveyors and materials. Prostitution has, however, flourished, as it appears to lack for neither service providers nor service purchasers. Indeed, the combination of expanding poverty among women, a shrinking job base for women with few technical skills or Latvian language skills, the fabulous profitability of prostitution for those who control the economic exchange of sex (less for the prostitutes themselves), and the current juridical status of prostitution, which neither prohibits nor formally regulates the sex market, offers little reason to believe that the sex industry will decline in the near future.

Conclusion

The (re)construction of normality in post-Communist Latvia has had important consequences for women. Perhaps in the field of gender roles and norms, more than any other area, the process of transforming and reasserting a "natural" order is readily apparent. Changes in this field have elicited comparatively little contestation or conflict. The return to a "natural" gender regime where women are defined by the private sphere and men by the public sphere is widely regarded as appropriate after the "overemancipation" of the Soviet period. Domestication marks both the normalization of the gender regime and a potential step toward the normalization of the demographic crisis of the nation. The shared sense that the Soviet period distorted gender relations and the common concern with the demographic position of Latvians help to explain the lack of contest between the narratives of change that dominate the political sphere.

The commodification of women, apparent in the booming pornography and sex trades, although not foreseen in any narrative of change, flows from the elevation of free markets and the power of the profit motive in post-Communism. The freedom of the sex trade is underscored by the lack of regulation in the area: prostitution is neither legal, where it could be controlled, nor illegal, where it could be potentially reduced. The supply of women for the sex trade is plentiful in a period of widespread economic dislocation, and the profits available to successful "entrepreneurs" in this trade are tremendous. The domination of prostitution by non-Latvian women is also arguably a factor in the lack of contest or interest in the public sphere; these are not, after all, the mothers of the nation.

In the chapter introduction, I suggested that both the domestication and commodification of women are linked to the broader transformation taking place in the post-Communist space. Women's experience of the transformation is affected by the social processes emergent from the dominant narratives of normalization as well as by the large-scale structural changes wrought by Latvia's entry into the capitalist marketplace. Both dominant narratives of change have shared a nation-centered orientation that reinforces and may even enshrine women's subjugated status in society. Hence, though the end of Communism has seen a clear expansion of rights and opportunities, not the least of which are the freedoms of speech and press and the creation of multiparty democracy, women as a group have been disproportionately affected by the negative processes engendered by the post-Communist transformation, including the deepening impoverishment of the population, the widespread loss of living-wage jobs, the open discrimination against women, and the expanding market in bodies for sexual consumption.

Transformation and Normalization: A Conclusion to the Study

On the eastern flank of the Freedom Monument, three dramatic figures labor to free themselves from the shackles that bind them. These are the *važu rāvēji* (chain breakers), and they represent

> humankind's yearning for freedom. . . . The muscular stance, strain-ing legs, hands pulling with iron strength suggest a will and respon-sibility before history: the power of the nation has awakened and it seeks to throw off the chains of subjugation. . . .
>
> They are three men bound together in their chains. Three, who are united in a common goal: supporting one another and each seek-ing to cast off the shackles, the figures represent an expressive rhythm, as if in a common step they work toward their objective.[1]

The notion of casting off a burden, dramatically described above, appeared in various guises in the period of opposition. Although Gorbachev's initiatives were recognized for their importance in opening the door to independent initiatives, those who rejected the Soviet order continued to feel bound by old constraints. Dainis Īvāns quoted the words of an Estonian villager, who commented that "restructuring *(perestroika)* has created new characteristics [in the order]: our chain is longer, [but] the bowl is further, and the dog continues to bark."[2] So the chain was extended, but it remained wrapped around state and society. The sense that the opposition was casting off a yoke was woven into the rhetoric of opposition leaders: "As we go forth at this moment, we must fight to throw off our shoulders the cross we bear as a vanishing and intimidated small nation. If we fail to do this, if we are not able to do this, our ideals can become the fall and graveyard of Latvians. . . . I believe we will be united. . . . We will triumph, if we believe, and we progress together with our beliefs. If our revolution will be and remain a revolution of song, love, and spiritual activity."[3]

I began the book with the assertion that dramatic changes in Latvia, and in Eastern Europe more generally, represent, among other things, a reimagination of the notion of revolution. On the one hand, revolution continued to be, as it has historically been, a vehicle of opposition against a despised social order. On the other hand, these revolutions represent something of a challenge to the way that the concept of modern revolution, born of the great revolutions, has been understood in both academic and popular literature. Together with the powerful imperative of progress—the hallmark of revolutionary radicalism—there is an equally powerful imperative of return. Revolution, hence, is realized in its dual meaning: a progressive rush forward and a return to a point of origin. In Eastern Europe, the opposition period accommodates both streams of change, but in the post-Communist period, the revolutions break apart.

These revolutions are also set apart from the great revolutions because they were born of visions that did not feature a "radiant future" such as humankind had not experienced, but rather the staid, mild goal of "normality" (these were, after all, "velvet" revolutions). For social scientists, this appears all the more odd in that Karl Marx, a founder of revolutionary theory, foresaw revolution as a vehicle of radical change that would be driven by the conflict between the oppressed proletariat and their bourgeois oppressors. He is understood as a conflict theorist because he, and his ideological and academic progeny, believed the normal tendency of modern societies to be inherently conflictual. Even apparently ordered societies, hence, mask latent clashes of interests among interest groups competing for positions, power, and limited resources. Tensions, as between classes in Marx's theory, may flame into revolution and radical change.

21   The chain breakers on the Freedom Monument

On the other hand, functionalist theorists (the bane of conflict theorists) have suggested that societies naturally tend toward order and equilibrium rather than conflict: *that* is the nature of society. To this point, it has been the common assumption of social theorists that functionalism cannot, consequently, accommodate events like revolutions: those, after all, seem to belie the notion that societies tend toward equilibrium. The revolutions in Eastern Europe, however, seem to straddle the two theoretical streams in an unusual way. The revolutions emerged from some of the conflicts that boiled beneath the surface of the seemingly placid Soviet society, yet they also seem to evidence a societal tendency toward equilibrium because their goals elevated notions of an organic "normality" and restoration of "normal" societal order.

I have sought to retain a degree of flexibility in my use of "normal" and "normality" because I wanted to highlight the multiplicity of understandings that are attached to the notion. In its quotidian incarnation, normality has a "commonsense" quality. It can appear as a hope and ambition during the period of change, as a description of places and times outside present-day Latvia, and as a template for transformation. The notions that help to define what is "normal" and "abnormal" also exist in a wide array of metaphors that can call forth binary opposites like authentic/false, truthful/deceptive, clean/polluting, democratic/totalitarian, or civilized/uncivilized. All of these appeared in the discourses and contests of opposition and change. The "common sense" of normality was the soil in which public narratives about normality grew, but it is not adequate as a research tool because it is a loose (and sometimes contradictory) amalgamation of ideas, hopes, visions, symbols, and discourses. Hence, this work attempted to theorize this notion before turning it back toward its place of origin as a lens of analysis.

I have relied on theorized notions of normality and ideal-typical narratives grounded in the particular conditions of post-Communism because, while these dramatic transformations surely qualify for a place among the great revolutions of the modern world, they also represent the reimagination and transformation of revolution's rhetoric, symbols, and aspirations. The singing, velvet, and gentle revolutions of this region represent a special and particular moment in global social change.

Beyond the scope of this work, which focuses on the early years of change, important to note is the way that notions of "normality" have become more complicated as the economic pain of competitive capitalism has become more pressing, especially for those on society's margins—among them, older people, unemployed people, and rural peasantry. Where normality once definitively marked that which was "not Soviet," the notion has taken on, for some, aspects of nostalgia for things Soviet: the oppressive political regime is not widely missed, but the broad welfare state and its relative equality can appear attractive to those occupying society's lower strata and gazing up with envy and longing at those who have, by hook or crook, managed to gather the trump cards of the capitalist order. At the beginning of the twenty-first century, notions about what constitutes a "normal" life continue to evolve as cultural and historical aspects are increasingly overshadowed by powerful economic forces.

New Roads, Old Maps

In this work I have sought to broaden understanding of post-Communist transformations by exploring the relation and contestation between narratives at different sites of change. As I have shown, the degree, nature, and stakes of contests vary across sites of change and even within them. In Chapters 3 through 5 in particular, I have endeavored to present the shadow cases of history that inform different narratives and to follow up to the early 1990s the way that those narratives have influenced social change in Latvia. These chapters show that there is no single logic of change that dominates post-Communist transformation; rather, change proceeds from the conflicts and complementarities between narratives in different fields.

The political field represents the most visible and contested field of change. The post-Communist elections and the case of citizenship law in Latvia offered prisms through which to view these contests. The stakes in this field were high: in a context where the state was widely seen as the most critical vehicle for change, legislative power was the key to realizing a particular vision of normality. The election campaign and its constituent rhetoric, platforms, and posters were part of a process of defining and disseminating different notions about change. As well, the examination of the path toward a citizenship law in Latvia highlighted the salience of the narrative contest and electoral outcome in anticipating change.

At the end of the first decade of post-Communist change, the political arena is still a site of intense and important change. In some respects, the picture at this point is not radically different from the picture of Latvia at the dawn of its renewed independence: the contest between those who seek to move Latvia rapidly toward European structures and a multicultural modernity and those who prioritize the restoration of a Latvia for Latvians that joins Europe on its own conditions is still apparent. In 1998, this contest was played out around a revised citizenship bill that was to extend the citizenship and the franchise to an increased number of (mostly non-Latvian) inhabitants. Though the result of the contest was, as earlier, a more rather than less inclusive bill, the powerful cleavage between those who sought to keep political power closely in the hands of the prewar citizenry and its descendants and those who sought a more "European" and integrative approach was again revealed. In 1999, the same cleavage marked the political fight over language legislation, proposed by a coalition of For Fatherland and Freedom and the Latvian National Independence Movement, which sought to mandate the priority use of the Latvian language at public events and even, to some extent, in the realm of private business.

Despite this, a more diversified ideological climate is apparent. The first post-Communist elections were very much about rejecting the past and choosing a path of change, but subsequent elections (in October 1995 and October 1998) have turned, to a greater extent, on perceptions about the prosperity or pain wrought by economic changes. These elections have also seen dramatic turnover in the Parliament: in the second elections to the Saeima, fully three-quarters of elected deputies were new. This, as well, has led to changes in the ideologies and interests of the governing body, though early cleavages will probably continue to be powerful for some time.

The discussion of change in spaces and places pointed to the various degrees of contest that attached to transformation in the changing of street names, the post-Communist borders, and the privatization and reprivatization of rural land. It also highlighted the point that land in post-Communist Eastern Europe is far more than just physical space: it is a symbol of history and the nation. The slow pace of land reform in this region is attributable, certainly, to the bureaucratic labyrinths that plague post-Communist countries—but it is also attributable to the politics, dreams, and fears that accompany changes in the status of this potent symbol. At a 2001 debate on land privatization in the Russian Legislature, deputies opposed to the plan unfurled a banner with the dramatic words, "To sell land is to sell the motherland!" In Poland, land restitution legislation has stalled for a decade. Even in countries determined to privatize and return land, the ghosts of history and the dreams of individuals and nations have had and continue to have powerful effects.

In Latvia, conflicts between individuals over rights to land continue to simmer, and countless hectares of land still stand fallow, overgrown, and untended as agricultural policy has failed to reverse the dual trends of underproduction and rural poverty.

I have argued that gender roles and norms have been a field of change that has evoked little contest in state and society after Communism. The combination of a complementarity of narratives has been underpinned, on the one hand, by a commonly held concern with national demographics that does not question the association between women and the private sphere, a location defined by mothering and care of the family. The domestication of women has been widely taken to be part of a general return to a normal gender regime that was distorted by the Soviet order. On the other hand, there has been a shared silence about the commodification of women in the new market economy. The domination of the sex market by non-Latvian women renders it a marginal concern for those who seek to protect the mothers of the nation. As well, the extraordinary profitability of the trade in flesh and the veneration of the modern free market, which underpins the dislocations as well as the wealth of the post-Communist period, render the sex market virtually unassailable at this time.

At the end of the 1990s, the status of women remained an open question. On the one hand, the problems of disproportionate female poverty, under-employment, and exploitation in the sex market have not been solved—in fact, they have largely not even been addressed in a context where the no-tion of "women's rights" has yet to make significant inroads. On the other hand, the 1999 parliamentary election of the president brought, for the first time, a woman, Dr. Vaira Vīķe-Freiberga, to the position. While the post is largely symbolic, the power of symbols, as this book has sought to show, should not be underestimated. The vision of a powerful woman in the public sphere may at the very least increase the legitimacy of female leadership in a post-Communist climate that has sorely lacked women's presence in posi-tions of authority. Only a changed climate is likely to bring to the fore the pressing women's issues that remain marginal in the post-Communist public sphere.

The span of this book, despite its focus on the early post-Communist period, runs the length of much of the twentieth century because the shadow cases of history—the interwar period of independence as well as the Soviet period—linger beneath the surface of the narratives and initiatives of social change. From these periods, post-Communist actors excavate meanings about what is normal, natural, and appropriate, as well as what is abnormal, unnatural, and contrary to a hoped-for way of life. In some cases there is broad agreement on these points, and in others there is fierce contestation. I have sought in this work to step into the spaces in which these excavations are taking place and to use the words and symbols and practices I find there to build a new and different prism for looking at social change in Latvia. I hope that I have succeeded in making a case for the utility of this prism in understanding the transformation there. More important, I hope that this book can convey the amalgam of elation, confusion, achievement, displacement, and complexity that has accompanied the early period of post-Communist transformation.

The River of Fate

> I crossed all the rivers,
> I could not cross the Daugava.
> I could not cross the Daugava—
> Its water full of souls.
> —Latvian folk song

The Daugava River has been a powerful symbol of the nation. From the Bearslayer who would, in the nineteenth-century epic, rise from the depths of the Daugava to overcome his foe and free the nation, to the myriad songs and poems dedicated to Latvia's "river of fate," the Daugava is a powerful poetic space and a link between the myths and histories of the past and the visions and hopes of the present and future. In the song above, the souls of the dead call out from the depths, imploring the living to seek freedom and to realize the desires of the nation. In the cultural canon, the Daugava also serves to protect. In a folktale of the Bearslayer predating Pumpurs's epic, the witch's three-headed son, who seeks to be the "strongest in the land," wishes to destroy the stronger Bearslayer. As the monster rushes to the Baltic to fulfill his quest, a terrible storm rises on the Daugava, and the waves on the river ripple and crash on the shore. Hearing the river's fury, the Bearslayer rushes to confront the enemy. It is even said that in 1920, as Latvia's army confronted the troops of Pavel Bermont-Avalov, who were preparing to occupy Riga, a poem, "Daugava," by Latvia's best-known poet, Rainis, inspired the soldiers to achieve decisive victory over the enemy troops. The Daugava, across time, is portrayed in the cultural canon as a site of battle, of mourning, of triumph, and of remembrance. In the 1980s, it was a site of national resistance and the rebirth of civil society, as thousands of residents fought the construction of the Daugavpils hydroelectric station and elevated the centrality of the Daugava for Latvian culture, history, and preservation. The river of fate is, indeed, an interesting prism through which to view Latvian history and social change because it has been a powerful symbol of national ideas, ideals, and aspirations across centuries.

> A thousand voices, a thousand sorrows—
> One Mother Daugava for all.
> —from Rainis's "Daugava"

In spring 1996, nearly a decade after the birth of the campaign to stop the Soviet authorities' construction of the Daugavpils hydroelectric station (HES), the City Council of Daugavpils passed a resolution calling for building of the HES, citing the need to improve the city's and region's economic situation and to create jobs for residents. In July 1999, a committee representing local governments, business interests, and Latvia's Agricultural University met to consider the possibility and to study the proposed plans. Though in 2001 the project had not yet come to fruition, it was still generating interest, particularly among those who would oversee its construction. Interestingly, some of the environmental impact studies being used to assess the project have been those used by the Soviet government (and condemned by the opposition) in the 1980s.

In a July 1999 article on the proposed project, the newspaper *Diena*, which printed the story on page 8, noted that at a meeting on the project in Daugavpils, almost no one offered objections to the plan. Only one man, presenting his personal opinion, suggested that areas with such unique and untouched natural beauty were few in number in Europe. On this basis, he expressed reservations about building the HES. Other local residents, in particular those in areas threatened with flooding by the HES, indicated to the newspaper that they also objected to the construction project.[4] Environmentalists, too, continue to reject the project, but their voices are whispers in the wind of post-Communist capitalism.

In view of the course of development, it does not come as a surprise that this project, harshly condemned as an affront to nature and the nation in the late 1980s, is elevated by many as a potential economic boon in the difficult circumstances of post-Communism. As in the electoral arena, the politics of symbols has largely given way to a politics of pragmatism and profit. This in itself is neither inherently negative nor positive. It is, however, indicative of a particular moment in post-Communist development. During this period of massive transformation, the visions and hopes of the opposition period and early post-Communism mingle with the social and economic dislocations and problems of the present, and the outcome of the processes of change is, like the ultimate fate of the Daugava, anything but certain. And so the Daugava, Latvia's river of fate, resting place of the Bearslayer, muse of Latvian poets and composers and storytellers, again reflects in its cascading waters the profound changes that have moved and continue to move Latvia toward its own uncertain destiny.

Notes

Chapter 1

1. Andrejs Pumpurs, *Lāčplēsis* (Riga: Sol Vita, 1995). All translations are my own.

2. In his book on the campaign against the building of the Daugavpils hydroelectric station on the Daugava River in the late 1980s, Dainis Īvāns also noted that "Latvia never has been and never will be a mono-religious land. Rather, deeply in our subconscious is etched the distrust of Pumpurs' Bearslayer toward the German-erected Church and the incompatibility between Rainis's Indulis and the cross-bearers." "Rainis's Indulis" refers to Rainis's book *Indulis un Ārija.* (Īvāns, *Gadijuma karakalps* [Riga: Vieda, 1995], 101.)

3. Īvāns, *Gadijuma karakalps,* 106–7.

4. Pumpurs, *Lāčplēsis.*

5. Quoted in Romuald J. Misiunas and Rein Taagepera, *The Baltic States: Years of Dependence, 1940–1990* (Berkeley and Los Angeles: University of California Press, 1993), 304.

6. Īvāns, *Gadijuma karakalps,* 53–54.

7. Interview with Īvāns in *Diena* (Riga), 2 May 1991, 3.

8. Quoted in *The Greatest Tyranny: Documentary Facts About the Organized Murder of the Baltic People,* pamphlet published by the Estonian National Committee in Canada, the Latvian Information Centre in Canada, and the Lithuanian National Federation in Canada, 8.

9. This figure is from *These Names Accuse: Nominal List of Latvians Deported to Soviet Russia in 1940–1941* (Stockholm: Latvian National Foundation, 1992), vi.

10. Alberts Ozols, *Latvijas vēsture, III daļa, 1914–1967* (New York: Ņujorkas Latviešu Ev. Lut. Draudzes Skolas Padome, 1967), 102.

11. Introduction in *Latvijas valsts atjaunošana, 1986–1993,* ed. Valdis Blūzma et al. (Riga: Latvijas universitātes žurnāls "Latvijas vēsture" fonds, 1998), 3.

12. Michael D. Kennedy, "An Introduction to East European Ideology and Identity in Transformation," in *Envisioning Eastern Europe: Postcommunist Cultural Studies,* ed. Michael D. Kennedy (Ann Arbor: University of Michigan Press, 1994), 3–4.

13. See, for example, *Debating Revolutions,* ed. Nikki Keddie (New York: New York University Press, 1995).

14. I am indebted to Istvan Rev for suggesting this point to me during his visit to the University of Michigan, Ann Arbor, in 1994.

15. Aleksandr I. Solzhenitsyn, *The Gulag Archipelago Two* (New York: Harper & Row, 1975), 91.

16. Stephen E. Hanson, *Time and Revolution: Marxism and the Design of Soviet Institutions* (Chapel Hill: University of North Carolina Press, 1997), 19.

17. "Between Utopia and Dystopia: The Labilities of Nationalism in Eastern Europe," in Kennedy, *Envisioning Eastern Europe,* 154.

18. "Culture in Action," *American Sociological Review* 51 (1986): 273–86.

19. Eduards Berklavs, *Zināt un neaizmirst* (Riga: Preses Nams, 1998), 416–17.

20. United Press International report, reprinted in Ojārs Kalniņš, ed., *Chautauqua/Jūrmala, 1986: A Latvian-American Perspective* (Rockville, Md.: American Latvian Association of the United States, 1987), 73.

21. The text of this letter is reprinted in Elmārs Pelkaus, ed., *Tauta: Zeme: Valsts: Latvijas Nacionālās neatkarības kustība dokumentos* (Riga: Latvijas Valsts arhīvs, 1995), 16–17.

22. The letter is reprinted in *Neatkarības atgūšana: Atmodas laiks dokumentos* (Riga: Latvijas Valsts arhīvs, 1996), 14–17.

23. "Ideologies and Social Revolutions: Reflections on the French Case," *Journal of Modern History* 57 (1985): 57–96.

24. *Gadijuma karakalps, 55.* The reference to "hearing" the Daugava recalls the story of the Bear-slayer because, according to the story, he has the large ears of a bear. In the struggle with the Dark Knight on the shores of the Daugava, he loses his ears to the sword of his enemy. As the Bearslayer is, of course, a symbol of the nation, the renewed ability of the nation to "hear" the call of the Daugava may be symbolic of a turn of fate. The Daugava as a "shield" also evokes the epic, as the Bearslayer is confronted on the river's shores by the Dark Knight wielding his sword.

25. I first introduced these labels in an article: Daina Stukuls, "Imagining the Nation: Campaign Posters of the First Postcommunist Elections in Latvia," *East European Politics and Societies* 11 (1997).

26. Jan Gross, "Poland: From Civil Society to Political Nation," in *Eastern Europe in Revolution,* ed. Ivo Banac (Ithaca: Cornell University Press, 1992), 68.

27. The quoted terms are used by C. Wright Mills, *The Sociological Imagination* (New York: Oxford University Press, 1959).

Chapter 2

1. Blūzma et al., *Latvijas valsts atjaunošana, 1986–1993,* 1.

2. Juris Dreifelds, "Latvian National Rebirth," *Problems of Communism* (July–August 1989): 79.

3. Jānis Taurens, *Latvijas vēstures pamatjautājumi un valsts konstitucionālie principi* (Riga: Latvijas Republikas Naturalizācijas pārvalde, 1996), 130.

4. Daina Bleiere, *Latvija, 1985–1996 gadā: Notikumu hronika* (Riga: N.I.M.S., 1996), 8.

5. Dzintra Bungs, "Zaļie sienāži: nemierīgā Latvijas jaunatne," in *Latvija šodien, 1987* (Rockville, Md.: World Federation of Free Latvians, 1987), 17–19.

6. Steven Pfaff, "Collective Identity and Informal Groups in Revolutionary Mobilization: East Germany in 1989," *Social Forces* 75 (1996): 99–100.

7. Andris Kolbergs, *Dumpis uz laupītāju kuģa* (Riga: Lauku apgāds, 1993), 17.

8. Berklavs, *Zināt un neaizmirst,* 416–17.

9. Andrejs Plakans, *The Latvians: A Short History* (Stanford: Hoover Institution Press, 1995), 147.

10. Michael Burawoy and Janos Lukacs, *The Radiant Past: Ideology and Reality in Hungary's Road to Capitalism* (Chicago: University of Chicago Press, 1992), 147.

11. Rasma Kārkliņš, *Ethnic Relations in the USSR: The Perspective from Below* (Boston: Allen & Unwin, 1986), 67.

12. Kolbergs, *Dumpis uz laupītāju kuģa,* 18–19.

13. Kolbergs, *Dumpis uz laupītāju kuģa,* 19–21.

14. Dzintra Bungs, "Zaļie sienāži: nemierīgā Latvijas jaunatne," 17.

15. This conceptualization is based in part on William A. Gamson and David S. Meyer, "Framing Political Opportunity," in *Comparative Perspectives on Social Movements: Political Opportunities, Mobilizing Structures, and Cultural Framings,* ed. Doug McAdam, John D. McCarthy, and Mayer N. Zald (New York: Cambridge University Press, 1996), 276–77.

16. Kalniņš, *Chautauqua/Jurmala, 1986,* 53.

17. Kalniņš, *Chautauqua/Jurmala, 1986,* 36–38.

18. Kalniņš, *Chautauqua/Jurmala, 1986,* 90.

19. Ļubova Zīle, "Latvijas atmodas ceļš (1986–1991)," *Latvijas vēsture* 4 (1993): 42.

20. "Opportunities and Framing in the Eastern European Revolts of 1989," in McAdam, McCarthy, and Zald, *Comparative Perspectives on Social Movements: Political Opportunities, Mobilizing Structures, and Cultural Framings,* 100–101.

21. Īvāns, *Gadijuma karakalps,* 89.

22. Ļubova Zīle, conversation with author, Riga, April 1997.

23. Abner Cohen, *Urban Ethnicity* (London: Tavistock, 1974), ix.

24. Cerulo, *Identity Designs,* 120–21, 129.

25. Zīle, "Latvijas atmodas ceļš (1986–1991)," *Latvijas vēsture* 4 (1993): 42–43.

26. Ļubova Zīle, "Neformālo organizāciju veidošanās un darbība," in *Latvijas valsts atjaunošana, 1986–1993,* ed. Valdis Blūzma et al., 99–100.

27. *Staburags '88: Vides aizsardzības kluba žurnāls* 1 (1988): 5.

28. Zīle, "Latvijas atmodas ceļš (1986–1991)," *Latvijas vēsture* 4 (1993): 44.

29. Zīle, "Latvijas atmodas ceļš (1986–1991)," *Latvijas vēsture* 4 (1993): 45.

30. Berklavs, *Zināt un neaizmirst,* 444.

31. Pfaff, "Collective Identity and Information Groups in Revolutionary Mobilization," 96.

32. Zīle, "Latvijas atmodas ceļš (1986–1991)," *Latvijas vēsture* 4 (1993).

33. Zīle, "Latvijas atmodas ceļš (1986–1991)," *Latvijas vēsture* 4 (1993).

34. Dreifelds, "Latvian National Rebirth," 82–83.

35. Pāvils Brūvers, "1988. gada 25. marts," in *Latvija šodien, 1988* (Rockville, Md.: World Federation of Free Latvians, 1988), 23.

36. Dreifelds, "Latvian National Rebirth," 83.

37. Brūvers, "1988. gada 25. marts," 23.

38. See, for instance, Jane I. Dawson, *Eco-Nationalism: Anti-Nuclear Activism and National Identity in Russia, Lithuania, and Ukraine* (Durham: Duke University Press, 1996).

39. Zīle, "Latvijas atmodas ceļš (1986–1991)," *Latvijas vēsture* 3 (1993): 3.

40. Quoted in Zīle, "Latvijas atmodas ceļš (1986–1991)," *Latvijas vēsture* 3 (1993): 5.

41. *Latvija šodien, 1988,* 28–31.

42. Mavriks Vulfsōns, *Nationality Latvian? No, Jewish: Cards on the Table* (Riga: Jumava, 1998), 81–83. In his book, Vulfsōns offered an interesting follow-up to this story: "During a break in the proceedings, [Boriss] Pugo hurried up to me. Flushed with anger, he hissed: 'Do you know what you have just done? You have killed Soviet Latvia!' "

43. Īvāns, *Gadijuma karakalps,* 124.

44. Zīle, "Latvijas atmodas ceļš (1986–1991)," *Latvijas vēsture* 3 (1993): 36.

45. The Lielvārdes belt is a folk relic in which, according to folk wisdom, the history of the nation is woven in symbols.

46. Īvāns, *Gadijuma karakalps,* 106.

47. Text reprinted in Pelkaus, *Tauta: Zeme: Valsts,* 28.

48. Pelkaus, *Tauta: Zeme: Valsts,* 48.

49. Dreifelds, "Latvian National Rebirth," 84.

50. Program reprinted in *Latvija šodien, 1988,* 84–87.

51. Zīle, "Latvijas atmodas ceļš (1986–1991)," *Latvijas vēsture* 1 (1995): 51.

52. Īvāns, *Gadijuma karakalps,* 139–40.

53. "Master Frames and Cycles of Protest," in *Frontiers in Social Movement Theory,* ed. Aldon D. Morris and Carole McClurg Mueller (New Haven: Yale University Press, 1992), 136–37.

54. Zīle, "Latvijas atmodas ceļš (1986–1991)," *Latvijas vēsture* 1 (1995): 51.

55. Snow and Benford, "Master Frames and Cycles of Protest," 140.

56. Snow and Benford, "Master Frames and Cycles of Protest," 140.

57. Dreifelds, "Latvian National Rebirth," 86.

58. Pelkaus, *Tauta: Zeme: Valsts,* 6.

59. Īvāns, *Gadijuma karakalps,* 139.

60. Bleire, *Latvija, 1985–1996 gadā,* 14–18.

61. Zīle, "Latvijas atmodas ceļš (1986–1991)," *Latvijas vēsture* 3 (1995): 30.

62. Dreifelds, "Latvian National Rebirth," 87.

63. Zīle, "Latvijas atmodas ceļš (1986–1991)," *Latvijas vēsture* 3 (1995): 58.

64. Zīle, "Latvijas atmodas ceļš (1986–1991)," *Latvijas vēsture* 3 (1995): 58–59.

65. Plakans, *The Latvians: A Short History,* 177.

66. Jack F. Matlock, *Autopsy of an Empire: The American Ambassador's Account of the Collapse of the Soviet Union* (New York: Random House, 1995), 235.

67. Tatiana Kukarina and Vladimir Tikhomirov, *Pochemu pogib Interfront? Istoriia odnogo politicheskogo uroka* (Riga: Latviiskaia assotsiatsiia sodeistviia vozrozhdeniiu Rossii, 1991).

68. Uldis Ģērmanis, *Latviešu tautas piedzīvojumi* (Riga: Jāņa sēta, 1990), 358.
69. Lieven, *The Baltic Revolution*, 193.
70. Kukarina and Tikhomirov, *Pochemu pogib Interfront?*
71. Bleire, *Latvija, 1985–1996 gadā*, 47.
72. Bleire, *Latvija, 1985–1996 gadā*, 43–46.
73. Bleire, *Latvija, 1985–1996 gadā*, 46–49.
74. Plakans, *The Latvians*, 179.
75. Bleire, *Latvija, 1985–1996 gadā*, 56.
76. Bleire, *Latvija, 1985–1996 gadā*, 56.

Chapter 3

1. Quoted in Vaidelotis Apsītis, *Brīvības piemineklis* (Riga: Zinātne, 1993), 135.
2. Apsītis, *Brīvības piemineklis*, 148.
3. At the time that the election took place, the English translation of the body's name was "Supreme Soviet." Later, "Soviet" was dropped, and the accepted translation came to be "Supreme Council."
4. For convenience, I refer to the contestants in the election as "political organizations" rather than "parties and coalitions."
5. Guillermo O'Donnell and Phillipe C. Schmitter, *Transitions from Authoritarian Rule: Tentative Conclusions About Uncertain Democracies* (Baltimore: Johns Hopkins University Press, 1986), 61–64. Their observations are primarily the product of research on Latin America and Southern Europe.
6. "Kandidātu programmas—balsotāju izvēle—Latvijas nākotne," *Diena*, 1 June 1993, 2.
7. "Solījumi 5. Saeimas vēlētājiem," *AP MP* (supplement in *Diena*), 14 May 1993.
8. "Solījumi 5. Saeimas vēlētājiem," 3.
9. Lisa Tickner, *The Spectacle of Women: Imagery of the Suffrage Campaign, 1907–14* (Chicago: University of Chicago Press, 1988), ix.
10. Sonya O. Rose, *Limited Livelihoods: Gender and Class in Nineteenth-Century England* (Berkeley and Los Angeles: University of California Press, 1992), 7–8. Rose does not explicitly name political posters in her list of cultural productions, which includes "rituals such as street demonstrations and parades, as well as speeches, newspaper articles and letters to the editor, pamphlets, scientific reports, photographs, drawings, and cartoons," but they are a logical addition.
11. Rose, *Limited Livelihoods*, 8–9.
12. Cerulo, *Identity Designs*, 119, 129.
13. Swidler defines culture itself as "symbolic vehicles of meaning, including beliefs, ritual practices, art forms, and ceremonies, as well as informal cultural practices such as language, gossip, stories, and rituals of daily life." I add that particularly in Eastern Europe and the former USSR, culture cannot be delinked from and is, in fact, permeated by, history. In the tool kit too, then, are "stories" of history, both as it *did* and as it *might have* occurred. ("Culture in Action," 273, 277.)
14. Bonnell, "The Representation of Women in Early Soviet Political Art," 270.
15. The word "nation" *(tauta)* here is not a synonym for country and is understood in the ethnically specific sense suggested by terms like the German *Volk* or the Russian *narod.*
16. Eduards Berklāvs, "Kādu gribam redzēt Latviju?" *Nacionālā neatkarība*, 12–18 May 1993, 2.
17. "Solījumi 5. Saeimas vēlētājiem."
18. For a discussion of this, see Aigars Jirgens, "3 D formulai nav alternatīvas," *Diena*, 6 January 1993, 2. The author was later a part of the coalition Our Land. A 4D formula, which included denationalization, was also discussed in some political circles. On this, see Jānis Freimanis, "3D vai 4D?" *Diena*, 14 November 1992, 2. The political organizations that more or less adhered to the 3D (or 4D) formula included Our Land, the Anti-Communist Union, For Fatherland and Freedom, and Latvia's Unity Party.

19. The life of Kārlis Ulmanis is documented in Edgars Dunsdorfs, *Kārļa Ulmaņa dzīve: Ceļinieks, politiķis, diktators, moceklis* (Riga: Zinātne, 1992).

20. Dreifelds, *Latvia in Transition*, 89.

21. "Solījumi 5. Saeimas vēlētājiem."

22. "Solījumi 5. Saeimas vēlētājiem."

23. Jānis Kampans and Ilmārs Punka, "Cik izmaksājusi priekšvēlēšanu cīņa?" *Tev*, 7 June 1993, 4.

24. "Solījumi 5. Saeimas vēlētājiem."

25. "Solījumi 5. Saeimas vēlētājiem."

26. "Kandidātu programmas—balsotāju izvēle—Latvijas nākotne," *Diena*, 25 May 1993, 2. The understanding of liberalism in Latvia reflects a European rather than an American notion of the term. The laissez-faire approach to the market is, in the United States, typically associated with conservatism, whereas liberalism embraces a stronger welfare state.

27. "Solījumi 5. Saeimas vēlētājiem."

28. Aivars Ozoliņš, "Bēgot no Eiropas, ieskriesim Krievijā," *Diena*, 20 June 1994, 2.

29. These preliminary census numbers are from the Central Statistical Bureau of Latvia, *2000. gada tautas skaitīšanas provizoriskie rezultāti* (Riga: Central Statistical Bureau of Latvia, 2001), 36.

30. W. Rogers Brubaker, "Citizenship Struggles in Soviet Successor States," *International Migration Review* 26 (1992): 277–79.

31. Brubaker, "Citizenship Struggles," 277.

32. "Politiķi par pilsonību: *Dienas* jautājumi," *Diena*, 22 January 1993, 2.

33. "Politiķi par pilsonību: *Dienas* jautājumi," *Diena*, 8 January 1993, 2.

34. *Alfa un omega: Enciklopēdiskā rokasgrāmata* (Riga: Latvijas enciklopēdija, 1992), 151.

35. Plakans, *The Latvians: A Short History*, 132.

36. The text of the law is reprinted in full in Richard Flournoy Jr. and Manley O. Hudson, eds., *A Collection of Nationality Laws of Various Countries as Contained in Constitutions, Statutes, and Treaties* (Littleton, Colo.: Fred B. Rothman & Co., 1983), 405–7.

37. The Peace Treaty of 1920 is reprinted in full in Alfreds Bilmanis, ed., *Latvian-Russian Relations: Documents* (Lincoln, Neb.: Latvian Legation, 1978), 73–74.

38. Jānis Rutkis, *Latvia: Country and People* (Stockholm: Latvian National Foundation, 1967), 239.

39. The text of the law is reprinted in full in Flournoy and Hudson, *A Collection of Nationality Laws*, 407–9.

40. Rutkis, *Latvia: Country and People*, 223.

41. Dreifelds, *Latvia in Transition*, 29.

42. Some might argue that referring to Latgalians as a minority population is problematic as this community is often identified with and identifies with the Latvian community. However, Latgalians retain their own language (or dialect) and religion (Catholicism). The region of Latgalia also has a history different from that of most of the northern and western areas of the country.

43. Agnis Balodis, "Latgales vaicājums," in *Latvija šodien, 1989/1990* (Rockville, Md.: World Federation of Free Latvians, 1990), 110.

44. Miķelis Bukšs, *Latgaļu atmūda: idejas un ceiņas* (Munich: Latgaļu izdevnīceiba, 1976).

45. Dreifelds, *Latvia in Transition*, 29.

46. Elmārs Pelkaus, "Latvijas valsts problēma Latvijas Republikas laikā," in *Latviešu nācijas izredzes: 1990. gada 28. septembra konference* (Riga: Zinātne, 1990), 115.

47. The well-known work of T. H. Marshall suggests that citizenship is composed of three dimensions that contain different sets of rights: civil, political, and social. Civil rights consist of a set of individual rights, including freedom of speech, equality in the eyes of the law, and the right to private property. Political rights are those rights that provide a voice in public decision making through suffrage. Social rights include the right to social welfare, education, and security. *Citizenship and Social Class* (Concord, Mass.: Pluto Press, 1992).

48. Levits also noted that election results were announced by the news agency TASS in Moscow twelve hours before the ballots were counted in Latvia. Egils Levits, "Latvija padomju varā," in *Latvijas valsts atjaunošana, 1986–1993*, ed. Valdis Blūzma et al., 44–45.

49. This was not always the case during the Soviet period, however. The 1924 decree on Union citizenship stipulated: "Every person in the territory of the Union of Soviet Socialist Republics is deemed to be a citizen of the [USSR] in so far as he does not prove that he is a foreign citizen," but the first Soviet Constitution, adopted in July 1918, categorized inhabitants into bourgeoisie (exploiters) and working people and denied the vote to the former category. Suffrage was extended to this segment of the population (which included clergy, entrepreneurs, and those who had enjoyed privilege under the tsars) only in the 1936 Soviet Constitution. The text of the Soviet law is reprinted in Flournoy and Hudson, *A Collection of Nationality Laws*, 511–15. On the Constitution, see John S. Reshetar Jr., *The Soviet Polity: Government and Politics in the USSR* (New York: Harper & Row, 1989), 173–75.

50. Ļubova Zīle, "Komunistiskās partijas krīze un šķelšanās 1989. Gadā," in *Latvijas valsts atjaunošana, 1986–1993*, ed. Valdis Blūzma et al., 192–93.

51. Reshetar, *The Soviet Polity*, 177.

52. O'Donnell and Schmitter, *Transitions from Authoritarian Rule*, 48.

53. Reshetar, *The Soviet Polity*, 177.

54. According to Smith, Lenin reasoned that "by granting Russia's minority nations the right to statehood he was in effect acknowledging national sensibilities for . . . if nations were not given this right, then, among peoples whose national consciousness was emerging as a political force, it would encourage a combative nationalism which would run counter to the establishment of socialism in Russia." On nationalities policy, see Graham Smith, "The Soviet State and Nationalities Policy," in *The Nationalities Question in the Post-Soviet States*, ed. Graham Smith (New York: Longman, 1996).

55. Balodis, "Latgales vaicājums," 110.

56. "The Soviet State and Nationalities Policy," 8–9.

57. Richard Pipes, "Introduction: The Nationality Problem," in *Handbook of Major Soviet Nationalities*, ed. Zev Katz (New York: Free Press, 1975), 2.

58. *Sblizhenie* was the precursor of what was eventually to be achieved: *sliyanie*, the merging of peoples.

59. Reshetar, *The Soviet Polity*, 176.

60. "Politiķi par pilsonību: *Dienas* jautājumi," *Diena*, 22 January 1993, 2.

61. "Politiķi par pilsonību: *Dienas* jautājumi," *Diena*, 5 February 1993, 2.

62. "Politiķi par pilsonību: *Dienas* jautājumi," *Diena*, 5 February 1993, 2.

63. "Politiķi par pilsonību: *Dienas* jautājumi," *Diena*, 8 January 1993, 2.

64. "Politiķi par pilsonību: *Dienas* jautājumi," *Diena*, 8 January 1993, 2.

65. "Politiķi par pilsonību: *Dienas* jautājumi," *Diena*, 26 January 1993, 2

66. A May 1993 poll, for example, asked voters to identify the three most pressing issues for the new Saeima to address: top choices included the economy (40.7 percent), unemployment (26.8 percent), agriculture (24.7 percent), and privatization (about 13 percent). Citizenship was in eighth place with just over 10 percent. (Einārs Semanis, "Atgrieztais spogulis jeb Ko vēlas vēlētāji Latvijā?" *Diena*, 12 May 1993, 2.)

67. Semanis, "Atgrieztais spogulis jeb Ko vēlas vēlētāji Latvijā?" *Diena*, 12 May 1993, 2.

68. As an example, according to the *PRB World Population Data Sheet*, in 1997, Latvia had a growth rate of –0.6, the lowest, together with Ukraine, in the entire world. (Population Reference Bureau, *1998 World Population Data Sheet* [Washington, D.C.: PRB, 1998].)

69. Ilze Ārkliņa, "LNNK Proposes Quota System for New Citizens," *Baltic Observer*, 17–23 September 1993, 2.

70. Ilze Ārkliņa, "Latvian Parliament Divided over Citizenship," *Baltic Observer*, 24–30 September 1993, 4; and idem, "Citizenship Law Won't Be Passed Before Christmas," *Baltic Observer*, 1–7 October 1993, 2.

71. Ārkliņa, "Latvian Parliament Divided over Citizenship," *Baltic Observer*, 24–30 September 1993, 4; and idem, "Citizenship Law Won't Be Passed Before Christmas," *Baltic Observer*, 1–7 October 1993, 2.

72. Gorbunōvs represented Latvia as chairman of the Supreme Soviet, and Yeltsin represented the Russian Federation as president.

73. Ilze Ārkliņa, "Nationalists Want to Cancel Treaty with Russia," *Baltic Observer,* 15–21 October 1993, 2.

74. "Van Der Stoel Opposes Quota Principle for Latvian Citizenship," *Baltic Observer,* 13–19 January 1994, 3.

75. Ilze Ārkliņa, "Latvia Will Remove Quotas from Citizenship Draft Law," *Baltic Observer,* 17–23 March 1994, 3.

76. "Moscow Plans to Seek Citizenship for Russians in Latvia and Estonia," *Baltic Observer,* 31 March–6 April 1994, 6.

77. Sanita Upleja, "Pilsonības likums var izšķirt koalīciju," *Diena,* 5 May 1994, 1.

78. LC subsequently opted out of supporting the bill, which in part underpinned the ultimate breakup of the ruling coalition.

79. Kaspars Kauliņš, "Pašvaldības ievēlētas, dienas kārtībā—pilsonība," *Diena,* 6 June 1994, 2.

80. According to some sources, the CSCE commissioner for National Minority Issues bluntly stated: "If the law isn't changed, [Latvia can] forget about the Council of Europe." (Ozoliņš, "Bēgot no Eiropas, ieskriesim Krievijā," 2.)

81. Ilze Ārkliņa, "Compromise Reached on Latvian Citizenship Law," *Baltic Observer,* 16–22 June 1994, 1.

82. Ilze Ārkliņa and Josh Karlen, "Latvian Parliament Turns Its Back on Council of Europe," *Baltic Observer,* 23–29 June 1994, 1 and 4.

83. Ozoliņš, "Bēgot no Eiropas, ieskriesim Krievijā," 2; and Pauls Raudseps, "EP vai NVS—Citu iespēju Latvijai nav," *Diena,* 21 June 1994, 2.

84. Ozoliņš, "Bēgot no Eiropas, ieskriesim Krievijā," 2.

85. Raudseps, "EP vai NVS—Citu iespēju Latvijai nav," 2.

86. Kaspars Kauliņš, "Neatstājiet mūs neziņā!" *Diena,* 27 June 1994, 2.

87. Ilze Ārkliņa, "Ulmanis Vetoes Citizenship Law," *Baltic Observer,* 30 June–6 July 1994, 1.

88. Josh Karlen, "Latvia's Citizenship Law Amended," *Baltic Observer,* 28 July–3 August 1994, 3.

89. Ilze Ārkliņa, "CE Reaffirms Opposition to Citizenship Quotas," *Baltic Observer,* 7–13 July 1994, 2.

90. "Latvia's Citizenship Law Angers Yeltsin," *Baltic Observer,* 11–17 August 1994, 1.

91. Josh Karlen, "Latvia's President Signs Citizenship Law," *Baltic Observer,* 18–24 August 1994, 3.

92. Rainis, *Uguns un Nakts,* 101.

Chapter 4

1. Before the opposition period, flowers were sometimes left at the base of the monument in the dark of night, only to reappear in the morning at the foot of the Lenin statue nearby.

2. Kubik, *The Power of Symbols Against the Symbols of Power,* 95. The sites to which he refers are Wawel Hill, Wawel Castle, and Wawel Cathedral in Krakow.

3. Quoted in Apsītis, *Brīvības piemineklis,* 153.

4. David Kertzer, *Politics and Symbols: The Italian Communist Party and the Fall of Communism* (New Haven: Yale University Press, 1996), 66. Kertzer is citing, in part, the work of Stanley Tambiah.

5. A similar imperative attaches to the restitution of urban property, but that issue has dimensions that I do not take up in this work.

6. Tuomas Forsberg, "Theories on Territorial Disputes," in *Contested Territory: Border Disputes at the Edge of the Soviet Empire,* ed. Tuomas Forsberg (Brookfield, Vt.: Edgar Elgar, 1995).

7. *The Ethnic Origin of Nations.*

8. *Language and Symbolic Power* (New York: Cambridge University Press, 1991), 105.

9. Mach, *Symbols, Conflict, and Identity,* 105.

10. Smith, *The Ethnic Origin of Nations,* 202.

11. Michel Foucault, *Power/Knowledge: Selected Interviews and Other Writings, 1972–1977,* ed. Colin Gordon (Brighton, England: Harvester Press, 1980).

12. *Outline of a Theory of Practice* (New York: Cambridge University Press, 1977).

13. The information in this and the former paragraph is from Jānis Stradiņš, *Trešā atmoda* (Riga: Zinātne, 1992), 270–76.

14. Stradiņš, *Trešā atmoda*, 284.

15. "East European Mass Media: The Soviet Role," in *The Soviet Union in Eastern Europe*, ed. Ode Arne Westad, Sven Holtsmark, and Iver B. Neuman (New York: St. Martin's Press, 1994), 110.

16. Ļubova Zīle, conversation with author, Riga, April 1997.

17. Stradiņš, *Trešā atmoda*, 268 and 277.

18. Imants Sudmals (1916–44) was a revolutionary and Soviet partisan. He participated in the underground Communist movement during the interwar period. He was posthumously honored as a Hero of the Soviet Union in 1957. (*Latvijas PSR Mazā enciklopēdija, PIE–Z* [Riga: Zinātne, 1970], 443.)

19. Stradiņš, *Trešā atmoda*, 269–71 and 281.

20. Stradiņš, *Trešā atmoda*, 281, 284, 272, 278.

21. Stradiņš, *Trešā atmoda*, 274–75, 280–81.

22. The street name *Stabu* (Stake) comes from a story about a stake erected in Riga to frighten those responsible for the city fire of 1677. (Stradiņš, *Trešā atmoda*, 274.)

23. Stradiņš, *Trešā atmoda*, 281–82. Pēteris Stučka participated in the revolutionary movement of 1917 in Russia and worked with Lenin in the first years of the USSR.

24. Ļubova Zīle, interviewed by author, Riga, April 1997, tape recording.

25. Stradiņš, *Trešā atmoda*, 283.

26. Stradiņš, *Trešā atmoda*, 282.

27. Stradiņš, *Trešā atmoda*, 284.

28. *Politics and Symbols*, 25.

29. Stradiņš, *Trešā atmoda*, 273.

30. *Language and Symbolic Power*, 105 and 127.

31. Photo essay in *Edinstvo*, 4 August 1989, 5.

32. Reprinted in Charles F. Furtado and Andrea Chandler, eds., *Perestroika in the Soviet Republics: Documents on the National Question* (Boulder, Colo.: Westview Press, 1992), 122–25.

33. Thongchai Winichakul, *Siam Mapped: A History of the Geo-Body of a Nation* (Honolulu: University of Hawaii Press, 1994).

34. Plakans, *The Latvians: A Short History*, 144.

35. Artūrs Mucenieks, "Cik precīzas ir Latvijas kartes?" *Rīgas balss*, 9 July 1996, 5.

36. Thongchai, *Siam Mapped*, 17.

37. Anderson, *Imagined Communities*.

38. "Kā Narva, Pečori un Abrene tika iekļauti Krievijas Socialistiskajā Federatīvajā Republikā," *Latvijas Vēsture* 1 (1991): 56.

39. The treaty is reprinted in Bilmanis, *Latvian-Russian Relations: Documents*, 71.

40. Census data cited in a special section on Abrene/Pitalovo: "Abrenes atgriezums," *Neatkarīgā cīņa* (n.d.): 2.

41. Andersons, "Kā Narva, Pečori un Abrene tika iekļauti," 55.

42. Andersons, "Kā Narva, Pečori un Abrene tika iekļauti."

43. Andersons, "Kā Narva, Pečori un Abrene tika iekļauti," 55.

44. Dītrihs A. Lēbers (Dietrich A. Loeber), "Krievijas un Latvijas teritoriālais strīds Abrenes jautājumā," *Latvijas vēsture* 5 (1996): 51.

45. Lēbers, "Krievijas un Latvijas teritoriālais strīds Abrenes jautājumā."

46. Andersons, "Kā Narva, Pečori un Abrene tika iekļauti," 56.

47. Nikonov, interviewed by Oskars Gerts, "1944. gada vasaras pārsteigums," *Neatkarīgā cīņa* (n.d.): 2.

48. Nikonov, interviewed by Oskars Gerts, "1944. gada vasaras pārsteigums," *Neatkarīgā cīņa* (n.d.): 2.

49. Bonifacijs Dauksts and Artūrs Puga, "Abrene," in *Contested Territory: Border Disputes at the Edge of the Soviet Empire*, ed. Tuomas Forsberg, 183.

50. Ernest Gellner, *Nations and Nationalism* (Ithaca: Cornell University Press, 1983), 1.

51. "The Collapse of the Soviet Union and the Historical Border Questions," in *Contested Territory: Border Disputes at the Edge of the Soviet Empire*, ed. Tuomas Forsberg, 28–31.

52. Dauksts and Puga, "Abrene," 183.

53. Jānis Silis, "Krievija brīdina LR kartogrāfus," *Diena*, 21 April 1992, 1.

54. Lēbers, "Krievijas un Latvijas teritorijālais strīds Abrenes jautājumā," 53.

55. Aivars Stranga, "Pro et contra, robežu velkot," *Neatkarīgā cīņa* (n.d.): 2.

56. Bilmanis, *Latvian-Russian Relations: Documents*, 70.

57. "Latvija atsakās no Abrenes," *Laiks*, 8 March 1997, 1.

58. Mark Kramer, "Why Is Russia Still Peddling This Old Soviet Lie?" *Washington Post*, 10 June 2001, B2.

59. *The Poetics of Space* (Boston: Beacon Press, 1969).

60. The process is at varying stages of completion in the region. For instance, in mid-2001, Poland has still not passed a law governing the return of private property; other states like the Czech Republic (then part of Czechoslovakia) and Latvia did so nearly a decade ago and have returned a substantial proportion of the land seized by the Communist governments.

61. Unlike the large cities, which are almost invariably Russian dominated, the countryside is predominantly Latvian; more than 75 percent of rural residents are Latvian.

62. Jānis Lauks, "Nolaupītais jāatdod īpašniekam un nevienam citam," *Diena*, 22 May 1992, 2.

63. Literally, kolkhozes were the collective farms of the Soviet period, and sovkhozes were state farms. When I speak of collectivized agriculture, I refer to both types.

64. Visvaldis Lācis, "Zemniecība un latviešu nācijas nākotne," in *Latviešu nācijas izredzes: 1990. gada 28. septembra konference*, 125–28.

65. Taurens, *Latvijas vēstures pamatjautājumi*, 101.

66. Lieven, *The Baltic Revolution*, 355.

67. Maija Krūzmētra, "Rural Women in Latvia," in *Fragments of Reality: Insights on Women in a Changing Society*, ed. Ilze Trapenciere and Sandra Kalniņa (Riga: VAGA, 1992), 133–34.

68. Verdery, *What Was Socialism and What Comes Next?* 134. For an excellent discussion of restitution in Romania, see chap. 6.

69. This was an actual case in southeastern Latvia. Pēteris Kalniņš, interviewed by author, Pļaviņas (Latvia), April 1997, tape recording. Kalniņš is the source of quotes in this subsection unless otherwise indicated.

70. The median and mode in this category are even lower: fully 64.8 percent of farms are only two to ten hectares in size. (*Latvia Human Development Report, 1997* [Riga: UNDP, 1997], 20, 69–71, 90.)

71. Plakans, *The Latvians: A Short History*, 124–25.

72. According to one historical source, "On agrarian questions the Social Democratic Party [in Latvia] did not demand that the manors be divided in to small farms, and yet, if the Latvian Revolution of 1905 had not been quelled, the division of the large estates would have been inevitable as happened later in 1920." (Spekke, *History of Latvia: An Outline*, 311–12.)

73. Spekke, *History of Latvia: An Outline*, 362–64.

74. Plakans, *The Latvians*, 124.

75. Article 1 of Part I (State Land Fund) of the reform act, quoted in Rutkis, *Latvia: Country and People*, 335.

76. Rutkis, *Latvia: Country and People*, 335–36.

77. Plakans, *The Latvians*, 125.

78. The latter figure is from the year 1897. Spekke, *History of Latvia: An Outline*, 364.

79. Plakans, *The Latvians*, 125.

80. Under the terms of the reform act, a maximum limit of twenty-two hectares of cultivated land was allocated to new farms. Rutkis, *Latvia: Country and People*, 340.

81. Spekke, *History of Latvia: An Outline*, 363–64.

82. Herbert Heaton, *Economic History of Europe* (New York: Harper & Brothers, 1936), 490.

83. Spekke, *History of Latvia: An Outline*, 363–64.

84. Spekke, *History of Latvia: An Outline*, 366.

85. Rutkis, *Latvia: Country and People*, 342.

86. Taurens, *Latvijas vēstures pamatjautājumi*, 101.

87. Plakans, *The Latvians*, 126.

88. Changes in land use and proprietorship took place again in the late 1980s but, as those were conducted under the auspices of the Supreme Soviet of Latvia and represented reformist initiatives, I do not include them in this category. These changes are discussed in other portions of this section.

89. E. Žagars, *Socialist Transformations in Latvia, 1940–1941* (Riga: Zinātne, 1978), 103.

90. Rutkis, *Latvia: Country and People*, 344.

91. Quoted in Žagars, *Socialist Transformations in Latvia*, 113.

92. Spekke, *History of Latvia: An Outline*, 390–91.

93. Žagars, *Socialist Transformations in Latvia*, 111.

94. Spekke, *History of Latvia: An Outline*, 344–45.

95. Spekke, *History of Latvia: An Outline*.

96. Cited in Žagars, *Socialist Transformations in Latvia*, 112.

97. Plakans, *The Latvians*, 156.

98. Spekke, *History of Latvia: An Outline*, 391.

99. This was not the only work that MTS undertook in the countryside: one source describes it as "the principal outpost of the Soviet regime in the rural areas." In 1950 a political department was set up in each MTS, the purpose of which was to disseminate "communist propaganda in the kolkhozes, set up primary party organizations within the kolkhozes, and in general, to see that directives of the Party were observed." In 1950, there were ninety-six MTSs in the Latvian countryside. Rutkis, *Latvia: Country and People*, 351–53, 369.

100. Spekke, *History of Latvia: An Outline*, 391.

101. Rutkis, *Latvia: Country and People*, 354–55.

102. The peak number was reached in this period because shortly afterward, in July 1950, the Soviet government ordered the consolidation of smaller kolkhozes. Thus, by the end of 1950, the total number of kolkhozes fell to 1,794, though they incorporated essentially the same land differently bounded. (Rutkis, *Latvia: Country and People*, 354.)

103. Rutkis, *Latvia: Country and People*, 371–74.

104. James H. Bater, *Russia and the Post-Soviet Scene: A Geographical Perspective* (New York: John Wiley & Sons, 1996), 193–94.

105. Bater, *Russia and the Post-Soviet Scene*.

106. World Bank, *Latvia: The Transition to a Market Economy* (Washington, D.C.: World Bank, 1993), 92–93.

107. World Bank, *Latvia*.

108. DOCEX Project, *Latvia: An Economic Profile* (Washington, D.C.: International Monetary Fund, 1992), 14.

109. *Brešu* is a play on the name of Vilnis Edvins Bresis, who, during the Gorbachev period, oversaw the legislation "creating" these farmers.

110. Central Statistical Bureau of Latvia, *Latvijas Statistikas gadagrāmata, 1999* (Riga: Central Statistical Bureau of Latvia, 2000), 49.

111. The laws are reprinted in *Par zemes reformu un zemes privatizāciju Latvijas Republikas lauku apvidos* (Riga: KIF "Biznesa komplekss," 1996).

112. At the time this legislation was enacted, the circulating currency was the ruble of the USSR. In May 1992, Latvia went over to a temporary currency, the Latvian ruble, and in March 1993, the Latvian *lat* was introduced. The currency changes and public uncertainty about the stability of currency in this inflationary period made cash an unattractive option.

113. World Bank, *Latvia: The Transition to a Market Economy*, 94.

114. In Estonia, large-scale farms predominate and account for about 60 percent of agricultural land. In Estonia's case, hundreds of collective and state farms have been transformed into about 1,000 farming enterprises that produce mostly milk and grain. Family farms of the type that predominate in

Latvia numbered about 13,500. In Lithuania, individual farms of this sort number about 135,000 and account for 34 percent of agricultural land. Another one-third of agricultural land is large-scale farms, and the final third is made up of household plots, typically smaller than three hectares. (Andrzej Kwiecinski and Vaclav Vojtec, "The Transformation of Baltic Agriculture," *OECD Observer* 202 [October–November 1996]: 31.)

115. World Bank, *Latvia: The Transition to a Market Economy*, 91. Indeed, though agriculture has, as noted, suffered severe declines over the past few years, the timber industry is doing reasonably well.

116. Dreifelds, *Latvia in Transition*, 131.

117. The story was related to me by Pēteris Kalniņš, my relative and a local Latvian farmer and district elected official and teacher at the local Russian school. He lives further along the road on which the dump is located. The interview took place in April 1997.

118. Latvian agriculture since the fourteenth century had, by and large, been based on a manorial order where noble landlords, mostly non-Latvian, held the land and peasant farmers, mostly Latvian, worked the land. Many of the peasant farmers were serfs. Serfdom was abolished in Latvia in 1817, but peasants remained tied to the land in a period known locally as the time of statute work *(klaušu laiki)*. In this period, peasant farmers did not own land, but leased it for payment in kind, which was normally given in the form of heavy farm labor. Most of Latvia's land at that time was owned by about 1,250 landlords and their families. Land began to come into the hands of peasants in the mid- to late nineteenth century when peasants were given the chance to buy land and gain full title. The process began slowly; by 1920, Latvian farmers had purchased about 39 percent of the territory formerly belonging to the manors. (Rutkis, *Latvia: Country and People*, 333–34.)

119. The Lithuanian couple occupying the small house (two rooms) at Juči remained in that house for quite a bit longer with Pēteris's consent. In 1997 after the husband drowned in an accident in a small pond at Juči, his elderly wife, who could not care for herself, went to live with the couple's son.

120. Farmers in the countryside are not the only ones to share this opinion. In a recent book based on lengthy interviews with the then-prime minister Ivars Godmanis, Godmanis expressed the opinion, with respect to the rural privatization process, that "we apparently did not understand some things. . . . It could well be that the privatization process was undertaken too early." His discussion of this issue can be found in Inga Utena, *Cilvēks Godmanis* (Riga: Apgāds Jāņa sēta, 1997), 153–55.

121. Andrejs Plakans, "The Tribulations of Independence: Latvia, 1991–1993," *Journal of Baltic Studies* 1 (spring 1994): 64.

Chapter 5

1. Peggy Watson, "Eastern Europe's Silent Revolution: Gender," *Sociology* 27 (1993): 471–72.

2. Anita Kalns-Timans, "Latvian Women: The Way Forward," in *Fragments of Reality: Insights on Women in a Changing Society*, ed. Ilze Trapenciere and Sandra Kalniņa, 32–58.

3. Inna Zariņa, ed., *News About Women in Latvia* (Riga: Latvian Women Studies and Information Center, 1994), 10–11.

4. Rutkis, *Latvia: Country and People*, 310–11.

5. Ilze Korlova and Ilze Trapenciere, "Women in Latvia: Some Significant Historical Data and Figures," in *Fragments of Reality: Insights on Women in a Changing Society*, ed. Ilze Trapenciere and Sandra Kalniņa, 232–55.

6. Zariņa, *News About Women in Latvia*, 11.

7. Velta Rūķe-Draviņa, "Studentes un studenti Latvijas Universitātē," in *Latvijas sieviete valsts 75 gados*, ed. Pārsla Eglīte (Riga: Zvaigzne, 1994).

8. Zariņa, *News About Women in Latvia*, 9–11.

9. *Karl Marx and Frederick Engels: Selected Works in Three Volumes* (Moscow: Progress Publishers, 1983), 1:120.

10. Frederick Engels, *Origin of the Family, Private Property, and State*, in *Karl Marx and Frederick Engels: Selected Works in Three Volumes* (Moscow: Progress Publishers, 1983), 3:245.

11. Engels, *Origin of the Family*, 240.

12. Engels, *Origin of the Family*, 245.

13. Buckley, *Women and Ideology in the Soviet Union*, 23.

14. Engels, *Origin of the Family*, 254.

15. Gail W. Lapidus, *Women in Soviet Society: Equality, Development, and Change* (Berkeley and Los Angeles: University of California Press, 1978), 41.

16. Buckley, *Women and Ideology in the Soviet Union*, 25–26.

17. Buckley, *Women and Ideology in the Soviet Union*, 108.

18. Buckley noted the interesting paradox that, in this period, the criminalization of abortion in some capitalist states was harshly criticized. The inconsistency of the position, however, was painted over with the assertion that in "socialism abortion was unnecessary, unhealthy, and rightly banned; under capitalism abortion was frequently needed by oppressed women, but wrongly denied." (Buckley, *Women and Ideology in the Soviet Union*, 109.)

19. Lapidus, *Women in Soviet Society*, 96.

20. Lapidus, *Women in Soviet Society*, 176.

21. Data cited by Einhorn show that in some countries women gained the right to vote only with the advent of socialist regimes. Poland and Czechoslovakia gave women the right to vote in 1918 (as Latvia did), one year after this right was extended in the USSR. In Bulgaria and Hungary, this came about only in, respectively, 1944 and 1945. (*Cinderella Goes to Market*, 274.)

22. Zariņa, *News About Women in Latvia*, 10–12.

23. Einhorn, *Cinderella Goes to Market*, 5.

24. Einhorn, *Cinderella Goes to Market*, 59.

25. Ārija Kārpova and Inta Kraukle, "Some Ideas About the Latvian Woman in the Present Sociopsychological Situation," in *Fragments of Reality: Insights on Women in a Changing Society*, ed. Ilze Trapenciere and Sandra Kalniņa, 72–80.

26. Anu Narusk, "Gender and Rationality: The Case of Estonian Women," in *Unresolved Dilemmas: Women, Work, and the Family in the United States, Europe, and the Former Soviet Union*, ed. Kaisa Kauppinen and Tuula Gordon (Brookfield, Vt.: Edgar Elgar, 1997), 115.

27. Lapidus, *Women in Soviet Society*, 169.

28. Rutkis, *Latvia: Country and People*, 297.

29. Cited in Trapenciere and Kalniņa, eds., *Fragments of Reality*, 242.

30. *Latvia Human Development Report, 1997* (Riga: UNDP, 1997), 87.

31. Lapidus, *Women in Soviet Society*, 166, 169–70.

32. Buckley, *Women and Ideology in the Soviet Union*, 137, 155–56.

33. Mikhail Gorbachev, *Perestroika* (Moscow: Progress Publishers, 1987), 117.

34. "Political Report of the CPSU Central Committee to the 27th Congress of the Communist Party of the Soviet Union, February 25, 1986," in Mikhail Gorbachev, *Selected Speeches and Articles*, 2d ed. (Moscow: Progress Publishers, 1987), 403.

35. Gorbachev, *Perestroika*, 117.

36. Susan Bridger, *Women in the Soviet Countryside: Women's Roles in Rural Development in the Soviet Union* (New York: Cambridge University Press, 1987), 133.

37. "Notes from the Underground," *New York Review of Books* 37, no. 9 (1991): 3–7.

38. Latvian National Preparatory Committee for the United Nations Fourth Conference on Women, *National Report on the Situation of Women* (Riga: Latvian Women Studies and Information Center, 1995), 10.

39. Dzidris Seps, "Women and Crime," in *Fragments of Reality: Insights on Women in a Changing Society*, ed. Ilze Trapenciere and Sandra Kalniņa, 185.

40. Hilary Pilkington, "Whose Space Is It Anyway? Youth, Gender, and Civil Society in the Soviet Union," in *Women in the Face of Change*, ed. Shirin Rai, Hilary Pilkington, and Annie Phizacklea (New York: Routledge, 1992), 112.

41. Seps, "Women and Crime," 187.

42. Zariņa, *News About Women in Latvia*, 38–39.

43. Latvian National Preparatory Committee, *Latvia Human Development Report, 1995* [cited May 1997]; available from http://www.undp.riga.lv/hdrs/engl95/chapter4.htm.

44. Pilkington, "Whose Space Is It Anyway?" 113.

45. Anita Millere, "Women in Latvia: They Endure All," in *Fragments of Reality: Insights on Women in a Changing Society,"* ed. Ilze Trapenciere and Sandra Kalniņa, 50–51.

46. Quoted in Verdery, *What Was Socialism and What Comes Next?* 81.

47. Watson, "Eastern Europe's Silent Revolution: Gender," *Sociology* 27 (1993): 472–73.

48. Einhorn, *Cinderella Goes to Market,* 40.

49. Sarmīte Hartmane, "Woman's [*sic*] Mood and Health Criteria," in *Fragments of Reality: Insights on Women in a Changing Society,* ed. Ilze Trapenciere and Sandra Kalniņa, 204.

50. Ārija Karpova and Inta Kraukle, "Some Ideas About the Latvian Woman in the Present Sociopsychological Situation," in *Fragments of Reality: Insights on Women in a Changing Society,* ed. Ilze Trapenciere and Sandra Kalniņa, 77, 80.

51. Jānis Mauliņš, "Pats galvenais—Dzīvīga gimene," in *Latviešu nācijas izredzes: 1990. gada 28. septembra konference* (Riga: Zinātne, 1990), 68–70.

52. Jēkabs Raipulis, "Latviešu tautu varam saglabāt tikai mēs paši," in *Latviešu nācijas izredzes,* 60.

53. In Latvia, women have, on average, more years of education than men. In addition, more are enrolled in universities: in 1999/2000, women made up 63 percent of university enrollees. (Ritma Rungule, "Izglītība," in *Dzīves apstākļi Latvijā, 1999. gadā* [Riga: Central Statistical Bureau of Latvia, 2001], 63.)

54. Narusk, "Gender and Rationality," 120.

55. Quoted in Einhorn, *Cinderella Goes to Market,* 79.

56. Raipulis, "Latviešu tautu varam saglabāt tikai mēs paši," 63.

57. In 1996, Latvia's Labor Code was revised, and the section of the code that foresees equal rights on the job and forbids the disqualification of individuals with appropriate work qualifications was modified to forbid discrimination based on gender or age. It is unclear how much effect this has had on real conditions of work.

58. Pārsla Eglīte, "Family Policy During the Transition Period in Latvia," *Humanities and Social Sciences Latvia* 2, no. 7 (1995): 28–47.

59. Latvian National Preparatory Committee, *National Report on the Situation of Women,* 25.

60. Figures from 1990 and 1993 are from Zariņa, *News About Women in Latvia,* 20. Data from 1995 are from *Latvia Human Development Report, 1996* (Riga: UNDP, 1996), 69.

61. Pārsla Eglīte, correspondence with author, April 1998.

62. The second child was to be entitled to 1.2 times the first child's allowance, and third, fourth, and fifth children were to receive 1.6 times the first child's allowance. For sixth and later children, the sum returned to that of the first child.

63. Zariņa, *News About Women in Latvia,* 18. Data from 1998 are from the Central Statistical Bureau of Latvia, *Latvijas statistikas gadagrāmata, 1999* (Riga: Central Statistical Bureau of Latvia, 1999), 64.

64. The figures cited include the influence of emigration as well as a declining birthrate. Pārsla Eglīte, "Population of Latvia: A Demographic Survey," in *Children and Families in Latvia: 1994 Situation Analysis,* ed. Anita Jakobsone (Riga: UNICEF Latvian National Committee, 1995), 22.

65. Women are underrepresented in the more remunerative private sector and constitute just 31 percent of employers. (*Latvia Human Development Report, 1997* [Riga: UNDP, 1997], 35–39.)

66. Latvian National Preparatory Committee, *National Report on the Situation of Women,* 13.

67. *Latvia Human Development Report, 1997* (Riga: UNDP, 1997), 32.

68. This statistic includes both women who are unemployed and seeking work and those who are not seeking paid employment outside the home. Statistics are for November 1995. (*Darbaspēks Latvijā* [Riga: Central Statistical Bureau of Latvia, 1996].)

69. *Darbaspēks Latvijā,* 38–40; and Zaiga Priede, "Nodarbinātība un darba apstākļi," in *Dzīves apstākļi Latvijā,* ed. Odne Oslands (Riga: Central Statistical Bureau of Latvia, 1996), 198.

70. The social tax collects funds for public welfare programs, including pensions. Wages are taxed at 37 percent, 28 percent of which is paid by the employer and 9 percent of which is paid by the

employee. Over time, the percentage paid by employees will rise: by 2001, it will be 15 percent. There is some incentive for companies and employees to contract unofficially because the tax is so high, but the state hopes to discourage this tendency by making pensions as well as other benefits contingent on whether and how much social taxes have been paid. (*Latvia Human Development Report, 1997* (Riga: UNDP, 1997), 34.)

71. Information on maternity leaves comes from Pārsla Eglīte, conversation with author, Riga, April 1997. Data on unemployment benefits come from *Latvia Human Development Report, 1997* (Riga: UNDP, 1997), 33.

72. Quoted in Daina Brila, "Is It Easy to Be Born in Latvia?" in *Fragments of Reality: Insights on Women in a Changing Society,* ed. Ilze Trapenciere and Sandra Kalniņa, 217.

73. Brila, "Is It Easy to Be Born in Latvia?" in *Fragments of Reality: Insights on Women in a Changing Society,* ed. Ilze Trapenciere and Sandra Kalniņa, 206–7, 213.

74. Exceptions are some private clinics that provide maternity services for pay, but these are out of reach for many patients. Even public facilities, however, have made some progress, for example, by allowing fathers to be present for the birth, which was not permitted in the Soviet period.

75. Līga Krapāne, "Pārkārtojumi ģimenes lietās, jeb Kas jāzina precēties un šķirties gribētājiem," *Diena,* July 1993, n.d., n.p.

76. Central Statistical Bureau of Latvia, *Latvijas statistikas gadagrāmata, 1999,* 60.

77. Eglīte, "Population of Latvia: A Demographic Survey," 25.

78. Unpublished data provided to the author by the Central Statistical Bureau of Latvia, May 2001.

79. Einhorn, *Cinderella Goes to Market,* 39–40.

80. Posadskaya, "Changes in Gender Discourses and Policies in the Former Soviet Union," 163.

81. Carol Delaney, "Father State, Motherland, and the Birth of Modern Turkey," in *Naturalizing Power: Essays in Feminist Cultural Analysis,* ed. Sylvia Yanagisako and Carol Delaney (New York: Routledge, 1995), 178.

82. The lower figure is an estimate from *Human Development Report Latvia, 1995* (Riga: UNDP, 1995). The higher figure is an estimate from the Morality Police, the body responsible for policing the sex trade until it was merged with the Criminal Police in 1998. In early 1997, at least 3,000 prostitutes were registered in the files of the Morality Police.

83. Statistics cited in this paragraph come from unpublished data prepared by the Morality Police for the Republic of Latvia's Cabinet of Ministers in 1995, and from Dzidris Seps, "Prostitūcija—sociāla parādība," in Noziedzības novirzīšanas nacionālais padomes kriminoloģisko pētijumu centrs, *Kriminoloģiskais biļetens nr. 26: Prostitūcijas sociālās, ekonomiskās un tiesiskās problēmas* (Riga: n.p., 1995), 40; and Andrejs Vilks, "Noziedzība, korupcija un ēnu ekonomika," in *Krīze Latvija: Ko darīt?* (Riga: Vērmaņparks, 1996), 37.

84. Egīls Šķēle, "LR valdību nomaina *Ledi Lukss,*" *Diena,* 17 April 1995, n.p.

85. "Čaka ielas republika," *Rīgas balss,* 5 December 1997, reprinted in *Laiks,* 10 January 1998, 12.

86. Andrejs Vilks, conversation with author, Riga, 23 April 1997.

87. Unpublished data prepared by the Morality Police for the Cabinet of Ministers in 1995.

88. "Labāk strādāt par prostitūtu, nekā dzīvot pusbadā," Baltic News Service report, 11 November 1997, reprinted in *Laiks,* 22 November 1997, 12.

89. Kligman, "Women and the Negotiation of Identity in Post-Communist Eastern Europe," 77.

90. Ailona Dārzniece, conversation with author, Riga, 30 April 1997.

91. Inta Mežavilka, conversation with author, Riga, 30 April 1997.

92. "Prostitūcija Latvijā: izplatības pakāpe, veidošanas mehānisms un kontroles iespējas (kriminoloģisko pētijuma materiāli)," in Noziedzības novirzīšanas nacionālais padomes kriminoloģisko pētijumu centrs, *Kriminoloģiskais biļetens nr. 26: Prostitūcijas sociālās, ekonomiskās un tiesiskās problēmas,* 53.

93. Inta Mežavilka and Aiva Soboļeva, conversation with author, Riga, 30 April 1997. Although earnings of prostitutes vary widely, the typical hourly earnings of a prostitute in Riga's sex clubs in 1995 was estimated to be fifteen to twenty *lati* per hour. For comparison, the typical monthly wage for

a state worker at that time was around sixty *lati* per month. (Seps, "Prostitūcija—sociāla parādība," 40.)

94. These data come from unpublished materials of the former Morality Police.

95. Pārsla Eglīte, correspondence with author, April 1998.

96. *Latvia Human Development Report, 1997* (Riga: UNDP, 1997), 40.

97. Elizabeth Waters, "Restructuring the Woman Question: Perestroika and Prostitution," *Feminist Review* 33 (autumn 1989): 4.

98. Inta Mežavilka and Aiva Soboļeva, conversation with author, Riga, 30 April 1997.

99. Seps, "Prostitūcija—sociāla parādība," 45 and 42.

100. "Jautājumi par prostitūcijas legalizēšanu vai noliegšanu (LR generālprokuratūras Metodikas nodaļas viedoklis)," in Noziedzības novirzēšanas nacionālais padomes kriminoloģisko pētijumu centrs, *Kriminologiskais biļetens nr. 26: Prostitūcijas sociālās, ekonomiskās un tiesiskās problēmas*, 107.

101. J. Raipulis, "Prostitūcijas sociālie un tiesiskie aspekti," in Noziedzības novirzēšanas nacionālais padomes kriminoloģisko pētijumu centrs, *Kriminoloģiskais biļetens nr. 26: Prostitūcijas sociālās, ekonomiskās un tiesiskās problēmas*, 32.

102. Latvian National Preparatory Committee, *National Report on the Situation of Women*, 30.

103. "Čaka ielas republika."

104. J. Raipulis, "Prostitūcijas sociālie un tiesiskie aspekti," 34.

105. Ailona Dārzniece, conversation with author, Riga, 30 April 1997.

106. The women's organizations represented in the council include organizations with interests in religion, charity, politics, and sports, among others. (Zariņa, *News About Women in Latvia*, 36–39.)

107. Latvian National Preparatory Committee, *National Report on the Situation of Women*, 20–21.

108. Odne Oslands, "Iedzīvotāji," in *Dzīves apstākļi Latvijā*, ed. Odne Oslands (Riga: Central Statistical Bureau of Latvia, 1996), 53.

109. Ole Noorgaard, Dan Hindsgual, Lars Johannsen, and Helle Willumsen, eds., *The Baltic States After Independence* (Brookfield, Vt.: Edgar Elgar, 1996), 150–57.

110. Moghadam, "Patriarchy and Post-Communism," 327.

111. Watson, "Eastern Europe's Silent Revolution," 472.

Chapter 6

1. Apsītis, *Brīvības piemineklis*, 119–22.

2. Īvāns, *Gadijuma karakalps*, 130.

3. Īvāns, *Gadijuma karakalps*, 179.

4. Māra Grīnberga, "Atkal grib celt Daugavpils HES," *Diena*, 24 July 1999, 8.

Bibliography

Anderson, Benedict. *Imagined Communities: Reflections on the Origin and Spread of Nationalism.* New York: Verso, 1983.

Andersons, Edgars. "Kā Narva, Pečori un Abrene tika iekļauti Krievijas Socialistiskajā Federatīvajā Republikā." *Latvijas vēsture* 1 (1991): 50–59.

Apsītis, Vaidelotis. *Brīvības piemineklis.* Riga: Zinātne, 1993.

Arato, Andrew. "Interpreting 1989." *Social Research* 60 (1993): 609–46.

Bachelard, Gaston. *The Poetics of Space.* Boston: Beacon Press, 1969.

Balodis, Agnis. "Latgales vaicājums." In *Latvija šodien, 1989/1990.* Rockville, Md.: World Federation of Free Latvians, 1990.

Baltic Observer (Riga). September 1993–June 1994.

Barner-Barry, Carol, and Cynthia A. Hody. *The Politics of Change: The Transformation of the Former Soviet Union.* New York: St. Martin's Press, 1995.

Bater, James H. *Russia and the Post-Soviet Scene: A Geographical Perspective.* New York: John Wiley & Sons, 1996.

Bebel, August. *Woman in the Past, Present, and Future.* London: Zwan, 1988.

Berklavs, Eduards. *Zināt un neaizmirst.* Riga: Preses Nams, 1998.

Beyme, Klaus von. *Transition to Democracy in Eastern Europe.* New York: St. Martin's Press, 1996.

Bilmanis, Alfreds, ed. *Latvian-Russian Relations: Documents.* Lincoln, Neb.: Latvian Legation, 1978.

Bleire, Daina. *Latvija, 1985–1996 gadā: Notikumu hronika.* Riga: N.I.M.S., 1996.

Blinkena, Aina. "Spīdola—Viena no trīspadsmit." In *Latvijas sieviete valsts 75 gados,* ed. Pārsla Eglīte. Riga: Zvaigzne, 1994.

Blūzma, Valdis, Ojārs Celle, Tālavs Jundzis, Dītrihs Andrejs Lēbers, Egils Levits, and Ļubova Zīle, eds. *Latvijas valsts atjaunošana, 1986–1993.* Riga: Latvijas universitātes žurnāls "Latvijas vēsture" fonds, 1998.

Bonnell, Victoria. "The Representation of Politics and the Politics of Representation." *Russian Review* 47 (1988): 315–22.

———. "The Representation of Women in Early Soviet Political Art." *Russian Review* 50 (1991): 267–88.

———. "The Peasant Woman in Stalinist Political Art of the 1930s." *American Historical Review* 60 (1993): 55–82.

Bourdieu, Pierre. *Outline of a Theory of Practice.* New York: Cambridge University Press, 1977.

———. *In Other Words: Essays Towards a Reflexive Sociology.* Stanford: Stanford University Press, 1990.

———. *Language and Symbolic Power.* New York: Cambridge University Press, 1991.

Bourdieu, Pierre, and Loic J. D. Wacquant. *An Invitation to Reflexive Sociology.* Chicago: University of Chicago Press, 1992.

Bridger, Susan. *Women in the Soviet Countryside: Women's Roles in Rural Development in the Soviet Union.* New York: Cambridge University Press, 1987.

Brila, Daina. "Is It Easy to Be Born in Latvia?" In *Fragments of Reality: Insights on Women in a*

Changing Society, ed. Ilze Trapenciere and Sandra Kalniņa, 205–20. Riga: VAGA, 1992.

Brubaker, W. Rogers. "Citizenship Struggles in Soviet Successor States." *International Migration Review* 26 (1992): 269–91.

Brūvers, Pāvils. "1988. gada 25. marts." In *Latvija šodien, 1988.* Rockville, Md.: World Federation of Free Latvians, 1988.

Buckley, Mary. *Women and Ideology in the Soviet Union.* Ann Arbor: University of Michigan Press, 1989.

Bukšs, Miķelis. *Latgaļu atmūda.* Munich: Latgaļu izdevniecība, 1976.

Bungs, Dzintra. "Zaļie sienāži: nemierīgā Latvijas jaunatne." In *Latvija šodien, 1987.* Rockville, Md.: World Federation of Free Latvians, 1987.

Burawoy, Michael, and Janos Lukacs. *The Radiant Past: Ideology and Reality in Hungary's Road to Capitalism.* Chicago: University of Chicago Press, 1992.

Cerulo, Karen. *Identity Designs: The Sights and Sounds of the Nation.* New Brunswick: Rutgers University Press, 1995.

Clemens, Walter C. *Baltic Independence and Russian Empire.* New York: St. Martin's Press, 1991.

Cohen, Abner. *Urban Ethnicity.* London: Tavistock, 1974.

Dauksts, Bonifacijs, and Artūrs Puga. "Abrene." In *Contested Territory: Border Disputes at the Edge of the Soviet Empire,* ed. Tuomas Forsberg. Brookfield, Vt.: Edgar Elgar, 1995.

Dawson, Jane I. *Eco-Nationalism: Anti-Nuclear Activism and National Identity in Russia, Lithuania, and Ukraine.* Durham: Duke University Press, 1996.

Delaney, Carol. "Father State, Motherland, and the Birth of Modern Turkey." In *Naturalizing Power: Essays in Feminist Cultural Analysis,* ed. Sylvia Yanagisako and Carol Delaney. New York: Routledge, 1995.

Diena (Riga). 1992–98.

Dreifelds, Juris. "Latvian National Rebirth." *Problems of Communism* (July–August 1989): 77–95.

———. *Latvia in Transition.* New York: Cambridge University Press, 1993.

Dunsdorfs, Edgars. *Kārļa Ulmaņa dzīve: Ceļinieks, politiķis, diktators, moceklis.* Riga: Zinātne, 1992.

Edinstvo (Riga). 4 August 1989.

Eglīte, Pārsla. "Family Policy During the Transition Period in Latvia." *Humanities and Social Sciences Latvia* 2, no. 7 (1995): 28–47.

———. "Population of Latvia: A Demographic Survey." In *Children and Families in Latvia: 1994 Situation Analysis,* ed. Anita Jakobsone. Riga: UNICEF Latvian National Committee, 1995.

Einhorn, Barbara. *Cinderella Goes to Market: Citizenship, Gender, and Women's Movements in East Central Europe.* New York: Verso, 1993.

Engels, Frederick. *Origin of the Family, Private Property, and the State.* In *Karl Marx and Frederick Engels: Selected Works in Three Volumes* 3. Moscow: Progress Publishers, 1983.

Flournoy, Richard, Jr., and Manley O. Hudson, eds. *A Collection of Nationality Laws of Various Countries as Contained in Constitutions, Statutes, and Treaties.* Littleton, Colo.: Fred B. Rothman & Co., 1983.

Forsberg Tuomas. "The Collapse of the Soviet Union and the Historical Border Questions." In *Contested Territory: Border Disputes at the Edge of the Soviet Empire,* ed. Tuomas Forsberg. Brookfield, Vt.: Edgar Elgar, 1995.

————. "Theories on Territorial Disputes." In *Contested Territory: Border Disputes at the Edge of the Soviet Empire*, ed. Tuomas Forsberg. Brookfield, Vt.: Edgar Elgar, 1995.

Foucault, Michel. *Power/Knowledge: Selected Interviews and Other Writings, 1972–1977.* Ed. Colin Gordon. Brighton, England: Harvester Press, 1980.

Furtado, Charles F., and Andrea Chandler, eds. *Perestroika in the Soviet Republics: Documents on the National Question*. Boulder, Colo.: Westview Press, 1992.

Gamson, William A., and David S. Meyer. "Framing Political Opportunity." In *Comparative Perspectives on Social Movements: Political Opportunities, Mobilizing Structures, and Cultural Framings*, ed. Doug McAdam, John D. McCarthy, and Mayer N. Zald. New York: Cambridge University Press, 1996.

Geertz, Clifford. *The Interpretation of Cultures*. New York: Basic Books, 1973.

Gellner, Ernest. *Nations and Nationalism*. Ithaca: Cornell University Press, 1983.

Ģērmanis, Uldis. *Latviešu tautas piedzīvojumi*. Riga: Jāņa sēta, 1990.

Gerner, Kristan, and Stefan Hedlund. *The Baltic States and the End of the Soviet Empire*. New York: Routledge, 1993.

Goban-Klas, Tomasz, and Pal Kolsto. "East European Mass Media: The Soviet Role." In *The Soviet Union in Eastern Europe*, ed. Ode Arne Westad, Sven Holtsmark, and Iver B. Neuman. New York: St. Martin's Press, 1994.

Gorbachev, Mikhail. *Perestroika*. Moscow: Progress Publishers, 1987.

————. *Selected Speeches and Articles*. 2d ed. Moscow: Progress Publishers, 1987.

The Greatest Tyranny: Documentary Facts About the Organized Murder of the Baltic People. Toronto: Estonian National Committee in Canada, Latvian Information Centre in Canada, Lithuanian National Federation in Canada, n.d.

Gross, Jan. "Poland: From Civil Society to Political Nation." In *Eastern Europe in Revolution*, ed. Ivo Banac, 56–71. Ithaca: Cornell University Press, 1992.

Hanson, Stephen E. *Time and Revolution: Marxism and the Design of Soviet Institutions*. Chapel Hill: University of North Carolina Press, 1997.

Harsanyi, Nicolae, and Michael D. Kennedy. "Between Utopia and Dystopia: The Liabilities of Nationalism in Eastern Europe." In *Envisioning Eastern Europe: Postcommunist Cultural Studies*, ed. Michael D. Kennedy. Ann Arbor: University of Michigan Press, 1994.

Hartmane, Sarmīte. "Woman's Mood and Health Criteria." In *Fragments of Reality: Insights on Women in a Changing Society*, ed. Ilze Trapenciere and Sandra Kalniņa. Riga: VAGA, 1992.

Heaton, Herbert. *Economic History of Europe*. New York: Harper & Brothers, 1936.

Hood, Neil, Robert Killis, and Jan-Erik Vahlne. *Transition in the Baltic States: Micro-Level Studies*. New York: St. Martin's Press, 1997.

Hosking, Geoffrey. *The Awakening of the Soviet Union*. Cambridge, Mass.: Harvard University Press, 1991.

International Monetary Fund. DOCEX Project. *Latvia: An Economic Profile*. Washington, D.C.: International Monetary Fund, 1992.

————. *IMF Economic Reviews: Latvia*. Washington, D.C.: International Monetary Fund, 1996.

Īvāns, Dainis. *Gadijuma karakalps*. Riga: Vieda, 1995.

Jakobsone, Anita. "Children in Families at Risk." In *Children and Families in Latvia: 1994 Situation Analysis*, ed. Anita Jakobsone. Riga: UNICEF Latvian National Committee, 1995.

Kalniņš, Ojārs, ed. *Chautauqua/Jurmala, 1986: A Latvian-American Perspective.* Rockville, Md.: American Latvian Association of the United States, 1987.

Kārkliņš, Rasma. *Ethnic Relations in the USSR: The Perspective from Below.* Boston: Allen & Unwin, 1986.

———. *Ethnopolitics and the Transition to Democracy: The Collapse of the USSR and Latvia.* Washington, D.C.: Woodrow Wilson Center Press, 1994.

Karpova, Ārija, and Inta Kraukle. "Some Ideas About the Latvian Woman in the Present Sociopsychological Situation." In *Fragments of Reality: Insights on Women in a Changing Society,* ed. Ilze Trapenciere and Sandra Kalniņa. Riga: VAGA, 1992.

Keddie, Nikki R., ed. *Debating Revolutions.* New York: New York University Press, 1995.

Kennedy, Michael D. "An Introduction to East European Ideology and Identity in Transformation." In *Envisioning Eastern Europe: Postcommunist Cultural Studies,* ed. Michael D. Kennedy. Ann Arbor: University of Michigan Press, 1994.

Kertzer, David. *Politics and Symbols: The Italian Communist Party and the Fall of Communism.* New Haven: Yale University Press, 1996.

Kligman, Gail. "Women and the Negotiation of Identity in Post-Communist Eastern Europe." In *Identities in Transition: Eastern Europe and Russia After the Collapse of Communism,* ed. Victoria Bonnell. Berkeley: Center for Slavic and Eastern European Studies, University of California at Berkeley, 1996.

Kolbergs, Andris. *Dumpis uz laupītāju kuga.* Riga: Lauku apgāds, 1993.

Korlova, Ilze, and Ilze Trapenciere. "Women in Latvia: Some Significant Historical Data and Figures." In *Fragments of Reality: Insights on Women in a Changing Society,* ed. Ilze Trapenciere and Sandra Kalniņa. Riga: VAGA, 1992.

Krūzmētra, Maija. "Rural Women in Latvia." In *Fragments of Reality: Insights on Women in a Changing Society,* ed. Ilze Trapenciere and Sandra Kalniņa. Riga: VAGA, 1992.

Kubik, Jan. *The Power of Symbols Against the Symbols of Power: The Rise of Solidarity and the Fall of State Socialism in Poland.* University Park, Pa.: The Pennsylvania State University Press, 1994.

Kukarina, Tatiana, and Vladimir Tikhomirov. *Pochemu pogib Interfront? Istoriia odnogo politicheskogo uroka.* Riga: Latviiskaia assotsiatsiia sodeistviia vozrozhdeniiu Rossii, 1991.

Kwiecinski, Andrzej, and Vaclav Vojtec. "The Transformation of Baltic Agriculture." *OECD Observer* 202 (October–November 1996): 31–32.

Lācis, Visvaldis. "Zemniecība un latviešu nācijas nākotne." In *Latviešu nācijas izredzes: 1990. gada 28. septembra konference.* Riga: Zinātne, 1990.

Laiks (New York). 1997–98.

Lapidus, Gail W. *Women in Soviet Society: Equality, Development, and Change.* Berkeley and Los Angeles: University of California Press, 1978.

Latvian National Preparatory Committee for the U.N. Fourth Conference on Women. *National Report on the Situation of Women.* Riga: Latvian Women's Studies and Information Center, 1995.

Lēbers (Loeber), Dītrihs A. "Krievijas un Latvijas teritoriālais strīds Abrenes jautājumā." *Latvijas vēsture* 5, no. 24 (1996): 50–59.

Levits, Egils. "Latvija padomju varā." In *Latvijas valsts atjaunošana, 1986–1993,* ed. Valdis Blūzma, Ojārs Celle, Tālavs Jundzis, Dītrihs Andrejs Lēbers, Egils Levits, and Ļubova Zīle, 42–63. Riga: LU žurnāla "Latvijas vēsture" fonds, 1998.

Lieven, Anatol. *The Baltic Revolution: Estonia, Latvia, Lithuania, and the Path to Independence.* New Haven: Yale University Press, 1993.

Mach, Zdzislaw. *Symbols, Conflict, and Identity: Essays in Political Anthropology.* Albany: State University of New York Press, 1993.

Marshall, T. H. *Citizenship and Social Class.* Concord, Mass.: Pluto Press, 1992.

Marx, Karl, and Frederick Engels. *The Communist Manifesto.* In *Karl Marx and Frederick Engels: Selected Works in Three Volumes* 1. Moscow: Progress Publishers, 1983.

Matlock, Jack F. *Autopsy of an Empire: The American Ambassador's Account of the Collapse of the Soviet Union.* New York: Random House, 1995.

Mauliņš, J. "Pats galvenais—Dzīvīga gimene." In *Latviešu nācijas izredzes: 1990. gada 28. septembra konference.* Riga: Zinātne, 1990.

McCarthy, John D., and Mayer N. Zald. *The Trend in Social Movements.* Morristown, N.J.: General Learning, 1973.

———. "Resource Mobilization and Social Movements." *American Journal of Sociology* 82 (1977): 1112–41.

Millere, Anita. "Women in Latvia: They Endure All." In *Fragments of Reality: Insights on Women in a Changing Society,* ed. Ilze Trapenciere and Sandra Kalniņa. Riga: VAGA, 1992.

Mills, C. Wright. *The Sociological Imagination.* New York: Oxford University Press, 1959.

Misiunas, Romuald J., and Rein Taagepera. *The Baltic States: Years of Dependence, 1940–1990.* Berkeley and Los Angeles: University of California Press, 1993.

Moghadam, Valentine. "Patriarchy and Post-Communism: Eastern Europe and the Former Soviet Union." In *Patriarchy and Economic Development: Women's Positions at the End of the Twentieth Century,* ed. Valentine Moghadam. New York: Clarendon Press, 1996.

Nacionālā neatkarība (Riga). May 1993.

Narusk, Anu. "Gender and Rationality: The Case of Estonian Women." In *Unresolved Dilemmas: Women, Work, and the Family in the United States, Europe, and the Former Soviet Union,* ed. Kaisa Kauppinen and Tuula Gordon. Brookfield, Vt.: Edgar Elgar, 1997.

Neatkarīgā cīņa (Riga).

Noorgaard, Ole, Dan Hindsgual, Lars Johannsen, and Helle Willumsen, eds. *The Baltic States After Independence.* Brookfield, Vt.: Edgar Elgar, 1996.

Oberschall, Anthony. "Opportunities and Framing in the East European Revolts of 1989." In *Comparative Perspectives on Social Movements: Political Opportunities, Mobilizing Structures, and Cultural Framings,* ed. Doug McAdam, John D. McCarthy, and Mayer N. Zald. New York: Cambridge University Press, 1996.

O'Donnell, Guillermo, and Phillipe Schmitter. *Transitions from Authoritarian Rule: Tentative Conclusions About Uncertain Democracies.* Baltimore: Johns Hopkins University Press, 1986.

Oslands, Odne. "Iedzīvotāji." In *Dzīves apstākļi Latvijā,* ed. Odne Oslands. Riga: Central Statistical Bureau of Latvia, 1996.

Par zemes reformu un zemes privatizāciju Latvijas Republikas lauku apvidos. Riga: KIF "Biznesa komplekss," 1996.

Pelkaus, Elmārs. "Latvijas valsts problēma Latvijas Republikas laikā." In *Latviešu nācijas izredzes: 1990. gada 28. septembra konference.* Riga: Zinātne, 1990.

———, ed. *Tauta: Zeme: Valsts: Latvijas Nacionālās neatkarības kustība dokumentos.* Riga: Latvijas Valsts arhīvs, 1995.

Pfaff, Steven. "Collective Identity and Informal Groups in Revolutionary Mobilization: East Germany in 1989." *Social Forces* 75 (1996): 91–118.

Pilkington, Hilary. "Whose Space Is It Anyway? Youth, Gender, and Civil Society in the Soviet Union." In *Women in the Face of Change*, ed. Shirin Rai, Hilary Pilkington, and Annie Phizacklea. New York: Routledge, 1992.

Pipes, Richard. "Introduction: The Nationality Problem." In *Handbook of Major Soviet Nationalities*, ed. Zev Katz. New York: Free Press, 1975.

Plakans, Andrejs. "The Tribulations of Independence: Latvia, 1991–1993." *Journal of Baltic Studies* 25 (1994): 63–72.

———. *The Latvians: A Short History*. Stanford: Hoover Institution Press, 1995.

Posadskaya, Anastasia. "Changes in Gender Discourses and Policies in the Former Soviet Union." In *Democratic Reform and the Position of Women in Transitional Economies*, ed. Valentine M. Moghadam. New York: Clarendon Press, 1993.

Priede, Zaiga. "Nodarbinātība un darba apstākļi." In *Dzīves apstākļi Latvijā*, ed. Odne Oslands. Riga: Central Statistical Bureau of Latvia, 1996.

Pumpurs, Andrejs. *Lāčplēsis*. Riga: Sol Vita, 1995.

Rainis, Jānis. *Uguns un Nakts*. Riga: Zvaigzne ABC, 1996.

Raipulis, Jēkabs. "Latviešu tautu varam saglabāt tikai mēs paši." In *Latviešu nācijas izredzes: 1990. gada 28. septembra konference*. Riga: Zinātne, 1990.

———. "Prostitūcijas sociālie un tiesiskie aspekti." In *Kriminoloģiskais biļetens nr. 26: Prostitūcijas sociālās, ekonomiskās un tiesiskās problēmas* (1995): 27–34.

Reshetar, John S., Jr. *The Soviet Polity: Government and Politics in the USSR*. New York: Harper & Row, 1989.

Rīgas balss (Riga). July 1996.

Rose, Sonya O. *Limited Livelihoods: Gender and Class in Nineteenth-Century England*. Berkeley and Los Angeles: University of California Press, 1992.

Rūķe-Draviņa, Velta. "Studentes un studenti Latvijas Universitātē." In *Latvijas sieviete valsts 75 gados*, ed. Pārsla Eglīte. Riga: Zvaigzne, 1994.

Rungule, Ritma. "Izglītība." In *Dzīves apstākļi Latvijā, 1999. gadā*. Riga: Central Statistical Bureau of Latvia, 2000.

Rutkis, Jānis. *Latvia: Country and People*. Stockholm: Latvian National Foundation, 1967.

Senn, Alfred Erich. *Lithuania Awakening*. Berkeley and Los Angeles: University of California Press, 1990.

Seps, Dzidris. "Women and Crime." In *Fragments of Reality: Insights on Women in a Changing Society*, ed. Ilze Trapenciere and Sandra Kalniņa. Riga: VAGA, 1992.

———. "Prostitūcija—sociāla parādība." *Kriminologiskais biļetens nr. 26: Prostitūcijas sociālās, ekonomiskās un tiesiskās problēmas* (Riga: n.p., 1995), 35–42.

Sewell, William J., Jr. "Ideologies and Social Revolutions: Reflections on the French Case." *Journal of Modern History* 57 (1985): 57–96.

———. "Historical Events as Transformations of Structures: Inventing Revolution at the Bastille." *Theory and Society* 25 (1996): 841–81.

Skocpol, Theda. *States and Social Revolutions: A Comparative Analysis of France, Russia, and China*. New York: Cambridge University Press, 1979.

Smith, Anthony D. *The Ethnic Origin of Nations*. Cambridge, Mass.: Blackwell, 1986.

Smith, Graham. "The Soviet State and Nationalities Policy." In *The Nationalities Question in the Post-Soviet States*, ed. Graham Smith. New York: Longman, 1996.

Snow, David A., and Robert D. Benford. "Master Frames and Cycles of Protest." In *Frontiers in Social Movement Theory*, ed. Aldon D. Morris and Carol McClurg Mueller. New Haven: Yale University Press, 1992.

Solzhenitsyn, Aleksandr I. *The Gulag Archipelago Two.* New York: Harper & Row, 1975.

Somers, Margaret R. "Narrativity, Narrative Identity, and Social Action: Rethinking English Working Class Formation." *Social Science History* 16 (1992): 591–630.

Somers, Margaret R., and Gloria Gibson. "Reclaiming the Epistemological 'Other': Narrative and the Social Construction of Identity." In *Social Theory and the Politics of Identity,* ed. Craig Calhoun. Cambridge, Mass.: Blackwell, 1994.

Spekke, Arnolds. *History of Latvia: An Outline.* Stockholm: M. Goppers, 1951.

Staburags '88: Vides aizsardzības kluba žurnāls (1988).

Stradiņš, Jānis. *Trešā atmoda.* Riga: Zinātne, 1992.

Stukuls, Daina. "Imagining the Nation: Campaign Posters of the First Postcommunist Elections in Latvia." *East European Politics and Societies* 11 (1997): 131–54.

Swidler, Ann. "Culture in Action: Symbols and Strategies." *American Sociological Review* 51 (1986): 273–86.

Szalai, Julia. "Some Aspects of the Changing Situation of Women in Hungary." *Signs* 17 (1991): 152–70.

Taagepera, Rein. *Estonia: Return to Independence.* Boulder, Colo.: Westview Press, 1993.

Taurens, Jānis. *Latvijas vēstures pamatjautājumi un valsts konstitucionālie principi.* Riga: Latvijas Republikas Naturalizācijas pārvalde, 1996.

Tev (Riga). June 1993.

Tickner, Lisa. *The Spectacle of Women: Imagery of the Suffrage Campaign, 1907–14.* Chicago: University of Chicago Press, 1988.

Tilly, Charles. *From Mobilization to Revolution.* Reading, Mass.: Addison-Wesley, 1978.

Tismaneanu, Vladimir. *Fantasies of Salvation: Democracy, Nationalism, and Myth in Post-Communist Europe.* Princeton: Princeton University Press, 1998.

Tolstaia, Tatiana. "Notes from the Underground." *New York Review of Books* 37, no. 9 (1991): 3–7.

United Nations Development Project. *Latvia Human Development Report, 1996.* Riga: UNDP, 1996.

———. *Latvia Human Development Report, 1997.* Riga: UNDP, 1997.

———. *Latvia Human Development Report, 1995* [cited May 1997]. Available from www.undp.riga.lv/hdrs/engl95.htm.

Ušackis, Uldis. "The Demographic Situation in Latvia: A Statistical View." *Humanities and Social Sciences Latvia* 2 (1995): 4–16.

Utena, Inga. *Cilvēks Godmanis.* Riga: Apgāds Jāņa sēta, 1997.

Verdery, Katherine. *National Ideology Under Socialism: Identity and Cultural Politics in Ceausescu's Romania.* Berkeley and Los Angeles: University of California Press, 1991.

———. *What Was Socialism and What Comes Next?* Princeton: Princeton University Press, 1996.

Vilks, Andrejs. "Noziedzība, korupcija un ēnu ekonomika." In *Krīze Latvijā: Ko darīt?* Riga: Vērmaņparks, 1996.

Vulfsōns, Mavriks. *Nationality Latvian? No, Jewish: Cards on the Table.* Riga: Jumava, 1998.

Waters, Elizabeth. "Restructuring the Woman Question: Perestroika and Prostitution." *Feminist Review* 33 (autumn 1989): 3–19.

Watson, Peggy. "Eastern Europe's Silent Revolution: Gender." *Sociology* 27 (1993): 471–87.

———. "Civil Society and the Politics of Difference in Eastern Europe." In *Transitions, Environments, Translations: Feminisms in International Politics,* ed. Joan W. Scott, Cora Kaplan, and Debra Keats. New York: Routledge, 1997.

Winichakul, Thongchai. *Siam Mapped: A History of the Geo-Body of a Nation.* Honolulu: University of Hawaii Press, 1994.

World Bank. *Latvia: The Transition to a Market Economy.* Washington, D.C.: World Bank, 1993.

Žagars, E. *Socialist Transformations in Latvia, 1940–1941.* Riga: Zinātne, 1978.

Zariņa, Inna, ed. *News About Women in Latvia.* Riga: Latvian Women Studies and Information Center, 1994.

Zīle, Ļubova. "Latvijas atmodas ceļš (1986–1991)." *Latvijas vēsture* 4–54 (1993–96).

———. "Latvijas komunistiskās partijas krīze un šķelšanās." In *Latvijas valsts atjaunošana, 1986–1993,* ed. Valdis Blūzma, Ojārs Celle, Tālavs Jundzis, Dītrihs Andrejs Lēbers, Egils Levits, and Ļubova Zīle, 190–206. Riga: LU žurnāla "Latvijas vēsture" fonds, 1998.

———. "Neformalo organizāciju veidošanās un darbība." In *Latvijas valsts atjaunošana, 1986–1993,* ed. Valdis Blūzma, Ojārs Celle, Tālavs Jundzis, Dītrihs Andrejs Lēbers, Egils Levits, and Ļubova Zīle. Riga: LU žurnāls "Latvijas vēsture" fonds, 1998.

———. "Pretestības kustība okupācijas režīma apstākļos." In *Latvijas valsts atjaunošana, 1986–1993,* ed. Valdis Blūzma, Ojārs Celle, Tālavs Jundzis, Dītrihs Andrejs Lēbers, Egils Levits, and Ļubova Zīle. Riga: LU žurnāla "Latvijas vēsture" fonds, 1998.

Index

LC. *See* Latvia's Way coalition (LC)
LDDP (Latvia's Democratic Work Party), 117
  campaign posters of, 87–89
  For Fatherland and Freedom coalition and,
    88–89
League of Women, 54, 59
Lenin, Vladimir, 139, 240 n. 54
Lenin Street, changing name of, 140
Levits, Egils, 239 n. 48
Liberal Alliance (LA), 84, 95, 97, 118
Liberal Party, 69
Lielvārdes belt, 45, 237 n. 45
Lieven, Anatol, 58
Lithuania, 6, 55, 244–45 n. 114
LKF. *See* Latvia's Cultural Fund
LL (Latvia's Luck) coalition, 95, 97
LNNK. *See* Latvian National Independence
  Movement (LNNK)
LTF. *See* Latvian Popular Front (LTF)
Lutheranism, 111
LZS. *See* Latvia's Farmers' Union (LZS)

Mach, Zdzyslaw, 134
Machine and Tractor Stations (MTS), 166–67,
  244 n. 99
mapping, 144–45
  nationhood and, 153
maps, 150–52
Marx, Karl, 194–95, 226
Marxism-Leninism, inequality and, 192–96
mass social movements, 22–23
maternity allowances, 213
Matlock, Jack, 33, 34, 56
Meierovics, Gunārs, 94
metro campaign, 42
minorities
  in interwar period, 111–12
  during Soviet period, 112–15
Molotov, Vyacheslav, 6, 44
Molotov-Ribbentrop Pact, 6, 39, 44, 49
Mother Latvia, 2
MZ (Our Land coalition), 68, 81–82, 103, 238 n. 18

naming, as creative power, 130, 133
narratives
  evolutionary, 73–74
  of normality, 71–72
  of transformation, 72–73
Narusk, Anu, 199, 207–8
National Independence Movement. *See* Latvian
  National Independence Movement
  (LNNK)

nationalism, 9
  in post-Communist politics, 17–18
  role of women and, 202, 205–10
  traditional rural life and, 156
nationhood, mapping and, 153
nation-states, as imagined communities, 145–46
naturalization policy, 105–8, 120. *See also* citizenship
natural order, 10
nature, use of, in campaign posters, 79–80
neotraditionalism, role of women and, 205–6
new-state model of citizenry, 106
normality
  concept of, 9–10, 12, 14–15
  increased complexity of, 228–29
  narrative of, 71–72
  political parties and, 71–72
  spatial, 16–17
  temporal, 17–18
normalization, social change and, 10–11
nostalgia, and social change, 190
November 18 demonstration, 40–41
November 18 Union, 74, 107, 118

Oberschall, Anthony, 34
OMON special forces, 59–60
On Agrarian Reform in Republic Latvia law,
  170–71
On Land Reform in country Districts of Republic of Latvia law, 171
opposition
  institutionalizing, 47–55
  spaces and places as aspects of, 129
Our Land coalition (MZ), 68, 81–82, 103, 238 n. 18

PA (Anti-Communist Union coalition), 82, 118
Panteļejevs, Andrejs, 73, 121
Parliament. *See* Saeima (Parliament)
Peace Treaty of 1920, 109–10, 146, 150, 151–52
perestroika, rural land and, 168–70
Peters, Jānis, 26, 41, 44, 48, 50, 51
Pfaff, Steven, 28
Pitalovo territory, 132, 145–46, 146–49, 149–50,
  183–84
  mapping of, 151
place, normalization of, 132
Plakans, Andrejs, 161, 182, 1663
political campaigning, 75–79
political opportunity, dimensions of, 32–33
political parties. *See also* specific political party
  campaign posters of, 100–103